CW00867879

I WANT YOU TO KNOW MY GLORY

Merlin H Oliver

WestBow Press books may be ordered through booksellers or by contacting:

WestBow Press
A Division of Thomas Nelson & Zondervan
1663 Liberty Drive
Bloomington, IN 47403
www.westbowpress.com
1 (866) 928-1240

ISBN: 978-1-4908-4177-9 (sc)
ISBN: 978-1-4908-4179-3 (hc)
ISBN: 978-1-4908-4178-6 (e)

Library of Congress Control Number: 2014911107

Printed in the United States of America.

WestBow Press rev. date: 09/02/2014

MY HEARTFELT THANKFULNESS TO

My parents, Henry (passed) and Susanna.
My mother for her steadfastness in the Lord.
My brothers, sisters, uncles, aunties, and cousins.
My family, Winnie, David, Hayley, Ruth, and Salome.
Winnie, you made this possible. I bless you.
David and Hayley, you were excellent in our store.
Ruth and Salome, you were my soldiers
in my Holy Spirit boot camp.

My pastor, counselor, and teacher, I especially thank you.
To the people of Niagara Falls, New York, for
the freedom to pray throughout the city.
To TCT TV, Orchard Park for allowing
me to be part of the prayer line.

POEMS BY DAVID OLIVER

I Belong to God

My body, mind, soul, and spirit belong to my God.
Don't you know? I wish you would understand.
My friend, it's better that you know.
God is the person I confide in, the person I lean on,
The person who brings me through any weather, any storm.
In every dream He is there. He makes the situations fair;
In doubt He makes me clear; I'm so glad that He's here.

Unconditional Love

We survive with air; it's a portion of love.
We survive with food; it's a portion of love.
We survive with clean clothes; it's a portion of love.
We survive with guidance; it's also a portion of love.
We survive in a paid job; it's a portion of love.
We survive with friends and family; it's also a portion of love.
We survive with grace; it's a portion of love.

We survive with mercy; it's also a portion of love.
We survive with blessings; it's a portion of love.
We survive in our environment; it's also a portion of love.
We live to survive by faith; it's also a portion of love.
There's a lot more we survive with; it's all a portion of love.

FOREWORD BY A FRIEND

It is with the greatest pleasure that I have come to know Brother Merlin Oliver over the last two years of his time in Niagara Falls, New York, and during the writing of this book. It seems my entire life in God has come to center on His glory, as Jesus prayed for us in John 17. I have found in Merlin the same heart's cry: "Glorify Your Son, that Your Son also may glorify You… Holy Father, keep through Your name those whom You have given Me, that they may be one as We are… that they all may be one, as You, Father, are in Me, and I in You; that they also may be one in Us, that the world may believe that You sent Me." (John 17:1, 11b, 21)

Reading this book and hearing the miracles Merlin has participated in has made me hungry for the Holy Spirit to manifest more of God's presence in my daily life, even though I have loved Him for years now. The revelatory insights he shares go hand in hand with his testimonies and are worthy of meditation so the Holy Spirit can expand His vision in you (and me), personalizing His working in us to will and do His good pleasure. As I have gone back and forth over these pages, I have been challenged to the very core of my being to more consistently live my whole life in the awareness of and hunger for His manifested glory, held by His limitless grace.

Moses knew what was important above all else—the *one thing* of utmost importance: His personal presence. "If Your Presence does not go with us, do not bring us up from here. For how then will it be known that Your people and I have found grace in Your sight, except You go with us?" (Exodus 33:15–16).

The glory of the presence of our Father God is where we truly live and move and have our being. We have been made out of Him, for Him, to be filled with Him, and to love and worship Him. He is truly the most worthy one in all creation—the Lamb of God. All the other blessings of God are of no value if He is not the one who is the very center of our being.

I trust as you climb into the pages of this book you will allow the Holy Spirit to personally challenge you to abandon your entire person to the one who knows and loves you best—the only one who will completely fulfill every longing and satisfy every desire He has created within you.

As you read of Merlin's life experiences, his walk with God, his honest struggles of faith, and his victories in the revelations of Father God and His kingdom, may you be stirred in the depths of your being to discover more of God yourself. I believe that would give Merlin the greatest pleasure for having penned these pages and poured his heart as an offering of love.

This book is an invitation into the one who is the greatest mystery and most thrilling adventure that exists. To be lovers of God, Jesus, and the Holy Spirit (as one) is the greatest reason for being in all of the universe. As lovers, we also can't help but share the love and glory of His person with others because we just can't contain Him!

> I do not pray for these alone, but also for those who will believe in Me through their word; that they all may be one, as You, Father, are in Me, and I in You; that they also may be one in Us… And the glory which You gave Me I have given them, that they may be one just as We are one: I in them, and You in Me; that they may be made perfect in one, and that the world may know that You have sent Me, and have loved them as You have loved Me. (John 17:20–23)

May the words and stories in these pages challenge you deeply to be renewed and revived in the fire of God every moment of every day and to be filled with His Spirit so you are ready at any moment to give an answer of the hope that lies within you—Christ *in you,* the hope, the knowing, of *glory*!

—Gloria Browne

CONTENTS

INTRODUCTION

> Then the Lord said: "I have pardoned, according to thy word; but truly, as I live, all the earth shall be filled with the glory of the Lord." (Numbers 14:20–21)

> It is the Spirit who gives life; the flesh profits nothing. The words that I speak to you are spirit, and they are life. (John 6:63)

Welcome! Imagine standing in a beautiful garden of assorted flowers: lavender, jasmine, daises, and others. Suddenly a yellow butterfly flies into the garden. It seems as if it's in a hurry. It lands on a flower and wastes no time. It finds what it wants, unwinds its proboscis, dips it in the nectar, and drinks to its heart's content. Then it rewinds its proboscis, and off it flies, whizzing out of sight. Its rapid action gives us reason to think, *My, that was quick!* After that fleeting display, just like an airplane's smooth approach on landing, into the garden flies a honeybee, and it lands on a jasmine. There are other flowers, but he chooses the jasmine. Do you notice how he first moves around the outside of the flower before he goes inside? After he goes inside, you turn to observe the lavender patch with the intention of returning to the honeybee…

Oh yes, the honeybee. Turning back to the honeybee, you are just in time to see it emerge out of the petal with its pollen baskets full. It stays on the petal a little while and then flies off. An afterthought comes: *Maybe he was saying, "Thank you, I appreciate the time you shared with me."* Gazing at the honeybee longer than the butterfly, but smiling, you say, "I know your honey is going to end up in some retail store for people to eat to their heart's content." There is also a personal observation while watching the honeybee—that peace and contentment have filled your heart.

The purpose and intention of the foregoing account is to produce the following result: to inform, to persuade, to call to action, and to gently help change attitudes in order to encourage us to live a glorious life in the Spirit, *now*.

In the late '80s and early '90s when shoppers used to frequent the retail store we owned, some of them spoke often of their personal mishaps. Their circumstances gave them compelling reasons as to why they purchased certain items, like alcohol and cigarettes. I never understood this until I experienced similar tragedies in my life. Remembering some of the reasons they gave for their addictions, I refused to succumb to similarly tormenting thoughts as I found myself a victim of the same type of circumstances they'd had. I reasoned that their methods only brought temporal relief. I concluded I wanted a better solution that would give me understanding and restored health. I needed to know what was affecting other people's lives and mine.

I decided to follow the path to victory many others had taken before me. Eventually, over the process of time, I also became victorious with the help of my best friend—the Holy Spirit. By

His leading, one can know God's glory. Due to His counsel and guidance, I was able to rise out of two common yet tragic disasters: the end of a marriage and the end of a business. Looking back, I take responsibility for much of the difficulty. Specifically, in my marriage, I did not fulfill my position as the male. I had no knowledge of my first role as a priest, which is to communicate with almighty God through prayer for myself and my household. There are other vital roles that we, as males, neglect due to ignorance and stagnant traditions. In reading this, you might wonder, *Did he love his wife?* Yes!

During my crisis I absolutely needed supernatural help because I did not know that the cross was bearing down on me. I became distressed and confused and suffered from spiritual exhaustion. I was close to insanity, but I rejected its projections. I believed there was an answer deep down beyond the anguish and incessant pain I was enduring. I held on to that thought. I began to search for an answer to what I firmly believed—that the visible world was somehow being affected by something out of the invisible world. I was convinced and unshakeable in my belief. That firm conviction became the anchor in my raging storm. It was a storm no one understood save the Holy Spirit, who became my teacher, friend, and guide.

My desired haven was the answer to my consuming question, which got closer at the end of each painfully dark and gloomy day. It came through a discipline for which I had little regard—prayer. Yes, prayer—that untapped electromagnetic sound pulse, my misperceived enemy. This brought me to my desired haven. Previously, I had literally run away from participating in it. I was petrified. Why? I have not diligently searched for an answer to this question. I was in a dilemma because I was unable to explain to those around me, who were concerned for me, what was happening—that the brilliance of my life had deteriorated into chaotic shambles. Well, maybe the situation turned out that way causing me to turn to the cross and Jesus crucified. If that was the case, then I humbly bend my knees.

On Wednesday, April 19, 1994, my life began to change radically for the better. I thank God because this thought was impressed upon my heart: *I want you to know My glory.* I will write more of this later. Even though I am writing a personal account, God's glory will be known globally.

This book is about a journey of practical encounters. Though they were of supernatural origin, the burning desire of my heart is to offer them so that wherever you, the reader, may be on your timeline, your response can consequently be, "I can do that too!" The spirit of boldness will come to assist in making your decisions real. The pathway you seek and some answers to your questions may be stated somewhere in these pages, specially framed in a way that would enrich your life. Our infinite Creator loves us all unconditionally!

Yes, humanity has been searching for answers to their questions since the dawn of time. Yet the answers are embedded deep in the annals of our subconscious minds; God placed eternity in the heart of man. From our hearts a firm belief emerges that there is much more to life than the sad scenes shown through the various media outlets. Some of these include: family conflicts, ethnic conflicts, nations at war, crumbling infrastructures, and global pollution. Have you ever wondered if there is something extraordinary or unusual that could be done to bring about a better life for yourself, your family, and your friends? Something that, when proven, works? Something that would be so dynamic that it compels you to tell your friends? Something that could help your community, put a sparkle in the eyes of children and adults, and even reverse moral decline? If any of these thoughts have ever crossed your mind, perhaps in the pages of *I Want You to Know My Glory* the answer will be found. Because I was the conduit for these manifestations, I know the methods work. So you can do these works… and greater!

There is nothing more convincing than when one personally proves a method works; it removes the veil of doubt. It gives individuals confidence and power in their delivery irrespective of those with whom they communicate. In my case, the results were so profound that they remain vivid in my mind: the healings, financial provisions, and relational manifestations. Further good news is that through these experiences, I have become a better person, abounding in confidence. By the empowerment of God's grace, I firmly believe I can do anything once I set my mind on its attainment. Painful as it was, I yielded to the process because it was not the usual, everyday humdrum. It was an enigma—a mystery. It was radically different and still is! I was ecstatic, amazed, and intrigued to see the sadness of individuals turned to joy as the Spirit of God worked through me, transforming their lives. I'm talking about cancer disappearing, a person coming out of a wheelchair through the spoken word, the dumb speaking, finances being provided, alcoholics becoming sober (some instantly and some by process), and the healing of multiple sclerosis, arthritis, fever, headaches, common colds, and many more by the power of prayer, the spoken word, and the presence and power of the Holy Spirit.

I will specifically explain in detail the healing of a lady who was in a wheelchair. This healing is connected with a later chapter in this book that gives credibility to the added power given when praying after midnight. These experiences span beyond twenty years. I sense the time is right to share these experiences, and my close friends have also encouraged me to do so.

The miraculous is only one facet in the plurality of God's glory. There has been a taboo on God's glory, as if it should be confined only to the miraculous, to having goose bumps, and to a theological niche. Far from it! Rather, its glorious splendor, beauty, and majesty should be made known. This glory should permeate every facet of society: family, education, government (law, politics, and military), economy (business, science, and technology), arts (entertainment and sports), media, and religion, more commonly known as the seven mountains of culture.

My awareness that the glory is for everyone who so desires and wants to be a partaker of it created an excitement in me to make my own experiences known. Not only that, but I realized the significance of Him saying to me personally, "I want you to know My glory!" He desires for us to enter into the glory of His presence. In addition, on my journey of discovery, I found in the Bible more than once where it validates the Sovereign's will in this matter:

> For the earth will be filled with the knowledge of the glory of the LORD, as the waters cover the sea. (Habakkuk 2:14)

> They shall not hurt nor destroy in all My holy mountain, For the earth shall be full of the

> knowledge of the LORD As the waters cover the sea. (Isaiah 11:9)

After reading *I Want You to Know My Glory,* you may be willing to step out of the box and venture into the secret place through the process shown in another chapter. There you will meet transcendent God by entering His glorious presence. In reading, you may discover a process for your God encounter. This is not for the hasty or the impatient. It is for those who want to know the glory now. Let me add, knowing the glory is available to all, isn't that good news? However, there are certain conditions to be met by those who have not made Jesus Christ their personal Lord and Savior. Yes, there are many ways into the supernatural. However, there is only one way into the supernatural presence of almighty God, and that is through Jesus Christ. Jesus paid the price on the cross for all humanity.

Dear reader, truth needs no defense or alibi. It rules supreme! It is infallible and unchangeable. Please read this entire book. It is for each of us to decide whether to embrace encountering His glory and eventually this lifestyle of living in His glorious presence. The choice is entirely yours.

The beauty of this journey is that God's love has no barriers or limitations; it's available to all. Give this invitation careful and prayerful thought, make your decision, and take action!

It is my privilege now to share my journey with you…

THE PURCHASE OF THE BUSINESS

My holy encounters in the glory began to increase after we bought our shop in London from a businessman who originally came from Pakistan. I admired him for his shrewdness and dedication in whatever he did from a business perspective. I used to help him redecorate his home since interior decorating was a hobby of mine. I was excellent in interior decorating (if I may boast just a little) as I had learned the art from my uncle, who was considered to be one of the best in the entire city of London. However, telecommunications was my own skill and true delight.

After we had been acquainted for some time, the businessman mentioned to my wife that he was selling the business. As we were part of his customer base at the shop, he asked us first if we wanted to purchase it. We considered the matter, had some discussions, and agreed to purchase the property. Well, all did not go according to our excited plan. Our concept of the people involved and our understanding of that business left some things to be desired. There was a steep learning curve, and thankfully, we had a panel of advisors who knew the intricacies in that field.

We found there was collusion between the seller and his solicitor where a large sum of money was deducted from the purchase price. Furthermore, there was no record of this. I found out that when it came to money, it seemed no one could be trusted! However, through determination to do things right in the sight of the Lord, we were able to recover the money through an excellent Christian solicitor.

Finally, the shop was in our possession, and this telecommunications man was the manager of a shop in a new field about which he knew very little. However, I knew I could make it work by utilizing the same principles and attitudes I had used to be successful in telecommunications. It helped tremendously to work alongside the seller day by day, learning the business procedures. As he introduced me to his customers and I became acquainted with them, an idea began to form in my mind.

A Brilliant Idea to Learn Their Language

Let me briefly tell you how the Turkish and Kurdish community who frequented our shop became our largest customer base. Ours was an international store with the idea of catering to everyone prior to these groups coming into the store. That type of inclusive thinking created the opportunity to learn at least the basics of a variety of languages. It was exciting and financially beneficial also.

After the purchase of the business, I noticed a couple of Turkish women entering the store together. They looked around and walked out. They came from a clothing factory not far from the store where many of the women worked. The following morning the same two came in again, did the same thing, and walked out. It happened repeatedly without them talking to me as they were unable to speak English. I then had an epiphany. It was my observation and realization that people usually came into the shop to purchase something. The idea was for them to leave with a purchased item. These ladies were not doing this, so I had an idea! Why not learn an introduction in their language, such as, "Good morning"? What made this easy for me was that we had a Turkish nanny who cared for our two younger children. I asked one of her daughters how to say good morning in Turkish. Armed with the words I needed, I was ready for when they came into the shop again.

The following morning, the two women came in again. I said, "*Gunayden.*" It means "good morning" in Turkish. Their eyes lit up, and with surprise on their faces, they looked at each other and ran out of the shop muttering, "*Arap kasap*!" Later I understood what it meant, "*Arab butcher.*" That evening many more people came along with the original two. The following morning, many more came. What grew to be our largest customer base was born. My next immediate move was to employ our nanny's daughter to help in the shop to communicate with the new customers and to teach me the Turkish names of the items and how to name our currency in their language. I thoroughly enjoyed that learning curve. I used the same technique with all the other nationalities that came to our shop too. Each nationality would tell me what items they liked, and when I brought the items into the store, they would come. I did exactly what they said, and they were true to their word. Not only did they bring their friends, but through their support, the store prospered until the Gulf War began.

As a result of the war in the summer of 1992, the majority of Turkish and Kurdish customers left. Because of the financial crisis this created, my wife also left and took our children. What was also devastating was that the business incurred a huge debt, and I worked myself beyond exhaustion trying to keep things afloat. I didn't take time to eat and rest properly. When I realized I was alone, I said to God, "It's you and me now."

During that summer, there was little rain, the atmosphere was dry, and the surrounding environment was steeped in political tension and apprehension for everyone as the Gulf War raged. What had started the previous year was affecting both residential and commercial businesses. The impact on our retail business was devastating because the majority of the customers were Turkish and Kurdish.

Living Alone and Not Knowing What to Do

I was now living alone above the shop. One morning I was standing in the middle of the sitting room with my hands in my pockets reflecting on something. I was all by myself, feeling helpless, and thinking, *How am I going to clear the huge debt amounting to thousands of pounds?* Suddenly I heard, "I want you to live by faith."

I blurted out an involuntary response: "But I've always had money in my pocket!" I didn't know where the command had come from, and I was shocked at my response. Then I heard it repeated a second time.

I gave it some thought and said, "Okay." Immediately the phone rang. I picked it up and said, "Hello!" The caller on the other end was a sister from another church I used to attend.

She said, "The Lord told me to call you and bring you some provisions. Can I bring them now?"

"Yes!" I said, thinking, *This must be that faith thing.* Later that day she brought the provisions. Briefly I related to her some of what was happening. I can't recall seeing her again after that. Thank you, wherever you are.

Sale of the Business for Fifty Thousand Pounds

Other events were unfolding, such as going to see my solicitor and counselor to try and figure out what to do next. One day while I was walking through the store on my way to Monday night's cell group at the church I attended, I heard, "Sell the business for fifty thousand pounds."

I believed what I heard was from God. I shared the information at the cell group. I made a pledge to give a fifty-pound offering as a step of agreement in faith. The following week I paid the pledge. During the same week, I also went to my solicitor's office. He was negotiating with creditors to whom the business owed monies. I went (without setting an appointment), opened the door, greeted everyone, and then said, "The Lord told me to sell the business for fifty thousand pounds." Then I immediately left his office.

As I said earlier, no one was buying any property, either residential or commercial, due to the Gulf War that year. However, I was advised to sell the business. It reminded me of Isaac in Genesis 26 where during the famine God told him not to go to Egypt. Rather God told him where he was to plant his seed. The Bible says what he planted yielded a return of one hundred fold.

Now I had this one persistent thought in mind: *Why has there been failure to achieve success in all I do? I'm honest and dedicated. I always go out of my way to help others and to go the extra mile like Jesus said in Matthew 5:41.* I just could not understand why there was such a lack of cooperation among those with whom I did business. I wondered if they didn't really want me to succeed.

In the month of August, an American evangelist held an annual event at Earls Court, London, called Mission to London. It was a large event, and many speakers usually accompanied him. Saints would attend from many nations: Switzerland, Austria, Holland, Denmark, Germany, and many others. The event created much excitement in the city and was beneficial to the business community, from the little hot dog stall to the superstores. All the sessions were well attended, and I believe it was due to the unending prayer sessions that were ongoing. Those prayer sessions would start half an hour before the event began each evening and end half an hour after the final event. There were seven prayer teams, each having a prayer captain. Each prayer session lasted for half an hour. At the end of each session, the next team took over to maintain continuity. In the final session, everyone could join in. It was dynamic. The anointing during and after those sessions could be felt beyond the perimeter of Earls Court itself. Many miracles took place, and many responded to the salvation messages. The meetings had a tremendous impact on the city. I decided to attend. I attended all the sessions, from morning until evening. I also got involved in the prayer sessions. I found this prayer exhilarating. I never knew there was such power in prayer! During those sessions, I developed an insatiable appetite for prayer. Later on I listened to one of the speakers, who talked about finances. He said something that caught my attention. He said, "When saints of God become wealthy, they stop walking in the Spirit."

That statement, "They stop walking in the Spirit," went through me like one of the many thorns piercing my bare feet as a youth tending to my grandfather's sheep. After I heard what he said, I was convicted. I repented, asking God's forgiveness. About three weeks after that meeting, three Kurdish men came to me. We negotiated the price, and they purchased the store at 136 Stoke Newington Road, London, N16, for fifty thousand pounds.

Upon signing of the contract, the solicitor had to interrupt my wife's protestations, informing her of how I walked into his office and said what God told me to do. He said he hadn't believed me, and still it happened. Unfortunately, the solicitor's response was a toxin for the venom that she was releasing. When anyone shows lack of trust in you without reason, there's nothing you can do to change the deception. Only God's mercy and grace will do it. However, we must continue to pray on behalf of these people until peace is restored to their broken hearts.

The deal was completed, the creditors were paid, and I became debt free! Hallelujah and glory to God! His word did not return to Him void. I was an extremely happy man! As the Lord had set me free from my own debtors, so I set free those who were debtors to me, canceling their debts. Their eyes would light up with glee as the burden was removed from their shoulders. They were released, and I was excited to be part of it!

The time had come to move from the store and apartment to what I called my Holy Spirit Boot Camp at 119 Lothair Road, Haringay, London N4, near beautiful Finsbury Park. I spent many hours in the park's flower gardens, admiring the beautiful flowers. Being there became extremely therapeutic for me.

It is sobering to think, and then know, that the Spirit of God has spoken to every individual on this earth at some time or another, often on more than one occasion. I discovered this fact while participating in evangelistic work and talking to various people groups all around the large cosmopolitan city of London, England. They did not know how to describe it, but they spoke of an inner voice instructing them of a particular direction or choice to make so they would not be harmed. Not knowing this inner voice as God's, they ignored the thought. At that point uncertainty set in, and not being sure, they decided on the action that incurred danger. The sobering truth is this—walls, either bad or good, are built brick by brick.

During the next step of my journey, the Holy Spirit began to communicate with me through counseling. One of the major things He said was that I had destroyed my own self. That was funny! For quite some time I thought it was crazy because I blamed almost everyone else for my demise. Yet He insisted I was to blame, not anyone else. It took some soul searching, and eventually the penny dropped with an involuntary response of my right hand touching my lips. My whole being at that time seemed to warp into abject stillness as the pieces found their rightful place. The profound recognition of this fact brought about a humbly whispered response: "You're right. I am guilty, and I'm sorry."

So what brought about that conviction of the truth? Simply put, I realized I had come into agreement with the words that were planted in my head by the enemy, even though I personally knew they were wrong. The primary phrase with which I had agreed was, "I can't." Do you want to know the eventual outcome of this agreement? I became a person who believed, "I can't," and my true identity became distorted. From the moment I imbibed those simpleton words (which were my way to plug the dripping tap of negative thoughts), I masterminded my own misery, doom, and destruction. I agreed with those negative words and began to confess them, giving them validity. What we say with our words is what we eventually become through our lifestyle. What I ignorantly did then was to give power to the adversary, not being in control of my person. After my epiphany, I stopped the blame game and began to search out how to recover.

I began to think about how to respond to those negative thoughts resident in my mind and how to break the loop of depression. I felt like a person being attacked by lots of blackbirds swooping down and squawking incessantly whenever they chose; I was very vulnerable. The attacks went on in the night also, like a bully stalking its victim whenever he chooses. My mind had no rest as I was being tormented day and night. Eventually the thought came to me to put out my hand in front of me with upheld palm and say, "From today forward, nothing but good comes my way."

During that time and still, I began to say good things about everyone, no matter how horrible people appeared to be. I began to see there's something good in every individual. This became the antidote to those horrible toxins embedded in my mind. This method worked for quite a while and brought much relief. In the midst of all this, the Spirit of the Lord was guiding me to help others in their troubles. That was therapy in itself as it took my mind off my own personal head games. It was when I was on my own that the mental cycle was devastating.

The next step in my progression was to move to new accommodations. This meant I had to get used to new surroundings. The mental attacks seemed to increase when earlier they seemed to be fading. Being from a Christian background and believing in a covenant-keeping God and Jesus Christ made no difference to the mind benders. Please understand, by this time the Bible became my refuge. In it I found 1 Corinthians 2:16, particularly the last part, where it mentions we have the mind of Christ. It applied to me as I had already accepted Jesus Christ as my Lord and Savior. I knew I could take it for my own and proclaim it. During those times, I began to speak these words to the mental giants in my mind. In the process of time, I noticed that the mind looping of negative, depressive thoughts began to fade. I didn't notice it until some months later. When I traced the thought back to that Scripture, it felt like electricity went through my body. I was ecstatic! From that moment forward, I began to speak the Scriptures with confidence and conviction. Hope of recovery became the inspiration in my actions.

The Power in Confessing the Word of God

The Scripture brought me much comfort day after day. During those times I would continue with daily Bible reading therapy through the epistles, latching on to any Scripture that would enlighten me and clear up the negative mind dominance that had me bound. I found another scriptural gem in Philippians 2:5, where the writer was admonishing us to let the mind be in us that was also in Christ Jesus. For quite some time, I pondered what was said and came to the conclusion it made sense. If I had accepted Jesus Christ as my Lord and Savior, it was true I had the mind of Christ. I accepted this fact and began to believe and speak it. With those two powerful Scriptures standing guard over my mind, speaking them daily, I noticed a drastic change in the attack on my mind. It began to fade away. Understanding came to me that as I increased in the power of confessing the Word of God, it had the creative ability to transform any situation. Let me emphasize—*any* situation. Through the grace of God and much practice, I gained total control over what I said and chose to say. As I said earlier, that inner voice speaks to each of us, which I have come to know as the Holy Spirit guiding us away from danger. In the midst of all that was unfolding, I had the thought lingering in my mind of going to Bible college. The thought of going to Bible college found residence in my mind and wouldn't leave.

Let's look back for a moment at my time in electronics college. It was coming to end, and I thought keeping my mind occupied would be good therapy. Somehow, through that emotionally unstable period in my life (the end of self), I managed to perform exceptionally well in my exams, scoring in the nineties. I remembered that while I was at electronics college in Earls Court,

London, I arrived home one afternoon and the Holy Spirit said to me I could earn As in all my subjects—micro-electronics, CCTV, VCR repairs, and color TV repairs. When I first heard, I doubted. Then He said it again, so I responded, "Show me."

I was guided to Exodus 31. Though I was a brilliant student, I didn't see the need to rack my brain to score well in exams. That was a challenge for me from the Holy Spirit because He knew I could perform much better than what I usually set myself to do. On that day I read the chapter and saw that God Himself filled Bezalel with the Spirit of God, in wisdom, in understanding, in knowledge, and in all manner of workmanship to design artistic works, to work in gold, in silver, in bronze, in cutting jewels for setting, and in carving wood and to work in all manner of workmanship. He went on to talk about Aholiab. On that day I read up to verse 11 and was astonished.

I prayed a heartfelt prayer. "Thank You, Holy Spirit, for what You said about my earning A's and guiding me to this Scripture. I believe what You have said. Now please fill me with the Spirit of God to bring about in my life all You have said."

Dear reader, from that day to the present I have scored exceptionally well and will always score well on exams. I would tell the teachers in whichever class I participated in, "I am an A student! Praise the Lord!"

Many more God encounters took place in my Holy Spirit Boot Camp at Lothair Road, North London, and it was from here I launched out to Bible college.

Two years had almost ended when, in 1994, it was impressed on my heart that the time had come to attend Bible college. There was much anticipation as to what to expect. I enrolled in the London Metropolitan College of Ministry with financial assistance from my mother. All my funds had been utilized to clear the huge debt that had encumbered me during the sale of the business. The amazing thing for me was my reception on the first day entering through the doors of the college. I received a welcome greeting, as if they had known me for quite some time!

ATTENDING BIBLE COLLEGE

The main reason I enrolled at Bible college was a feeling I had that I needed some sort of systematic pattern and knowledge of how to help others from a practical standpoint. As I said earlier, the Holy Spirit was directing me to help others, and I would act spontaneously on what I heard, just being obedient. As I followed the instructions I heard from Him, I was always successful. As an example, I obeyed when the Holy Spirit told me to tell a certain male student to allow his wife to speak; otherwise she would leave him. I didn't really know him well and neither had I met his wife. My only connection with him was through Bible college. However, on a particular day we were at a wedding reception for one of the college students, and the Lord instructed me it was time to talk with him and what to say to him. Thankfully, he was responsive.

Fasting with a Brother at Bible College

I went to him, called him aside, and told him the word of knowledge I had from the Lord. He acknowledged the word and agreed he was trying to allow his wife to speak more. Glory to God! Unfortunately, he spoke with me at Bible college a while after our meeting with the sad news that she had left him.

Of course I said to him, "What did the Lord tell you?"

"I really tried," he said.

However, he asked if I would agree to fast with him, so I did. After all, he was and is my brother in the Lord. I agreed that we could pray over the phone at midnight. Come to think of it, I never gave it a thought then. I just agreed. I can imagine what he must have been encountering as they had a young baby at that time. My word to him then was that he was in boot camp and had a great opportunity to make some personal adjustments for when his wife returned. I wasn't just speaking to make him feel good. The Spirit of the Lord gave me instructions for him, and I knew He cared for and loved them. I could only have spoken the words of encouragement and reassurance that the Lord gave me. The funny thing was that I was still so personally broken myself. I could see I was being put back together as I reached out to help others.

Our nightly prayer went on for some time, and suddenly, during the conversation one night I said to him, "God showed you that your wife would leave more than once."

"No," he said

"Yes, He did." I said, "Think back into the past."

Eventually he remembered and pointed out that God did tell him in a dream. In the dream he related that a demon entered their home and dragged his wife out by her long blond hair.

I said, "That's it! We have to go into the spirit realm and find her. When we find her and set her free in the realm of the spirit where she's held captive, she will come home."

"We Got Them!"

I got really excited about pursuing those evil invisible kidnappers, knowing they could be overpowered through the delegated authority we've been given by working in harmony with the Holy Spirit. You see, I lost everything because I had no prior knowledge of demonic activities affecting people's lives. Yes, I was learning fast. So that night I said to him, "Can you remember how the Americans released heat-seeking missiles that would zero in on the target no matter how much the enemy's plane zigzagged in the air?"

"Yes," he said.

I said, "Great! We will release a prayer in agreement. Our prayer will be like those heat-seeking missiles. Wherever that demon or demons are having a celebration, they'll be zapped, and your wife will return home at such and such a time." I heard myself speaking and knew that was a word to him from the Lord—a word of knowledge.

We prayed in what we called tongues or an unknown language to us but known to almighty God. According to 1 Corinthians 14:2, he who speaks in an unknown tongue does not speak to men but to God because no one understands him. However, in the spirit he speaks mysteries. That is a valid statement as I have encountered many other demonic spirits, and it's that speaking in tongues they acknowledged. Sometimes they acted rather surprised when that language was spoken, but they obeyed and left every time. I am also inquisitive as to what was actually said, but the Lord has never given me the interpretation. I have heard from others it's called tongues of angels. Whatever it is called, those demonic spirits recognize its validity. Also, there's power in the name of Jesus in both the physical and spiritual realms.

While we were praying over the phone that night in tongues, the fun part came when, after some time, my colleague shouted, "We got them!"

One could estimate that there were more than one thousand demons and less than ten thousand. Alone he wasn't strong enough to overpower them, but when the two of us agreed and prayed, they were overpowered as the Scripture states, "One will put a thousand to flight and two will put ten thousand to flight," or "A thousand will fall at your left and ten thousand on your right." The latter is specifically in Psalm 91:7.

Sometime after that midnight prayer encounter, his wife returned home at the stated time. What, you might ask, was the most beautiful reward? When his wife phoned to thank me for joining her husband in securing her release. My heart melted, and I cried tears of joy. I had forgotten all about the matter and never expected any response because it was done, finished. As the family of God, we should look to one another's needs. She was grateful, and her saintly response was beautiful. Our God is super-loving and cares for us beyond what we could ever imagine. He always will. Let's give Him thanks.

Learning Humility

There was another good thing about being at Bible College, and that was learning humility from a practical standpoint. As part of our daily activities, on a rotational basis, each student took turns at cleaning toilets, vacuuming the carpets, washing cups, and other menial tasks. I thought, *Why can't they employ a cleaner?*

After my first cleaning session I said to myself, "Merlin, you didn't expect this, did you?" My response was, "No." Then I thought, *You had better get used to it and look for the benefit.* Gradually my heart began to soften toward doing those chores. What I once considered below my intellectual, academic, and telecommunications brilliance because I acted like a "toffee nose" (colloquial jargon for high-mindedness and misperceived elevated standards) became a pleasure because I began to envisage Jesus. He went about doing things with an unusually graceful manner, never refusing to do anything or go anywhere. He was obedient in everything, from healing the sick to washing the disciples' feet.

In healing the centurion's servant, Jesus never hesitated because the centurion was not a Jew. Rather, He demonstrated His willingness to act in meeting anyone's need. Because of the centurion's faith in Jesus' authority and ability to heal, all Jesus had to do was speak the word and the servant would be healed. Although Jesus was willing to go to his house to heal his servant, the centurion believed it was not necessary, so great was his faith.

Another example is Jesus washing the disciples' feet. Foot washing was an ongoing custom. In the eastern culture during Christ's time, a servant did the tasks that were classed as lowly. Chores that were regarded in high society as an insult to those of position and standing, Jesus adopted. Foot washing was the lowest of all, and next up was undoing the sandal straps, as John the Baptist indicated in his statement addressing Jesus. John recognized Jesus' regal position and felt he wasn't worthy for even such a menial task.

Nothing about Christ Jesus coming to earth was coincidental. He chose to humble Himself and take the position of a servant, being born of lowly parentage in very sparse surroundings. He came into a period when spiritual pride was at its height. The teachers of the Word had departed from the Law and the Prophets and were teaching the traditions of men. Sectarianism became normal, and "I am better than you" was the norm. Today, aren't we hearing a similar echo?

In our fast-paced modern society where haughtiness seems to be the dominant factor, it's hard to imagine someone in high society, like a billionaire, washing the feet of some unknown dropout who never had any formal education. Yet Jesus demonstrated the power in humility, not the way we perceive humility to be—as a weakness. Rather, He demonstrated humility as divine strength carved out of an obedient life to almighty God. Power and authority were given to Him (in the giving of all things), and He knew it, so He rose up and girded Himself. The contrast here is like that of a king to a common peasant. Yet the King of glory bent His knees with towel in hand to wash His disciples' feet, setting us a kingly example in John 13:3–5.

> Jesus, knowing that the Father had given all things into His hands, and that He had come from God and was going to God, rose from supper and laid aside His garments, took a towel and girded Himself. After that, He poured water into a basin and began to wash the disciples' feet, and to wipe them with the towel with which He was girded.

The Servant-Heart of our Lord and Savior

At Bible college I began to see the servant-heart of my Lord and Savior to be one of humility, devoid of all arrogance and self-exaltation. Literally, it is a person who is willingly submitted to God and His will. Years later, in 2004, I was given a revelation of how His humility destroyed the kingdom of darkness. Out of it I taught a series of messages entitled, "Christ, the King of Humility," focusing on how Jesus' life and mission were totally opposite of Satan's, where pride ruled supreme. That paralyzing pride, cunningly injected into Eve and willingly accepted by Adam, was and is the undoing of the entire human race.

In the process of time, I developed a little habit to use when certain folks are getting obnoxious with me over the phone. I'll share my little secret with you. This is what I do to abate the verbal storm. While they're talking, I quietly kneel if I'm indoors. If outdoors I would say, "My friend, I bow my knees" instead of kneeling in public. After giving this subject some thought, it appears that this characteristic of humility isn't often taught in the churches, at least in most of which I am aware. Yet Jesus taught much about humility throughout the gospels. Here are a couple of examples:

> At that time the disciples came to Jesus, saying, "Who then is greatest in the kingdom of heaven?" Then Jesus called a little child to Him, set him in the midst of them, and said, "Assuredly, I say to you, unless you are converted and become as little children, you will by no means enter the kingdom of heaven. Therefore whoever humbles himself as this little child is the greatest in the kingdom of heaven." (Matthew 18:1–4)

There are numerous Scripture references on humility, and what may appeal to me may not to someone else. Even so, it doesn't change the meaning or purpose. In January 2013, I bought a little book by Andrew Murray titled *Humility*. I've read it twice, and I am now on my third reading. This is my humble opinion—every Christian needs to read it!

Another highlight of Bible college was the morning prayer sessions. The Spirit of God would come among us powerfully. We prayed for ongoing current events in government, families, missions, and natural disasters. There were so many answered prayers that it would take up a lot of pages to share the unfolding of each and how God gave sight during the prayer sessions. There is one, however, that instantly pops into my mind.

Group Prayer for Holland

One morning one of the professors said that the dykes (an embankment built as a barrier against the sea) in Holland were not holding back the water anymore. The North Sea was overflowing them and getting onto the land. We needed to pray that it would cease. I understood what he said, as I had spent time in Terneuzen on more than one occasion, where we walked on those dykes along the seashore. I thought about the family I knew there. Holland is a beautiful country with flat terraces. It would be devastating if water should overflow the dykes. So that morning, we prayed fervently. In a vision God showed me one of the dykes, and the water was about a foot above the top of the dyke. A transparent wall that looked like glass was preventing the water from flowing over the top of the dyke. I thought, *Wow! The miracle worker has intervened due to the serious intercession this morning.* I knew in my heart what I was shown was the answer to our prayers. I saw the tides rushing in and hitting against the transparent glass that was above the top of the dyke, but it never spilled onto the land.

In those days, I didn't really give any thought to what others might think of me or about being considered weird because of the revelations I shared in the class. That morning I believed God showed His love to the people in that part of Holland. Since then, to my knowledge, I've not heard of any disaster to befall that nation. It is a country worth visiting just to see its manicured beauty. After our prayer time, we began our morning lessons.

At the Home of a Student from Bible College

One Sunday after church, at the invitation of one of the Bible college students, I visited her home. The reason was because she accommodated foreign students and asked me to come and witness to them. I lived a fasting lifestyle, at the time fasting three days each week. On that particular weekend, the fast would end on Sunday night. After church service, I took the bus to her home in Clapham. On arrival, I knocked on the door and was greeted by a beautiful Japanese girl with long black hair.

She asked, "Are you Merlin?"

I said, "Yes. Who are you, and where is Esther?" (Esther is not her real name.)

She said, "My name is Jane, and Esther said to let you in. She went to visit a neighbor and will be back shortly."

I agreed to enter and wait for her. Since I was fasting, I expected someone would give his or her heart to the Lord. Normally that's what happens during or at the end of the fast.

Tell Me about the Holy Spirit

I sat on a sofa in the waiting room while she sat on a chair facing me. I had nothing to say as we were just waiting for Esther's return. All of a sudden Jane said to me, "Tell me about the Holy Spirit."

I looked at her and studied her facial expression due to the seriousness of the statement. I perceived her question was genuine.

I said to her, "I cannot tell you about the Holy Spirit until I first talk to you about Jesus."

She agreed. I began to tell her about Jesus coming to earth to teach us about God the Father and His passionate love for us. His purpose was to pay the price with His life to ransom us back from Satan. While I was talking, she was absorbing every word. I also talked about how Jesus took our place by dying on the cross and paying the ultimate price for our sins; that included the entire human race. She was absorbing every word.

Again, after a long pause, she said, "Now tell me about the Holy Spirit."

I said to her, "Jesus said the Holy Spirit is our teacher and that He would tell us about Jesus." I talked to her about salvation through Jesus and that she must become born again to know more about the Holy Spirit and Jesus. After the presentation of the gospel, I asked her if she would like to accept Jesus as her Lord and Savior. She said no. I felt her resistance. I immediately looked at this beautiful young Japanese girl with long flowing black hair sitting on the chair. Her entire demeanor portrayed one of gentleness and calmness, yet she responded with this gruff no.

Immediately I internally asked the Holy Spirit why she had such an abrupt response. He said to look on her right hand. I looked and saw an ankh, an Egyptian bracelet (shaped like a cross with the top part formed in a loop) that honors Osiris. Seeing the bracelet, I then understood the gruff response. It wasn't the response of that beautiful young girl but rather a personality associated with the bracelet. That bracelet was the barrier to her salvation.

My next task was to have her remove the bracelet of her own free will. On removing the bracelet, I knew she would quickly accept Jesus as her Lord and Savior because I could see she was ready. Now knowing what the problem was, thanks to the Holy Spirit, I had another problem. It was inconceivable for me to talk to her about the bracelet or assist with its removal in a one-on-one situation.

I Waited for Esther

I questioned her about family-related things, such as her home. She was from Kyoto in Japan.

Our church normally spent one entire week praying for a nation. Ironically, as the overseas prayer coordinator, I had felt impressed to pray for Japan over the past two weeks. During that time Japan was experiencing a lot of earthquakes and rising tides. It caused some concern for the prayer team. Prior to praying I would carry out extensive research on the selected country[1] that included demographics, population, political affiliation, agriculture, etc. One of the exciting discoveries was that the people originated from mainland China. They first settled in Kyoto. It became their first capital, not Tokyo. Later some of the people migrated to Tokyo, which then became the capital city.

During our conversation to pass the time, Esther came anxiously rushing into the room. "Merlin, Merlin! I have been trying to witness to Jane all morning, but her response to the gospel is always negative, even after much persuasion."

Here is a little background about Esther. I loved Esther. She was very generous and loved helping others. For instance, the Spirit of the Lord would instruct me that I needed to go to America for further studies on spiritual matters, especially on the subject of fasting. I did not have sufficient funds but was always giving thanks to the Lord by faith for the release of resources. Esther was one of the saints who responded to my need and contributed financially each time I solicited for funds to go abroad or when I was in Bible college.

During the time of her great generosity, we became good friends. She was married to a brilliant man who worked as the chief engineer in the design department for a large motor vehicle company. Through a puzzling set of legalities, the company released him without compensation. The trauma of the dilemma eventually led to his being diagnosed with Parkinson's disease. Through further legal complications, he wasn't allowed to stay in his own home. All these events, which she was unable to understand, caused Esther much stress. Eventually her husband came to live with me, and that was some comfort to Esther in the midst of all their troubles.

Now back to Esther's friend, Jane, who rejected the good news of the gospel when Esther ministered to her.

I was eager to lower Esther's anxiety, so I beckoned her to come closer to me and whispered in her ear, "There's a bracelet on Jane's right hand that must be removed. Please take her upstairs and gently speak to her about removing it." Esther looked and saw the bracelet, and now she too understood why there was resistance.

Esther and Jane marched off in the direction of the upper room. Shortly they both came back with the bracelet removed. Time was passing quickly, and Jane had to leave to go to Heathrow Airport to get back to Japan. Esther asked if I would accompany Jane to the airport and also help carry her suitcases. I agreed. To my surprise, the suitcases were extremely heavy. As I was carrying them, I thought of the two weeks our church had prayed for Japan. I literally struggled to carry those two suitcases. We finally got to the train station (tube). We both bought tickets and were on our way to the airport.

While we were on the tube traveling to the airport, she repeated her now-familiar statement, "Tell me about the Holy Spirit."

She Accepted Jesus as Her Lord and Savior

The Piccadilly tube was filled with passengers heading to Heathrow Airport. She started the dialog again, so I had to act quickly before we parted company. I looked around at the travelers and thought, *I wish there were fewer people.* I quickly abandoned the thought and stepped out in boldness. I knew she wanted an answer, and the barrier to her accepting the salvation call was in my favor. She was sitting on the opposite side of the tube facing me. I leaned forward and asked if she was ready to accept Jesus as her Lord and Savior. Then I could tell her about the Holy Spirit.

She replied, "I'm ready."

I led her in the sinner's prayer, and from that moment on, she became my spiritual sister. Next I said to her I would ask Jesus to baptize her with the Holy Spirit because Jesus is the Baptizer. She agreed. On asking Jesus to baptize her, I watched a reddish glow descend on her from the top of her head, transforming her skin into a glow that spread down to her chest where the skin could be seen. It was marvelous to watch this phenomenon. Its occurrence was warm because she put both hands to her face, feeling what was happening with a beautiful smile on her face.

Jesus is so marvelous! I cannot recall what I said to her about the Holy Spirit, but I likely would have said something like this: Jesus said the Holy Spirit is the teacher, and He would teach her about Jesus. He is our teacher, comforter, and friend. Ask Him to be your best friend. That was what I did; I asked the Holy Spirit to be my best friend.

We finally got to Heathrow and got her checked in on time. I waved good-bye to my new sister in the Lord and never saw her again.

Reading the Book *Dark Angels*

Some years later while I was reading the book entitled *Dark Angels* by C. Peter Wagner (page 122) I noted his concern in wondering why it was so difficult to evangelize in Japan. I felt I had an answer to his concern, so a few years later I wrote to him about it. Following is my letter in its entirety.

> August 29, 1996
> Dear Mr. Wagner
>
> Re: Warfare Prayer, P 122/3—The Challenge of Japan[1]
>
> Inspiration has been gained from each book I've read, but few have motivated me to write to the authors with maybe some useful insights. Cindy Jacobs, Dick Eastman, and you have been compelling.
>
> In Cindy's case she was here in London in 1993 at Kensington Temple, where I was able to hear lasting insights on prayer and purchased her prayer manual, *Possessing the Gates of the Enemy.* This became the foundational tool since the Lord called me into intercession in February of that year. By trade I function as a telecommunications technician.

---

1 Prayer for Japan—research information came from Moorgate Library, London, England.

In Dick Eastman's case, I wrote to him after reading his book *The Jericho Hour.* He wrote about "Praying the King Back." Now to that I could give wholehearted support. The Spirit of the Lord gave me a revelation of such in Anaheim, California, while attending one of Morris Cerullo's World Conferences. The conference had ended, and my intercessor friends were heading back to Baton Rouge early on the Sunday morning when the Holy Spirit spoke in my heart repeatedly, "Go read Acts." I finally responded around 3:00 p.m. I was missing my friends. Sitting in my hotel room alone, I started from Acts 1. On reaching Acts 3:18, I was taken into what I call a spiritual location where time disappeared. (The surroundings didn't look any different than normal, but what seemed like a moment lasted three hours.) There I saw the body of Christ must come together and pray in this Kairos time (set time); thereafter the King will return. Since then I have sought the Lord and also included it as a prayer point to the intercessors spread across the United States and Europe.

In your case, two years ago I read your book *Dark Angels.* I ask your forgiveness. I should have written then. My journey into spiritual warfare began on June 9, 1993. I was on my way to a house group and had to travel through Finsbury Park, North London. I was speaking in tongues. On reaching the top of the hill in the park, I stopped for some unknown reason, looking up into the sky, and suddenly did a full circle. This Scripture seemed to fall from the sky: Colossians 2:15. I was scared because I come from a Seventh Day Adventist background. I knew the text. I eventually prayed and asked to be directed to a cassette, book, or video with information about what to do. Two weeks later I came across your book *Territorial Spirits*. Glory to God, I have never had so much fun in my life! Please forgive my last statement, but you get to know your position and spiritual warfare is definitely my slot!

I should have written regarding Japan and how it may be taken. In the book *Dark Angels*, you were pondering why Japan was so difficult to evangelize. In a flash the Spirit gave me a strategy for Japan. As we continued to expand our prayer bases to ultimately have one in every nation linked by computer, we gave a command one day to initiate synchronized prayer directed at Kyoto in Japan.

Why Kyoto, you may ask? After the migration of the people from China through Korea to Japan, Nara (now Kyoto) was the first stop-off point or first capital. Thought processes were formulated in that place that became the foundational pattern for future city developments. The longest period of imperial reign was in that city from around 794 till 1868. By the middle of the twelfth century, effective power was in the hands of a warrior household—the Taira. Their great rivals were another family—the Minamoto.

In 1185 the Minamoto annihilated their enemies by a bloody coup. Thereafter the leader of the Minamoto, Yoritomo, set up a new system of government known as Bakufu, literally "camp office," at Kamakuru in the east of the country far from the imperial capital. The emperor gave Yoritomo the title Sei-I Tai *Shogun,* or "Barbarian—Subduing, Generalissimo," usually abbreviated in Western use as *Shogun*.

Where is my focal point, you may ask? Well, I lead prayer for the nations at our church, and while praying for Japan over a two-week period, I saw in the Spirit this animal-like creature releasing a massive amount of black spores. The wind was taking them over North America. Since then I have sought the meaning from the Lord. After reading *Warfare Prayer*, on June 8, 1996, it suddenly dawned on me—motor vehicles were the spores! All over America and Europe is the vehicle called *Shogun* with the symbol of a sword above the name. This was birthed by much bloodshed between two feuding families. Could this then be a demonic point of contact, thus enlarging their territory?

During those two weeks of prayer over two specific areas, finance and exports, the Spirit said to sever the link between big and little brother—the United States and Japan. I began to inquire. After Icyasu, during the Tokugawa Rule (base now Tokyo, formally Yedo), a rule of isolation was imposed upon the nation from 1628 to 1854, which ended when Commander Matthew Perry's squadron of US warships paid a visit to Yedo Bay (now Tokyo). Even today that spirit of isolation still seems to be on the people. On his second visit, Perry secured Bakufu's consent to open up two of the ports and acceptance of a future date to form a resident consul.

The question was, "What was it that Perry did for the Bakufu to open up that paved the way for General Douglas MacArthur, who represented the Allies about one hundred years later, to make a decision without President Truman's consent? Also, why did he uphold that the monarchy should stay and that it was a stabilizing influence?" Could it be that Matthew Perry and Douglas MacArthur were in the same camp as Dardo Rocha? Could it be that though the agreement was political on the surface, the real intention tends toward a long-term spiritual implications?

In the process of time, I asked the Lord, "How can this thing be when I don't even know one Japanese person, much less have a prayer base in

Japan? On the third day of a three-day fast, I went to the house of a friend and met a Japanese girl there who was getting ready to go back to Japan. She had an ankh bracelet on her hand, which she removed after we prayed for her. I accompanied her to Heathrow Airport, and on the way, she gave her heart to the Lord Jesus Christ on the crowded tube on October 23, 1995. She was then baptized with the Spirit. I have written since then without any response due to the description of her background, which caused me concern.

(I omitted the address she gave me.)

It has been many years since that encounter took place. I would like to believe she has grown in the Lord and is leading some thriving ministry, advancing God's kingdom. Meeting that Japanese girl demonstrated to me that Father God was directing what I was doing, that I was listening and acting out my concerns to Him—praises to the Lord. God answers prayers. May we continue passionately to exalt His name!

Sincerely,
Merlin Oliver

Much activity was taking place on a regular basis in the supernatural because I was living a fasted lifestyle. As I fasted, I became available for the Lord to work through me. In this case, one morning on April 19, 1994, after a fervent prayer time and just before occupying my seat in class, I heard in my heart, "I want you to know my glory."

I Want You to Know My Glory

As I stated earlier, I cannot recall the events of that morning, but my prayer time was always exciting. I thought about prayer quite often, a topic that usually occupied my thoughts on my way to Bible college. The journey to the college was from Haringay, North London. Often I would walk from my home or take the bus to Manor House tube station, where I could ride on the Piccadilly tube to King's Cross, St. Pancrass. From there I would walk across to a choice of terminals: Circle, Hammersmith & City, Metropolitan, and Northern. I would take the Northern tube, as it was more convenient for my final destination to Moorgate terminal. On exiting the station, the distance to the college was a short walk.

On my way to college, prayer time was my dominant thought. I was also thinking about the other students and what the final outcome of prayer time might be like. Each prayer session would vary as students each had the opportunity to lead in prayer. Through that discipline, each student's confidence increased as we learned to pray in the presence of others. It helped in removing fear, misperceived intimidation, not wanting to make mistakes, and wondering what others might be thinking. I've come to realize it's a fear common to many people—having to speak or pray in public! Through a gradual process, I made the decision to pray what needed to be said, so with all my heart believing, I gave it my best. There are times when you know you are in that zone where the Holy Spirit takes over and the words just flow out of your heart.

This kind of flow in prayer is like a beautiful symphony—such as Isaiah 40 from Handel's Messiah when the London Symphony Orchestra performs it, conducted by Sir Colin Davis (more on this later). I have many new songs, but one in particular is "Heaven Came down to You Through the Son." I had learned to keep a tape recorder at the ready after having missed many songs previously. This one I was able to capture, and I desire the London Symphony Orchestra or London Philharmonic Orchestra to perform this song at some point in time. My mind is ablaze with the melodious beauty of this song. It must be done! This song is around fifteen minutes long. It flowed from the Spirit, both words and melody. Let's take a moment and worship the Lord.

> I worship and adore You, *El-Elyon,* the Most High God who is the First Cause of everything, the Possessor of the heavens and the earth. You are the God of love, the everlasting God, the great God, the living God, the merciful God, the faithful God, and the mighty God. You are truth, justice, righteousness, and perfection. You are *El-Elyon*—the highest sovereign of the heavens and the earth. Hallowed is Your Name! Let that in which You delight fill the earth—loving-kindness, justice, and righteousness. Allow it to manifest to the glory of Your name. Since You have shown me what is acceptable, I will do what You require of me by grace—to do justly, to love mercy, and to walk humbly with You, my

> heavenly Father. Bless Your holy name. Father, show me now how to help spread Your glory over all the earth as You have said it will, in Jesus' name. Amen.

Oftentimes an individual who wanted to know if God speaks or how He speaks would ask the question, "How does God speak?" Well, let me give an example of how God speaks by His Spirit to my spirit. I personally call it override—a sensitivity that supersedes the normal—and it usually generates a spontaneous response. It does not go to the head but to the heart area. Some call it your "knower." You just know that you know. Spontaneous speech becomes a byproduct. It was a similar outcome to the latter I experienced while attending Metropolitan College of Ministry in London, UK, on April 19, 1994, when the Spirit of the Lord spoke into my heart: "I want you to know My glory."

That morning this was what happened. I froze for an instant just before sitting down, amazed at what I had clearly heard. Since then, I have checked every text I can find on glory, glorify, glorious, or things in that category. Out of that a new song came from my spirit about light pouring out from His face, sparkling light, radiant light, a beauty to behold! That song caused my thoughts to transcend time and space to the vision Habakkuk saw,

> O Lord I heard Your speech and was afraid; O Lord, revive our work in the midst of the years! In the midst of the years make it known; In wrath remember mercy. His glory covered the heavens, and the earth was full of His praise. His brightness was like the light; He had rays flashing

> from His hand, And there His power was hidden. (Habakkuk 3:2–4)

I believe it was a foreseeing of the futuristic event about Jesus' experience on the holy mount, a prelude or preparation to encounter the cross. His inner glory was revealed, and He was seen as the Deliverer of all mankind. That was His life's mission—to seek and to save that which was lost. Preparation was necessary. He completed the assignment because He made mention of it on the cross. Later on Paul was given revelation of the finished work of salvation when he wrote in Titus 2:11, "The grace of God which brings salvation has appeared to all men." In my understanding, that meant all the children of Adam with no distinction between believers and nonbelievers.

Webster's Dictionary Definition[2]

Here's Webster's Dictionary definition of *glory*:

> Praise, honor, or distinction extended by common consent: renown; worshipful praise, honor, and thanksgiving to God; something marked by beauty or resplendence; the splendor and beatific happiness of heaven: eternity.

The meaning clearly refers to someone greater than man in the use of "thanksgiving to God" as the defining indicator. It is

---

2 Definition of glory: A Merriam Webster, *Webster's New Collegiate Dictionary*, Springfield, Massachusetts, U.S.A. 1977, Page (490).

referring to someone who is awesome. In simple terms, it is the glory, honor, and majesty that belongs to a Supreme Being. God is the only one who qualifies. I believe it would be safe for me to specifically use the word *Elohim*. Here's my reasoning. Jesus, during His intercessory prayer in John 17, mentioned the glory He had with His Father before the world was. This prayer gives validity to what God said through the prophet Isaiah in Isaiah 42, that He would not give His glory to another. In other words, all those who walk on the earth who God created and has given the breath of life can only share in His glory if they are born again of His Spirit. This brings up an interesting thought. Partakers of the glory must manifest Jesus' love, and humility must permeate their being. In my opinion, pride is the most destructive element in the entire universe.

Therefore, getting to know God in His glory won't happen overnight. It calls for pushing persistently against negative hindrances: ignorance, darkness, foolishness, and disobedience, all those things that are ungodly. In my reading I also doubled certain scriptural incidents for emphasis, coaxing my mind to break through the familiar patterns. Adopting that new habit, I increased my time in prayer and Bible reading. One day while praying, I received a revelation of the transfiguration recorded in Matthew 17:1–3. Immediately I asked the Holy Spirit if I could have what I saw in this revelation. The following chapter was the outcome of His response.

LET HOLINESS CONSUME US

I had recently moved from the business and was living in new accommodations I called my Holy Spirit Boot Camp. One day in early 1993, while praying, I received revelation on this Scripture:

> Now after six days Jesus took Peter, James, and John his brother, led them up on a high mountain by themselves; and He was transfigured before them. His face shone like the sun, and His clothes became as white as the light. And behold, Moses and Elijah appeared to them, talking with Him. (Matthew 17:1–3)

I asked the Lord for an impartation, but He told me it wasn't His timing yet. I asked the Holy Spirit, "Why not?" The answer was, "There must be deliverance, and then holiness, before what you ask can come." Out of that statement I saw the body of Christ, not just an individual, coming into fullness. There is a true beauty in holiness that I began to see. From that time I began to pursue the first stage of holiness in prayer. Deliverance ministries near and far seemed to become more prominent in my mind.

We are at the position in (spiritual) time where we must recognize the need for holiness before God will allow this manifestation of the Spirit of his Son in us to break forth in us as laid out in the following Scriptures:

> To them God willed to make known what are the riches of the glory of this mystery among the Gentiles: which is Christ in you, the hope of glory. (Colossians 1:27)

> But we all, with unveiled face, beholding as in a mirror the glory of the Lord, are being transformed into the same image from glory to glory, just as by the Spirit of the Lord. (2 Corinthians 3:18)

I termed this indescribable treasure within us *reflections of inner beauty*. It emerged from one of the new songs from the Spirit.

After receiving the revelation of holiness, two years later on July 26, 1995, two new songs came to me the from the Spirit: "Know Your Spiritual Position" and "Heaven Came Down to You through the Son," in that order. I asked God for an understanding of holiness in prayer, with supplication and intercession relentlessly, until it radiates from the body of Christ at His appointed time. There must be a burning desire in our hearts for this attribute. It will not come by wishing or just talking about it. Action must be adopted and pursued with all diligence because the forces of darkness will not sit idly by and let it happen.

Even so, God wants us to progress from our type of holiness. I believe this present position the body of Christ is in is not what He wants. We have made advances. Streams of the body are flowing together, and we are embracing the truth that the church could only be established by revelation and not programs. We must seek Him to know our spiritual position and then walk in holiness. There must be a desire burning within our hearts to know Father God intimately. He meant what he said when more than a thousand years after He spoke to Moses, He gave Peter and Paul the revelation that we should be holy and without blame before Him in love.

As follow up to what I have just said, I believe He put the two aforementioned songs into my spirit after an intense time of worship and prayer in July 1995. I was astounded by the amount of information in the songs; they were prophetic. The words and music came from the Spirit simultaneously. My part was to pick up the guitar, turn the recorder on, and sing by faith. I sensed something was going to happen. May God be glorified at all times through us!

God was questioning Job about creation and where was he when the morning stars sang together and all the sons of God shouted for joy (Job 38:7). That spontaneous adoration of God should be our daily lifestyle. Let's do it! He's worthy of all our praise!

A very simple definition of holiness is to live a sanctified life daily, being set apart to the Lord. We are rapidly approaching the season where our conversation must align with the Word of God. Jesus said He and the Father are one. His Spirit is in us. Jesus is coming back for a church without spot or wrinkle—free from both original and personal sin. We, as the Body of Christ, must begin to take seriously whatever Jesus said in the red writing. The last days began when Jesus appeared on earth, as He said.

> God, who at various times and in various ways spoke in time past to the fathers by the prophets, has in these last days spoken to us by His Son, whom He has appointed heir of all things, through whom also He made the worlds; who being the brightness of His glory and the express image of His person, and upholding all things by the word of His power, when He had by Himself purged our sins, sat down at the right hand of the Majesty on high. (Hebrews 1:1–3)

All the way through His ministry, every word He spoke was in truth, with power and authority. He was speaking His Father's words. Jesus often made it known that the words He spoke weren't His own, but the Father Who sent Him told Him what to say. Jesus was showing us how totally dependent He was on God. I believe we can glean that His heart was set on being obedient to God.

While making out this message, this beautiful song came to mind.

> Lord you have my heart and I will search for Yours,
> Let me be to You a sacrifice.
> Lord You have my heart and I will search for Yours,
> Jesus, take my life and lead me on.

Giving our hearts is of great importance because the one who gave us the best He has asks of us the best we have—our hearts.

Many years ago I attempted to prepare a message on the heart, and I experienced opposition from unseen forces. I wasn't as aware of spiritual hindrances (demonic opposition) then as I am now. Thank God for the authority He's given us through His Son, Jesus Christ. There is a short allegorical paragraph in the next few pages where God gave me a full understanding of this battle and how to overcome. Hallelujah!

Take hold of the following statement: "When God speaks to us, He speaks according to His divine plan for our lives." If we decide to walk in ignorance to His plans, when the revelation comes and we miss the answer, that's our fault. However, we have the audacity to hastily blame God! Shouldn't we slow down and think on bended knees? We are supposed to be in a position to understand the message and obediently do what Jesus did. In John 5:30 Jesus clearly says of Himself that He can do nothing on His own. Rather, as He hears, He judges, and His judgments are righteous because He doesn't seek His own but the will of the Father who sent Him. So we see Jesus wasn't exalting or promoting Himself at any time whatsoever. Neither was He seeking recognition. He was the Messenger with a message whose main purpose was to first direct Israel back to the Father.

The majority of us think God is complicated, but He is rather simple. Jesus made a profound statement in Matthew 18:1–5, where He told His disciples of the prerequisites for entering the kingdom of God—to become as little children. Children are trusting, and their faith is steadfast. They believe quite easily and are quick to act upon the instructions they are given without numerous questions. (I am speaking about the type of children with which I am most familiar.)

With this thought in mind, I purposed to present this message in a way that was easy to understand. I felt long, analytical excursions would defeat the whole purpose and were not necessary whatsoever. Because it is written:

> We know that we all have knowledge. Knowledge puffs up, but love edifies. (1 Corinthians 8:1b)

The latter part of this verse is desperately needed today. Grace empowers us to live sanctified lives that lead to holy living on a daily basis. Irrespective of the evil encroaching upon us, we have the victory through Jesus. He overcame the world. Saints, Satan and his principalities were defeated at the cross, once for all. We aren't facing a victorious foe. It doesn't mean we drop our guard and walk about unguarded because Jesus told us to be alert and to be watchful. Peter talks about the adversary who goes about like a roaring lion, seeking whom he may devour and to resist him in the faith.

During prayer time another day, I asked the Holy Spirit how it was possible for Jesus Christ to operate in such power, and His answer was, "Holiness unto the Lord."

I could imagine Jesus setting His will to live a sanctified life so He could fulfill the purpose for which He was born. He understood the role of the priest and what he needed to do before going into the temple to perform the priestly duties. For example, washing at the laver was compulsory. Otherwise the priest would die. Also, the priest could not touch unclean things that would defile.

Therefore, it is imperative that we make every effort to live a holy life. I know there are countless distractions. However, on the last day of account, we won't be able to give anything as an excuse. He has already seen our fruit. He stressed often that he who overcomes and endures to the end would enter into rest—living in the Spirit. This means we must adhere to the Scripture that admonishes us:

> Pursue peace with all people, and holiness, without which no one will see the Lord: looking carefully lest anyone fall short of the grace of God; lest any root of bitterness springing up cause trouble, and by this many become defiled. (Hebrews 12:14–15)

Why did the writer exhort the people to holiness? He was asking them to renew their spiritual vitality. They seemed to have been getting tired and weary.

> Therefore strengthen the hands which hang down, and the feeble knees, and make straight paths for your feet. (Hebrews 12:12–13a)

In the previous chapter of Hebrews, it was all about faith. So what was happening to the believers that they had to be reminded with so many witnesses?

Isn't it true when a plan we have fails or what we expect to happen does not occur we become discouraged and show disappointment in God? We then set about reverting to our old ways of operating in the flesh. We depend on our seeing, hearing, smelling, touching, and tasting and abandon the walk which is by faith.

In ignorance we continue to pray our little prayers according to how we think they ought to be prayed and nothing happens, so we give up! Giving up isn't the right thing to do, and furthermore, God will never answer your prayer in that adverse mind-set. We need to humble ourselves. Almighty God told us to call upon Him, and He will show us mighty things.

Consider this little allegorical story. Seeing no answer came, Doubt intervened and said, "I told you this faith thing doesn't work, and fancy denying yourself all those worldly pleasures, which you long for anyway. Why don't you go and have them right now? No one cares what you do." Being drawn into agreement, you begin to think, *That's right, why should I deny myself? Furthermore, I have lost so many friends.* Immediately the phone rings, and it's an old friend from the past offering to invite you back into the old habits. Reverential Fear enters your heart but Rebellion and Defiance say, "You are old enough to do what you like. Nobody can stop you. It's the twenty-first century, modern times—come out of your shackles!" Agreement is reached again, and you think, *It was boring anyway.* Defiance comes again, "They don't read the Bible. They don't pray. Look how happy they are, and I am so miserable! Don't you think you've been a bit silly?" Suddenly, Reverential Fear overtakes every thought, bringing a simple solution to oppose and throw out those negative thoughts. Open your mouth and shout aloud, "No, help me, Holy Spirit! I need You now!" Right at that moment, bend your knees to the Father of glory.

We also know the cornerstone of holiness unfolding—that is, to get up into the high mountains in prayer as we see in the Scripture.

> As He prayed, the appearance of His face was altered, and His robe became white and glistening. And behold, two men talked with Him, who were Moses and Elijah, who appeared in glory and spoke of His decease which He was about to accomplish at Jerusalem. But Peter and those with him were heavy with sleep; and when they were fully awake, they saw His glory and the two men who stood with Him… And a voice came out of the cloud, saying, "This is My beloved Son. Hear Him!" (Luke 9:29–32, 35)

The Trustworthy Prophetic Word

Peter was obedient to Jesus' command not to mention what they saw on the mount until after the resurrection. After Jesus' ascension Peter confirmed that he saw the glory radiating from Jesus on the holy mount. He also confirmed it to Cornelius after he arrived at Cornelius's house while preaching his salvation message in Acts 10. They were witnesses, as we see here:

> For we did not follow cunningly devised fables when we made known to you the power and coming of our Lord Jesus Christ, but were eyewitnesses of His majesty. For He received from God the Father honor and glory when such a voice came to Him from the Excellent Glory: "This is

> My beloved Son, in whom I am well pleased." And we heard this voice which came from heaven when we were with Him on the holy mountain. And so we have the prophetic word confirmed. (1 Peter 1:16–19a)

Jesus' Destiny Finalized by Supernatural Visitation

I would like to point out that Jesus knew He was going to the cross prior to this epic encounter. He repeatedly told His disciples He was going to die. Peter unknowingly went as far as to deter Him from a human perspective. However, Jesus had discernment and rightly rebuked Peter for agreeing with Satan in his cunning attempt to manipulate Jesus through Peter's ignorance.

Aspects of the Glory

There are other types of glory, like wealth and position, as spoken of by Joseph while in Egypt. However, that is not the focal point of this pursuit. I am pursuing the *Doxa* (Greek for the excellence and perfection of the divine nature)—that is, the knowledge and understanding, to know by experience this glory. Jesus understood the *Doxa* that dwelt in Him; He embraced it, knew how to activate it and live in the fullness of it while praying the intercessory prayer to the Father in John 17. The *Doxa* is the same glory He had before the foundation of the world. It is this manifestation of His glory that will reveal the love of the Father, cause the world to recognize the uniqueness of Jesus Christ in us, and bring the fullest expression of unity within the body of Christ as we love one another. This expression of God's glory *will* be known globally.

Remember, the law says that in the mouth of two or three witnesses, a matter is established. Jesus had three witnesses with Him. Peter, James, and John always appeared to be His inner circle. Jesus usually took those three on special assignments, as in the case of bringing Jairus's daughter back to life in Mark 5:37. On the way down from the mount, Jesus charged the three not to make known what they saw until He was raised from the dead. As we study the lives of these three apostles, we notice the manifestations of the glory operating through them in the form of miracles, signs and wonders, and love. In James's case, he glorified God in the form of martyrdom. King Herod saw fit to divert attention from the main cause, and James became the target at that time. It's ironic that a while after, King Herod died himself after displaying his oratory skills with pride.

The Unfolding of the Glory

What I am searching for by revelation is to be in the know about God's glory and in what given time it will come into effect. The main way it will happen is already known. We also know from the Scriptures that the wise will receive this glory (Proverbs 3:35).

In John 17:5 lies the essence of what I am looking for, and the process of how to bring into reality is stated in these two examples—Proverbs 2:1–8 and 2 Peter 2:1–8. The desire to produce the glory must become a burning desire, energized by the power of the Holy Spirit. Communing with God through prayer, praise, and worship must become a priority and passion for every born-again believer.

The body of Jesus Christ has drastically neglected prayer. Christ Jesus showed us the pinnacle of prayer on the mount and the profusion of glory that followed. That dedication and obedience created the spiritual atmosphere enabling Moses and Elijah to appear at that high point of righteous spirituality. Words were spoken securing our entrance back into oneness with Father God. Hallelujah!

We, as a chosen people, are living well below the potential of what God has provided for us. We have no idea of what we've been given, but we need to quickly become cognizant. For instance, in John 17:22 Jesus said He's given the disciples the glory, and this glory is applicable to us also who hear the gospel message, which culminates in salvation. Today the main reason why it is important to know the glory of God is because of the encroaching immoral lifestyles that are darkening the seven mountains of society. The glory of God is what should be encroaching instead. Therefore the body of Christ needs to find out how to enter into the glory because there are many benefits. The greatest benefit of all is love for one another causing the world to see God is alive. We are not impacting the world as we should, but we can if we set our hearts on God as Jesus did. "Help us, Holy Spirit, to know Jesus."

The Significance of Worship

High praises from our mouths accompanied by a two-edged sword in our hand (Psalm 149:6) should be proclaimed from the place of spiritual domain where true worship begins in the Spirit. Later this location will be revealed. We should voluntarily praise God, just like in the case of the making of incense to place before the ark of testimony. It was the perfumer who determined, by the amount of salt he used, how sweet an aroma was exuded. Therefore, the yielding of our wills magnifies the tenure of our praises. At that point we then settle our minds or make a decision to praise the Lord. It is in unity that the anointing for worship comes. In other words, the mind under the leading of the Holy Spirit enters in to pleasing the Lord. Where reverential submission or obedience is agreed upon by the individual to praise, there comes a state of quietness in his soul. The Holy Spirit then releases the anointing to worship. With that impartation, the worshipers worshiping in spirit and truth create a holy habitation to enthrone King Jesus.

Here the Scripture would be fulfilled where Jesus said, "We worship in spirit and truth." At that point, an act of the Spirit is in operation, no more yielding the will but a moving of the Spirit. It is an effortless offering from spirit to Spirit in adoration, love, and intimacy. Through observation it has been noticed that the worship normally stops just after entering in. But there is a "beyond" where the real tenderness exists, where your spirit becomes still. In reaching this place, it is necessary to establish a holy intimacy with God so He can speak. Communion is prolonged as we worship, singing new songs and melodies in tongues (or as is said in the nature of couples in love, with starry eyes they speak sweet nothings to each other). Here, revelation of Him unfolds wave after wave. His billows rush over us. Wave upon wave is encountered as described in Psalm 42:7. The word from the Spirit for the body of Christ today is: *intimacy, be still and know*. This then, my friend, brings in the glory. True repentance, gratitude, thanksgiving, and love are demonstrated out of the ocean of agape love. Later on you will discover the pathway I found to enter God's presence daily after mining in John 6:63 for twenty-one years.

I've been thinking, and it appears to me that the Body of Christ is like a tender plant in this area, and it's time for it to be nurtured into maturity. Would a miracle like the former and latter rain in the first month according to Joel 2:23 need to take place for this type of worship to bear fruit all over the earth? Or would sudden persecution be required? Whatever the pathway, the Father would be pleased by this kind of worship.

I believe heaven's atmosphere is glory. Heaven came down to you through His Son, Jesus Christ. Wherever Jesus went, He brought change or affected someone's life. I believe this is in motion presently by those saints who have the revelation that the only way for the glory to come is to crucify the flesh. Next, yield your soul so the reality can burst forth from our hearts and the glory will come out of us. When the alabaster box was broken, it sent forth a sweet perfume. Heaven's treasure is in earthen vessels, according to 2 Corinthians 4:7—that is, the body of Christ. Holy Spirit, please teach us how to die to self. Father, we want to see Your glory today!

Prayer and Worship Birth New Songs

I neither write lyrics nor compose songs. As I made known earlier in these writings, prayer wasn't a priority in my life. Now I will tell you of the power in prayer and worship that births new songs beyond the lampstand. Before these encounters, it was rather like having to go to the dentist with the thought, *I hope they are extra careful with me.* You know that misperceived fear I'm talking about, believing in some mishap? If you could avoid going that route, you would. Yet it's amazing to know that most of the time, our apprehension as to what may happen only gives the mind an opportunity to play tricks, telling you of all the horrors that await you that never actually happen. That is when the twin spirits of flight and fright show up.

Prayer was my fear phobia dominated by flight and fright. Anyway, I never expected that I would have to face my phobia. How did that come about? When you helplessly watch all you held dear burn down or walk out the door and people's talk turns to whispers as you pass by, where can you find the courage to hold your head up? What do you do when the friends you nourished by pouring your life into them suddenly become too busy to answer your call? Yes, you thought you had friends, and you get a sudden shock, realizing you're all alone. You suddenly discover the reality of silence—no one to talk to. Thinking becomes your sole vocation as you try to summarize your life, desperately trying to find an answer as to what went wrong. Your days of contemplation turn to weeks of despair without any sign of improvement. The simple involuntary action of maintaining your daily appearance doesn't enter into your thinking process. You cannot understand why others are avoiding you. Neither are you able to understand why you're staying in bed all day. The daily social and cultural modes of existence have gone deep into the sediments of the mind and been forgotten; you have come to the end of the yourself.

In that state of mind, all inhibitions are removed because the acceptable social norms are inaccessible. Therefore, offenses are far removed, and the behaviors of others toward you are meaningless. It doesn't enter the mind that you're in another world beyond flesh and soul. The only evidence that life exists is the ongoing pain and the flicker of light deep down in the ravine of the mind. Every so often it flickers, illuminating the mind with the thought that there must be purpose to life. Yet out of the darkest gloom comes the greatest hope and glory. It is similar to when John was on the Isle of Patmos on the Lord's Day. The adverse trials necessitated him being in the Spirit, which enabled him to see a door opened in heaven noted in Revelation 4:1. Pause and think of that! The world thought they were getting rid of John, not knowing they had executed God's plan to separate him from the hustle and bustle to an obscure place to show eschatological revelations of Jesus Christ.

Jesus was heading toward his crucifixion when reflections of inner beauty manifested through Him on the mount. In that moment of glory, reassurance came by way of Moses and Elijah. Like Isaiah, Jesus, and John, the body of Christ is moving in the same direction by the shaping of global circumstances.

Israel was in a crisis after the death of king Uzziah. Despair and darkness enveloped the people when Isaiah made that renowned cry,

> I saw also the Lord sitting upon a throne, high and lifted up, and his train filled the temple. Above it stood seraphim; each one had six wings: with two he covered his face, with two he covered

> his feet, and with two he flew. And one cried to another and said: "Holy, holy, holy is the LORD of hosts; the whole earth is full of his glory!" And the posts of the door were shaken by the voice of who cried out, and the house was filled with smoke. (Isaiah 6:1b–4)

In verse 3, the prophet speaks of the *Lord* of hosts, meaning a captain of a vast army. Does that mean a spiritual battle will be fought to keep the Enemy away to allow the saints time to enter into the glory? Is it in the midst of persecution that this seeking after God would forge the ability to manifest the glory? Though Satan was defeated at the cross, none of his power was taken.

As prophesied by the prophet Isaiah, "All flesh together shall see the glory of the Lord."

> And the glory of the LORD shall be revealed, and all flesh shall see it together: for the mouth of the LORD hath spoken it. (Isaiah 40:5)

What I am gleaning so far is that this glory will not become a reality if we persist in walking in disobedience to God's commands. You can clearly see that disobedience was the devastating obstruction to the spreading of the glory of God. Isn't disobedience still a thorn in our sides today? How about rebellion? What of witchcraft? Neither will He command a blessing if we continue in disunity. You may think He's using these Scriptures too many times. What? That's what I used to think until I took note of how often God reminded Moses to make sure he built the tabernacle as it was shown to him on the mount.

It appears to me that the body of Christ is still looking on the outward appearance of man and either forgets or doesn't grasp that unity is in the Spirit.

> There is one body and one Spirit, just as you were called in one hope of your calling; one Lord, one faith, one baptism; one God and Father of all, who is above all, and through all, and in you all. But to each one of us grace was given according to the measure of Christ's gift. (Ephesians 4:4–7)

We could then confidently say that obedience to His word of loving one another is the key to realizing the glory. We could also consider this sequence to entering the glory.

1. Having knowledge of the glory.
2. Unity comes by understanding the purpose of the glory.
3. We must become one with Father, Son, Holy Spirit, and body.
4. We must have awareness of the unity; like light attracts light and a sunflower bends to the sun, so the world will see and recognize the Spirit of Christ in us—God's love.

There are sequences of this type of progression in Scripture to realize God's purpose for humanity. Just like learning the discipline of becoming a great basketball player. In the early stages the basics are taught—its history and rules of the game. Later on you progress to the basic movements and positions and so forth to finally getting the ball in the net time after time—the all-important goal.

It is no different here in the acquisition of wisdom and godliness. In these two examples cited, a sequence should be discovered in each that holds true to coming into a deeper relationship with almighty God and the Lord Jesus Christ:

a. The acquisition of wisdom as seen in Proverbs 2:1–7. Applying all your powers to the quest of it. Cry out for insight, and raise your voice for the understanding of it. It would be worthwhile to read the Scripture slowly.

   My son, if you receive my words, And treasure my commands within you, So that you incline your ear to wisdom, And apply your heart to understanding; Yes, if you cry out for discernment, And lift up your voice for understanding, If you seek her as silver, And search for her as for hidden treasures; Then you will understand the fear of the LORD, And find the knowledge of God. For the LORD gives wisdom; From His mouth come knowledge and understanding; He stores up sound wisdom for the upright; He is a shield to those who walk uprightly. (Proverbs 2:1–7)

b. This must be considered. Peter, of all the apostles, is telling us what God has bestowed upon us—that is, all things suited to life and godliness. He called us by and to His own glory and excellence. Remember Peter who denied the Lord Jesus three times? There's nothing richer than when the grace of God transforms a life. Old things are sure to pass away. This is the Peter who emerged out of the upper room, who preached a sermon and three thousand people responded to the message of salvation.

> As His divine power has given to us all things that pertain to life and godliness, through the knowledge of Him who called us by glory and virtue, by which have been given to us exceedingly great and precious promises, that through these you may be partakers of the divine nature, having escaped the corruption that is in the world through lust. (2 Peter 1:3–8)

Fruitful Growth in the Faith

> But also for this very reason, giving all diligence, add to your faith virtue, to virtue knowledge, to knowledge self-control, to self-control perseverance, to perseverance godliness, to godliness brotherly kindness, and to brotherly kindness love. For if these things are yours and abound, you will be neither barren nor unfruitful in the knowledge of our Lord Jesus Christ. (2 Peter 1:5–8)

It is with this diligence and fervency in prayer that the knowledge of the glory would become known. In other words, our thinking must accelerate to enable us to take that quantum leap into spiritual bliss. "Come up hither!" is the call.

"Father, let Your glory be known and produced in us today to fulfill Your Word to give You glory, in Jesus' name." This is only scratching the surface of the radiance, splendor, and majesty of this topic.

For the prophetic word about the glory to be fulfilled, and it will (Isaiah 55:11), for man's pitiful condition to change from flesh to soul to spirit and for what Jesus prayed to be answered, mustn't mankind become aware of his helplessness without God Almighty? When that anguished state is reached, God will hear the cry for help as it was for Israel in Egypt. At that point, God is the answer, deliverance is imminent, and we will see His glory.

Water Sparkling like Crystals

In the process of time, I have been seeking revelation knowledge so I could understand more clearly the marvelous manifestations He performed through me relating to His glory over the years. Near the end of January 2001, I had a beautiful dream where I saw the water in Niagara Falls sparkling like crystals a little ways up, just before it cascades over the falls. The volume of sparkling waters rose above the bank and flooded the city. It did no harm to the land but rather was softening it. According to my interpretation, I took it as a symbol of the Holy Spirit flooding the land, preparing it for seed sowing. I began to write on February 18, 2001, as information came from the Spirit of God. I constantly sought the Lord for understanding of the glory because it was extremely important to me since my time in Bible college.

It appears to me as if only a small number of saints really know of the glory of God and what to do to make its manifestation a reality. However, many have entered into a position of the hope of the glory as stated in Colossians 1:27 through the only way possible, and that is accepting Jesus Christ as Lord and Savior. If we had the knowledge, would the body of Christ be in unity today? Isn't that one of the things the glory produces? Isn't it then the Lord would command the blessings? It may be the majority of us say it quite often as a mere cliché. However, the tides of evil are swiftly sweeping through the seven mountains of society. Now is the time for us to know and experience the glory of God.

In the distant past, the God of Abraham, Isaac, and Jacob told Moses that His glory will fill the whole earth. Had there been unity, or one heart, when the twelve came back from their successful scouting of the Promised Land, I believe God would have manifested His glory to all Israel that day. Instead, He declared that as truly as He lived, His glory would fill the whole earth.

On that occasion, after scouting the land, it never took place. I would say it was hindered by the reason for Adam's downfall and by what is still hindering us today—disobedience. However, know for certain it shall surely come to pass. I take this position, seeing God said it and I believe it. Yet as extravagant, abundant, and overflowing as His glory is, obedience is absolutely necessary in keeping our desire focused to enter into the fullness of the glory of God. Moses, the master deliverer of the nation of Israel in his exploits through God in Egypt working signs, wonders, and miracles, had one quest—his desire to see God's glory according to Exodus 33:18. The glory is what emits from God Himself. It is what surrounds, radiates, or exudes from Him—a visible presence of Him.

I would say that wherever the glory is, God was and is there, present in the sense of His omnipresent ability. God Himself is within the glory, within the unapproachable light. For example, the haze around the sun isn't the sun but what it emits. Seeing the haze causes one to look deeper at the sun but only for a moment because there is a danger. Looking directly at the sun for more than a moment immediately causes a black dot effect in the eye. Here is a profound gratification. Getting to know the glory is an elevation or ascension of thought to a higher plane. The thinking is transported beyond the confines of earth's limitations and boundaries of gravity or magnetic attraction or the composition of earth, water, and space. It is an example of rarified illumination or speed of thought, or instantaneous occurrence, or as one writer puts it, in the twinkling of an eye. It causes spontaneous worship induced by the Holy Spirit. Ponder this: He left His home in glory.

Let's pause and think of this now. Our atmosphere is air; heaven's atmosphere is glory. To put it another way, heaven came down to you through the Son. Our senses cannot comprehend such statements without revelation or visitation. Therefore, the end-time call to Zion is to come up here, to know. Historic literature documented that the Romans wanted to rid themselves of the disciples of Jesus Christ. John was high on the list. It is said they tried to destroy him by throwing him alive into a cauldron of hot boiling oil but to no avail. Due to their ineffectiveness, they banished him to the Isle of Patmos. John himself testified of his presence in the isle of Patmos and the reason why he was there in Revelation 1:9.

He talked about being in the Spirit on the Lord's Day; every day is the Lord's. From that expression one could glean that seeing God's glory would not be accomplished from the natural aspect of things but rather from the spiritual dimension by knowing how to be in the Spirit. While in the Spirit, John heard the call to "come up here" into the realm of glory. In these writings you will be shown the way of what Jesus meant in John 14:6.

Take note of the similarity of these two texts when minds and hearts are united in cause or purpose.

Praising and Thanking the Lord

> Indeed it came to pass, when the trumpeters and singers were as one, to make one sound to be heard in praising and thanking the Lord, and when they lifted up their voice with the trumpets and cymbals and instruments of music, and praised the Lord, saying: "For He is good, For His mercy endures forever," that the house, the house of the Lord, was filled with a cloud, so that the priest could not continue ministering because of the cloud; for the glory of the Lord filled the house of God. (2 Chronicles 5:13–14)

The Upper Room Prayer Meeting

> These all continued with one accord in prayer and supplication, with the women and Mary the mother of Jesus, and with His brothers… When the Day of Pentecost had fully come, they were all with one accord in one place. And suddenly there came a sound from heaven, as of a rushing

> mighty wind, and it filled the whole house where they were sitting. Then there appeared to them divided tongues, as of fire, and one sat upon each of them. And they were all filled with the Holy Spirit and began to speak with other tongues, as the Spirit gave them utterance. (Acts 1:14, 2:1–4)

God Is Seeking an Obedient Generation

God is seeking obedient generation. Could this be the generation? It must be a generation with a desire to love the Lord Jesus wholeheartedly. That's the heart of Jesus. You could understand why this manifestation of the glory burst forth so profusely on the mount through Jesus only. Jesus' life was one of total obedience to His Father. His obedience culminated in Him being glorified and exalted to the highest place at the right hand of God the Father and given a name that is above every other name. In the following Scripture, Jesus spoke of giving them the glory, and that same glory extended beyond the twelve disciples to anyone who believes in Him through their witness, and so it continues.

> I do not pray for these alone, but also for those who will believe in Me through their word; that they all may be one, as You, Father, are in Me, and I in You; that they also may be one in Us, that the world may believe that You sent Me. And the glory which You gave Me I have given them, that they may be one just as We are one: I in them, and You in Me; that they may be made perfect in one, and that the world may know that You have sent

> Me, and have loved them as You have loved Me.
> (John 17: 20–23)

We will examine the overwhelming beauty of God personified through Jesus Christ in this statement later. I have given them the glory.

FOLLOWING A STREAM—GOD'S DIVINE ORDER

Through careful observation of looking at biblical patterns of individuals, God has chosen significant figureheads from Abram through to Saul of Tarsus. We see their way was not one strewn with roses and carnations or lilies and orchids. They had to make life-changing decisions. Saul, who became Paul, went so far as to say he would encounter woe if he didn't preach the gospel.

For some strange reason, we of the modern era think the call of God on certain individuals today should feel like a cool, refreshing breeze on a hot summer's day. Friends, do not be deceived. If the price were reduced, the goods (anointing, tangible presence) would lose their value.

Looking at some of the difficulties they had to overcome, if we were to really delve into their experiences (because of the stock of which we are part of Gentile nations—foolish nations in relation to divine things, which is the greater part of the body of Christ) we would possibly find ourselves in surreal moments similar to what affected a nation recently.

Those forerunners followed an order or pattern they called "the Way" and with it manifestations of the glory of God were, it seems, a normal occurrence. We of the modern church need to get back to the old pathway of the divine order of "consecrated, Lord, to Thee." It literally means you are no longer your own. You are bought with a price—the precious blood of Jesus Christ. The process to get to that honorary state I will pick up in a different book. Father God desires for us to spend more time with Him. If we respond, we will walk by revelation of Him that leads us to life and peace and not by suppositions. These are the Devil's pathways (broad and wide) that lead to heartaches, pain, anguish, and untimely death!

As I am writing, the presence of God is all around me as a witness to the truth. While we are in this area, we will briefly touch on sanctification also. This is a requirement or process to holiness for proceeding to Him in the most holy place. The specially prepared anointing oil sanctified even the earthly tabernacle. This oil was a preparation for the visitation of almighty God, who then sanctified the tabernacle a second time by His glory, resulting in everything associated with the tabernacle, both man and articles, being soaked, saturated, and permeated in Him. Hallelujah! Now if we stay in that sanctified state, read carefully what God said He would do in the daily offerings.

> Now this *is* what you shall offer on the altar: two lambs of the first year, day by day continually. One lamb you shall offer in the morning, and the

> other lamb you shall offer at twilight. With the one lamb shall be one-tenth *of an ephah* of flour mixed with one-fourth of a hin of pressed oil, and one-fourth of a hin of wine *as* a drink offering. And the other lamb you shall offer at twilight; and you shall offer with it the grain offering and the drink offering, as in the morning, for a sweet aroma, an offering made by fire to the Lord. *This shall be* a continual burnt offering throughout your generations *at* the door of the tabernacle of meeting before the Lord, where I will meet you to speak with you. And there I will meet with the children of Israel, and *the tabernacle* shall be sanctified by My glory. So I will consecrate the tabernacle of meeting and the altar. I will also consecrate both Aaron and his sons to minister to Me as priests. I will dwell among the children of Israel and will be their God. And they shall know that I *am* the Lord their God, who brought them up out of the land of Egypt, that I may dwell among them. I *am* the Lord their God. (Exodus 29:38–46)

Read what Jesus said and did for us and the essence of His Word.

> Sanctify them by Your truth. Your word is truth.... And for their sakes I sanctify Myself, that they also may be sanctified by the truth. (John 17:17, 19)

> It is the Spirit who gives life; the flesh profits nothing. The words that I speak to you are spirit, and they are life. (John 6:63)

Another area I believe we have not given much attention to, and therefore can't get into a flow with, is seeing the significance of strategically positioning the tribes around the tabernacle. They were protecting the tabernacle from outside intruders and learning how to hear and dwell in God's presence. This was for moving out from His holy presence and then spreading out in all four directions—north, south, east, and west, literally taking dominion in a righteous way. He is not a containing God but one who likes the increase of His glory. Therefore the church has missed the purpose or misunderstood Scripture about the glory. Perhaps somewhere along its controversial, meandering pathway, someone misunderstood the revelation and kept the church contained in its tabernacle seclusion, hidden among the tribes. Like the king hiding among his army propagating defeatist rhetoric to a beleaguered army, we are not able. Isn't it ironic that the spirit of the ten showed its ugly head again as "we aren't able"? Wouldn't you say the church is in that cowering position today? Let's get real and change this global mind-set!

Still, praise is to our God! He always had a warrior or warriors on the fringes—seen yet hidden. "I have seven thousand who have not bent the knee to Baal," as was said to Elijah. Through Him, with one word spoken or one stroke of a pen, what seemed like certain defeat is miraculously turned to undaunted victory. We see this being lived out in the life of David, the anointed shepherd king. The modern church was birthed out of that cowering mentality where evangelism is seen as if it is only for the missionaries and radicals. Let me assure you by my testimonies that everything is available for all born-again believers today! It is said we overcome the world by our faith. Each church is supposed to take the ground based upon its jurisdiction. With so many churches around today, there should easily be an overlapping from church to church or shore to shore.

There is a King upon a throne, and His realm has no limits. He is the Alpha and Omega. What is relevant for today? How could we now make amends? From what has been said, does it seem we now need to more seriously consider our walk representing the Most High God? He is the God who said, "Go!" He has not changed! If your church is only a ten-by-ten building, the mentality of the group should be to pack the place out, to train and then go with boldness to perform miracles; to enforce righteous justice among the judges in their jurisdictions! Strategy number one is prayer. It is the scepter extended by the King to every home by every saint in his or her locality. Every house in the city would be constantly covered with prayer. One will put a thousand to flight and two will put ten thousand to flight holds true. A plan was given back in 1997 to divide the city into four sections: north, south, east, and west, symbolic of the four rivers in the garden, flowing its route to the sea. Water flows from top to bottom or high point to low point, which meant Eden was a high place. A careful look at the text reveals the source of the flow started in Eden, a higher point, and flowed into the garden where it parted into four rivers—Pishon, Gihon, Hiddekel, and Euphrates.

> Now a river went out of Eden to water the garden, and from there it parted and became four riverheads. The name of the first is Pishon; it is

> the one which skirts the whole land of Havilah, where there is gold. And the gold of that land is good. Bdellium and the onyx stone are there. The name of the second river is Gihon; it is the one which goes around the whole land of Cush. The name of the third river is Hiddekel it is the one which goes toward the east of Assyria. The fourth river is the Euphrates. (Genesis 2:10–14)

Can you see the mist coming down from the mountain or the dew from Mount Hermon symbolic of the anointing? The churches in each sector would take that territory. Then all would come together on a quarterly basis and give a progress report of the advancing. Can you see this being implemented throughout each city and then the nations? With this there are two keys: intercessory prayer and worship. The former is the major tool or key to open the city, nation, and people groups locked by darkness. The latter will follow to invade with the Holy Spirit as the singers sing and the musicians play in harmony, and the glory will come in as a testimony. Have you noticed of late that the word spoken seems to be of little worth? God, it seems, must now show up with a stretched-out arm as in the days of old for the hardened and seared consciences to yield to the call to repent!

God's Steadfastness with Abraham

God's plan and purpose will come to pass even though we mess up. When His time (Kairos) is ripe, irrespective of the situation we are in, the demand will be placed on us as it was in the case of Abram.

> When Abram was ninety-nine years old, the LORD appeared to Abram and said to him, "I am Almighty God; walk before Me and be blameless. And I will make My covenant between Me and you, and will multiply you exceedingly." (Genesis 17:1–2)

He came and disarmed Abram of all his preconceived thoughts of what God would or would not do. Remember, Abram and Sara reasoned in their decision (no revelation—valley mentality) to have a son their way. Maybe we could argue that Sara had reason to convince Abram to exclude her from the child-bearing process because her name wasn't specifically mentioned in the discourse between the Lord God and Abram. Sara, considering she was past the age for bearing children, possibly concluded the female would have to be someone else. We also need to consider that Sara respected Abram. Therefore if Abram told her the Lord God said there would be a child, she believed him. Sara, in her desire to see the word of God manifest, was eventually given a third-party idea. It is often this type of idea or thought that causes marriages and relationships to take a turn for the worse, as it was in this case. I am talking about the intervention of Satan. It is my belief that Satan put that idea into Sara's thoughts to make such a suggestion to Abram. Neither was Abram guiltless. He dwelt on the idea until it manifested. I am saying this—Abram forgot to build an altar like he did on previous occasions. In the neglect, the Lord God wasn't consulted, and Satan's appeal to the flesh succeeded. After all that, God came and did what Abram never expected, and in so doing, Abram caught the purpose of God. He was showing Abram that He, almighty God, could be trusted. He is faithful to His word.

Almighty God, communing with Abraham, said,

> After these things the word of the LORD came to Abram in a vision, saying, "Do not be afraid, Abram. I am your shield, your exceedingly great reward." But Abram said, "Lord GOD, what will You give me, seeing I go childless, and the heir of my house is Eliezer of Damascus?" Then Abram said, "Look, You have given me no offspring; indeed one born in my house is my heir!" And behold, the word of the LORD came to him, saying, "This one shall not be your heir, but one who will come from your own body shall be your heir." Then He brought him outside and said, "Look now toward heaven, and count the stars if you are able to number them." And He said to him, "So shall your descendants be." And he believed in the LORD, and He accounted it to him for righteousness. (Genesis 15:1–6)

The culmination of this trust developed in Abraham toward almighty God was lovingly performed in the sacrificing of Isaac, the promised son. Abraham developed that trust due to almighty God's gentle admonition after the miscommunication that brought about the birth of Ishmael. It wasn't God's purpose that caused the birth of Ishmael but rather human reasoning. As an intercessor, this is my belief. Abraham did not pray to ask for God's guidance. In other situations where he sought God, the Bible says he built an altar. Nowhere during this incident is it recorded he built an altar to the Lord. Yet in Genesis 17:1, almighty God told him to walk before Him and be perfect. God's gentleness is overwhelming as we see David echoing similar praise to almighty God in Psalm 18:35.

Therefore, after that demonstration of understanding and reprieve toward Abraham, almighty God changed Abram's name to Abraham. The meaning of the new name was Father of a Great Multitude or Exalted Father.

I believe Abraham's love and trust in almighty God increased beyond description. I could imagine Abraham saying that anything God required of him, he would do it. The test came later when almighty God asked Abraham to sacrifice the promised son, Isaac. The Scriptures give no indication of any hesitation on Abraham's part. Rather, there was willing obedience, even when Isaac asked his father where the lamb was. Abraham's faith and confidence in almighty God providing the lamb was mentioned to his son, Isaac.

The amazing encounter of the entire incident that took place on Mount Moriah, where Abraham was about to slay his son, the ultimate intervention by Almighty God, and providing the sacrificial lamb in place of Isaac can be read in Genesis 22:1–18.

Abraham's Faith in Almighty God

That sacrificial act proved Abraham's faith in almighty God had matured. God's end result is to bless! Let me insert this statement here: Don't expect to come into the abundance of God's blessings without first being tested or proven! Wake up, Zion! It may be well worth reading Deuteronomy 8. There's a statement there regarding the latter end. I believe He was hinting about it to Israel then and also to whosoever. Well, a similar demand is being placed upon Abraham's in-grafted children of Zion to come out of the valley (the world's way of doing things) and get up into the high mountains of revelation into the unfolding of a divine lifestyle. The prophets spoke of the highway that is the lifting up of a standard. Jesus has said that's how His church would be built, upon revelation of the Rock, who is Jesus. Peter spoke of us being called to glory and virtue. It was in that sanctified state, and when unison of worship was offered to the Lord, that the cloud appeared as the covering of His presence. Somewhere in the midst all that I hear, "*Holiness unto the Lord*!"

Folks, we are well beyond the time of watching from the wings to see what happens next. Be careful not to agree with the spirit of Jezebel who operates this way, watching from afar off to see where she can make trouble. It is time for the intimacy of our head resting on His chest as in the case of John being able to hear the heartbeat of his Lord, or like Mary sitting at the feet of her Master. Presently, where does your head rest, and what are your ears hearing and at whose feet are you sitting? This is not a group thing. Rather, a one-on-one relationship. Only your spirit man can enter the holy of holies. The flesh must be offered as a sacrifice and the soul yielded. From that encounter or experience, the group is then formed and the unified conversation would be about their Lord. Can you perceive for one moment that divine love would be flowing among the saints? If that would be the case, do you think the world would notice? I believe so.

We must live free from sin and guilt, staying anointed, and walking in obedience by embracing the cross and going beyond the flesh into the realm of the spirit. The glory of God would become a lifestyle by constancy in worship, by knowing and practicing God's way into the holy of holies. Does one think for a moment that His kingdom would expand through an overwhelming influx of souls? Does one think there is a price to be paid for all this? Would we be willing to pay the price? When a man is hungry for natural food, he would pay any price to obtain it. Esau demonstrated the natural power of hunger. The Master said, "Blessed are those who hunger and thirst after righteousness." If you were part of the latter, you also would pay any price to be close to your Lord, desirous to be part of His inner circle. Presently, I wonder what position the Body of Christ occupies.

Fellow saints, I believe we must choose the inner circle lifestyle because it's attainable. The days are coming when we will wish we had pressed in a little deeper when the Holy Spirit was prompting us. Instead, we risk ignoring Him and wasting precious time watching cunningly devised distractions dubbed as entertainment.

What inexpressible love we would encounter! The request made by Jesus to His Father on behalf of the "they" (those God points to the Son as Savior) is so deep it calls for some very serious meditation by many of the "they" out there! This kind of love has no barriers. It transcends time and space and takes you into the eternity of the eternities. When your meditation ends, you may find yourself resting in the arms of love because of the desire for your Lord.

There are some restless saints who are weary of the form. They want reality. They want the Lord Jesus Christ in all His fullness. This passion has been placed in them, and they must find their

Lover, as it was in the case of the Shulamite and Mary. Are you faint with love for Him? Are you lovesick? Do you have a magnificent obsession? Then you must seek your Jesus encounter.

A sanctified lifestyle prepares the entrance into almighty God's presence. As the singers and musicians made one sound in singing, "For He is good; for His mercy endures forever," then the house was filled with a cloud, even the house of the Lord, so that the priests could not stand to minister by reason of the glory of God that filled the house of the Lord. Then what about you, the living temple? What type of cloud are you allowing to enter your temple? Only you know the answer.

MY TRIP TO ISRAEL

It was foretold many years ago that I would visit the land of Israel. I didn't rush out and buy a plane ticket and dash off to Israel. At that time in my walk with the Lord, I had learned from experience to wait for more confirmation through the spoken word. There was much excitement in my heart at the thought of going to Israel and placing my feet on the soil. It meant much to me. Let me share with you why.

As a young boy in the islands, I grew up with my grandparents. Our parents had immigrated to the United Kingdom, so we were left with our grandparents taking care of us. Though I was young, less than five years old at the time, I felt my mother should have stayed with me. My little world crashed in. I remember holding onto my mother's dress with a tight grip. It was difficult to undo my little fingers locked onto her dress. You could imagine the crying I did, saying, "Mammy, don't go." She still talks about it today! I have forgiven her. She is a precious lady and the best mother in the entire world. I pray God's presence and power to sustain her daily.

They had gone, and my little world was devastated. I was lost in a vast world of uncertainties. I loved my grandmother. She was a gentle woman, and I stuck closely to her. She would give me little things to do. I remember one particular task she had me do was crushing rock salt in a mortar with a pestle. I remembered pounding the salt inside the mortar with the pestle until the salt was extremely fine. That activity became a crucial metaphor for me while I was developing and writing *Fervent Prayer Releases the Anointing*. That pounding action gave me understanding of the instruction God gave to Moses about how to finely crush the incense to place before Him. In a later chapter, we will see the importance of crushing to bring out the fragrance of the compound. A good example of this is found in Exodus 30 regarding intercessory worship.

The story I want to bring forth is how I got involved with the Jewish nation from this time in the Islands. One morning before going to school, I was reading the Bible. My grandmother had a Bible, which I used. I was little, but I loved to read (and still do). I remembered distinctly which book I was reading. It was the book of Exodus. And while I was reading, I got caught up in the drama and could feel the pain the people in the book were feeling. It was too emotional for me, and not really understanding what was happening to the people, I went and asked my grandmother who the people were that the book was talking about. She said it was the Israelites, but they were not God's people anymore. What she said to me that morning—that they were not God's people anymore—was too traumatic for my little mind. I was brokenhearted. I couldn't fathom what she said. From that moment, instantly, their pain and anguish overwhelmed me and became mine. From that morning, something got locked into my spirit that never got released until January 10, 1994. The release came after I returned from San Diego where the Jewish sister had told me about her encounter with Jesus as the Messiah (more about this later).

On the same day I returned to London, England, the Lord asked me this question, "What did Moses' rod do to the Egyptians' rods?" The answer to this question and the outcome is in the following chapter.

My life was one of being able to identify with the Jews. I could feel their pain and understand the anti-Semitism and all the other undesirable things they had suffered. It wasn't easy to hear the replacement theology, and however I tried to understand how their thought processes were germinated, I could not come to believe that God had cast His people away. The Deliverer will come out of Zion at the appointed time. The watchmen on the walls in Isaiah 62 will eventually pray the Holy Spirit–induced prayer, and the God of Abraham, Isaac, and Jacob will respond. It is for that reason the church needs to add all night prayer to their itinerary. You see, dear reader, the apostle Paul had to get a revelation concerning Israel's salvation to comfort his heart after his magnum opus: Romans.

> There is therefore now no condemnation to those who are in Christ Jesus, who do not walk according to the flesh, but according to the Spirit. (Romans 8:1)

Immediately after, in Romans 9, he sank back into, "Wait a minute! What about my people?" His prayerful petition began for an answer when he let us know, "Brethren (Gentiles, you to whom I'm called to minister salvation), I'm happy now because God hasn't cast away His people." One could detect a change in his epistles; there was a seemingly effortless flow in his writing style. About five years later, we are blessed with the revelatory book of Ephesians laying out the blueprint for a thriving, Holy Spirit–led church or body of Christ.

The Deliverer will come, who will turn away ungodliness in Jacob. To continue, as the years roll by, one of my goals was to visit all the synagogues in London, both Messianic and Orthodox. I accomplished that goal. One of the benefits of attending their services is that they all follow the same annual reading of the scroll. Irrespective of which synagogue you may visit, you will recognize identical pattern of worship, and it's global. It causes me to wonder why the Gentiles don't adopt the same system. I find the system in the synagogue to be more harmonious because of the annual cycle through the Scriptures.

Just my inquisitiveness, for instance, has anyone looked at Leviticus 23 and followed the pattern outlined? In it I see Jesus' ministry as humanity's road map. Reading through the gospels, a pattern can be seen. What I'm proposing is the removal of confusion from the body of Christ—a more-cohesive way of gathering to worship with Him at the center. There tends to be a touch of the days of the book of Judges occurring among us right now.

Anyway, over the years I've studied the history since the destruction of the temple in AD 70. Wherever the Jews were dispersed, the nations prospered. The Scripture to which the statement relates is:

> Thus says the Lord, your Redeemer, The Holy One of Israel: "I am the Lord your God, Who teaches you to profit, Who leads you by the way you should go." (Isaiah 48:17)

That, in and of itself, eventually became a problem. Instead of the resident nation showing appreciation, jealousy, vindictiveness, and hatred ensued. We know that no development where there's disagreement is one sided. Therefore I can't understand why a particular group in those days would burn the synagogues. In the area of London where I lived, that was common. I remember listening to a particular group who wore big boots; their heads were shaved, and they were chanting anti-Jewish slogans. In those days, of course, I didn't understand why they would be saying such things. They seemed so young and innocent, yet their vocabulary was amazing. Their message projected what they were led to believe. Maybe I only saw the opposition and couldn't understand why they would be saying those things.

I could tell where the Jews lived. Their dwelling places stood out. The area had a pleasant atmosphere and was kept in good condition. In addition, they had really beautiful homes in the best part of London. Whenever we wanted to look at homes to get ideas of what a dream home should look like, where did we look? You got it! We would drive through those areas of Southgate, Golders Green, and Muswell Hill. The houses were exceptionally beautiful, with well-kept, manicured gardens.

We also shopped in their retail stores due to the kosher products. The Jews also owned jewelry stores in the city. They were excellent businesspeople in relation to banking also. Whatever they did prospered! My uncle was an excellent interior decorator. I rated him one of the best in the city of London. I felt he was so good because he used to decorate their homes. I could go on endlessly about the benefits they provided wherever they went through associating with them. This richness of activity in whatever they do brings to mind what Moses said to all Israel.

> For you are a holy people to the Lord your God; the Lord your God has chosen you to be a people for Himself, a special treasure above all the peoples on the face of the earth. The Lord did not set His love on you nor choose you because you were more in number than any other people, for you were the least of all peoples; but because the Lord loves you, and because He would keep the oath which He swore to your fathers, the Lord has brought you out with a mighty hand, and redeemed you from the house of bondage, from the hand of Pharaoh king of Egypt. (Deuteronomy 7:6–8)

Of course, persecution was inevitable.

I had no problem identifying with the Jewish people to the extent I even attended one of their colleges to learn the Hebrew language so I could participate in the Sabbath services. The synagogue I attended most was a progressive one in Stamford Hill, North London. The cantor there sang like an angel. Amidst all that was taking place, visiting all the synagogues and so forth, I knew one day I would visit Israel.

I was trying to establish an identity that was difficult due to my ethnic background, yet I felt comfortable among the Jews. I knew it was due to that Jewish disposition that got locked in my mind when I asked my grandmother the question of who the people were in the book of Exodus. I felt out of place in society even though I was brilliant as a telecommunications technician. As time unfolded, I eventually came to America on a missionary assignment to the Niagara Falls area. It was due to a dream I saw the year before that I came. I knew the scene wasn't my home country. My prayer was, "If You want me to be involved in what You showed me, please get me to the location." I arrived in the area I was shown in the dream on April 12, 1997. It was in America that the second word came that I would visit Israel. This was my confirmation.

I continued my all-night prayer sessions, as that was a Friday night weekly event back in UK. New songs would be given to me during my prayer time. One such song was Psalm 65:1–2 with accompanying melody.

> Praise is awaiting You, O God, in Zion; And to You the vow shall be performed. O You who hear prayer, To You all flesh will come. (Psalm 65:1–2)

As I can play the guitar somewhat, I would add the chords to the tune I heard—beautiful. God is absolutely magnificent. There were many new songs. I never sat down and worked out the lyrics; they just came from the Spirit. Other beautiful songs were Psalms 19, 42, 45, 122, and 148. Let me extract Psalm 122 from the above. This was unique and set the tone for what is to follow.

On June 22, 2004, after returning home from work as a computer technician, I was reciting Psalm 122 verbatim with my guitar resting on my lap. The next thing I knew, I was playing and singing it simultaneously. After that I played it verbatim because the melody stuck in my memory. Realizing what was happening, I said, "Jesus, I believe You want me to sing this song to you going through the gates of Jerusalem." I believed it, so I made the statement. Get ready for what I'm about to write next. Let's have a praise break. Glory to the Righteous One!

King Jesus, You are beautiful, and Your love is beyond compare. You are marvelous and amazing, and we love You with all our hearts flowing like a fountain. Thank You for knowing how to tenderize our hearts, making all this possible. Amen.

A Call from International House of Prayer, Kansas City

Praise God! Two months later I had a surprise call from the International House of Prayer, (IHOP) Kansas City. Prior to this call I had some wonderful prayer time in the prayer room praying for Israel. I had traveled there from Niagara Falls, New York, to participate when I found they were praying 24–7. I was ecstatic! Glory to God! So the call went something like this…

"Merlin, IHOP is sending a missionary team to Israel in November. We have one spot left, and we are looking for someone to take it. Do you want it? Think about it, and call me back on this number with your decision."

I could have given her an answer there and then, on the spot, done! During the call I agreed to call her back with my decision. Friend, I couldn't hang up the phone quickly enough to celebrate with my Jesus to let Him know I knew He had done it. This was confirmation that He wanted me to sing Psalm 122 going through the gates of Jerusalem as I said to Him. This song is absolutely beautiful, with an upbeat melody. David was happy; he said he was glad when they said to him, "Let us go up to the house of the Lord." Of course, I'd been praying for peace in Jerusalem, like countless others. I memorized Isaiah 62 to integrate with it:

> I have set watchmen on your walls, O Jerusalem;
> They shall never hold their peace day or night.
> You who make mention of the Lord, do not keep silent, And give Him no rest till He establishes
> And till He makes Jerusalem a praise in the earth.
> (Isaiah 62:6–7)

Concentrating on the day and night vigil and noticing how the various dreams over the years were integrating to form a picture, I saw a plan unfolding. What do I mean? I noticed that the majority of the dreams involved all the saints or all people, even the dream where the angel showed all the nations in a cave weeping, wailing, and mourning because they rejected salvation because of unforgiveness. While he was leaving the scene, he said, "Last call, last call." I woke up weeping that morning. I slid off my bed onto my knees, interceding for the nations, asking Father God to forgive them, for they know not what they do, and for Him to stretch forth His hand and save them. The two musical prayers and the others merge into the vision with the body of Christ, both Jews and Gentiles, praying the King back,

> Repent therefore and be converted, that your sins may be blotted out, so that times of refreshing may come from the presence of the Lord, and that He may send Jesus Christ, who was preached to you before, whom heaven must receive until the times of restoration of all things, which God has spoken by the mouth of all His holy prophets since the world began. (Acts 3:19–21)

The command Jesus gave is for us to pray, fast, forgive, and engage in day-and-night prayer vigils.

After giving God thanks, later on I called IHOP letting them know I would take the spot to go with them to Israel. I had to show up at the prayer center one week early to integrate and have team meetings for the journey. It was also mandatory to spend time in the prayer room, which was sheer delight. What was also exciting for me was being able to mix Hebrew into my prayer time while praying for Israel, petitioning the God of Abraham, Isaac, and Jacob.

On November 15, 2004, the team flew out from Kansas City to Chicago O'Hare Airport. We changed onto an El Al airline and eleven hours later landed at Ben Gurion Airport, Tel Aviv, Israel. When we landed, it was an impactful, emotional moment. Almighty God had confirmed His word.

After landing, we went through immigration, collected our luggage, and were welcomed by our tour guide. He then took us to the waiting coach. From Ben Gurion Airport, we traveled to our first accommodation in Galilee. All that time my mind was overwhelmed with gratitude for how almighty God had guided my life continuously since the morning in Bible college when I heard, "I want you to know My glory." Since my Bible college days many people's lives, both near and far, had been enriched through various kinds of healings, some by laying on of hands and others through the spoken word. And now I was in Israel. You just never know where His glory will carry you. How exciting!

On arrival at our destination, we collected our luggage and then had a time of thanksgiving. The attendant showed us to our various rooms. The place overlooked the Sea of Galilee. How marvelous! We had an excellent team leader. She was the lady who made the initial call inviting me on the trip, bringing this purpose of God to fullness in my life. I am sincerely grateful to her. I pray the God of Abraham, Isaac, and Jacob will favor her, including her family, always. I very much appreciate her.

I quickly noticed after prayer that after all these years, His presence was still in the Galilee. It was amazing! I don't know if I was the only one who noticed or if it was because I was in a highly charged emotional state! I had to voice what I was sensing—the presence of God in Galilee. During our stay there, He never left Later, we visited a synagogue in Capernaum and Peter's house nearby. We also visited Bethlehem in the West Bank. (These visits are in no particular order.)

I remembered us visiting Caesarea Philippi. As we stood in the area, I could imagine what it must have been like when Jesus asked His disciples the question, "Who do men say that I, the Son of Man, am?" As I stood there and looked at the backdrop, bear with me. I could imagine the demons lined up on the top of the ridges looking down eagerly, waiting for the answer. They were waiting to confirm whether Jesus' identity as Son of God was true. Some of us climbed up to the top of the ridges and looked down to the area where Jesus and the disciples possibly stood. There the revelation would unfold to give confirmation of who He is and strike fear and terror into the enemy's camp—He is the Son of God! Their doom was sealed. Jesus' response to Peter's "You are the Son of the living God," was "Peter… my Father has revealed this to you. On the rock of this revelation I will build my church, and the gates of hell will not prevail against it."

From there we went on to the Golan Heights overlooking Syria. We stayed in that location for some time, touring the bunkers used during the Six-Day War back in 1967. It was rather dark inside. From there we traveled up to Northern Israel into King Jeroboam's realm. We looked at the artifacts of the tribe of Dan. No one seems to know what has become of the tribe of Dan. His name isn't in the book of Revelation. Could it be because of the prophetic word spoken over his life by his father, Jacob, in Genesis 49:16? I would like to know the answer to that mystery.

We also went on to Mount Carmel and saw a statue of the prophet Elijah. From the lookout at Mount Carmel we were able to see vast plains in that region that span for miles. We drove past Megiddo and noticed lots of birds in that area. We did much touring, visiting many locations that made the Bible come alive with new meaning, making it more real and appreciating its authenticity. I thoroughly enjoyed the tour.

Our next place of interest was Joppa in the region where Peter had the vision on the rooftop and eventual meeting with Cornelius.

Acts 10 came alive here. Imagine what it must have been like for Peter to see the Holy Spirit given to the Gentiles. This is still happening today, praise the Lord. We accompanied Tents of Mercy[3] ministry led by Eitan Shishkoff, who was establishing a ministry in the area of Joppa. I enjoyed the prayer time as our team helped set the foundation for that branch, praise the Lord. We also had the opportunity to minister to some of the Russian Jews who were part of his ministry. God is amazing as I recalled some of the dreams relating to what was happening. Many times I guess many of us say, "I wonder what that dream meant?" Knowing that most of us haven't the unique ability to interpret dreams like Joseph and Daniel, that's as far as we go. We give no thought of praying to God about the dream to make it a reality, it seems.

To see our dreams unfold is so awe-inspiring that you cannot but give God thanks. For example, one of the dreams was fulfilled when Father God gave favor to a Muslim man by directing him to His Son, Jesus. He accepted Jesus as his Lord and Savior on resurrection morning in April 1994. Times like that are extremely emotional for me, and I rejoice that Father God is glorified. I love You, Father God, with all of my heart.

The Last Week of the Tour

We had a new tour guide. He and his wife had a ministry in Beer Sheba. It's a beautiful place with lots of green foliage in the midst

3 Tents of Mercy ministry led by Eitan Shishkoff—http://www.tentsofmercy.org.

of a dry landscape. The team spent quality time with them at their ministry sharing and worshiping. His wife gave the team copies of one of her beautiful songs entitled, "Remove the Veil So We Could See." I sensed it was a genuine cry from her heart regarding her people. That's why the watchmen on the walls of Jerusalem can only make a cry of abandonment if they have a deep, unfeigned love for Israel flowing out of their hearts like a fountain. Anything less would not suffice. Remember what Paul said.

> I tell the truth in Christ, I am not lying, my conscience also bearing me witness in the Holy Spirit, that I have great sorrow and continual grief in my heart. For I could wish that I myself were accursed from Christ for my brethren, my countrymen according to the flesh, who are Israelites, to whom pertain the adoption, the glory, the covenants, the giving of the law, the service of God, and the promises; of whom are the fathers and from whom, according to the flesh, Christ came, who is over all, the eternally blessed God. Amen. (Romans 9:1–5)

I'm eager to tell you what happened going through the gates of Jerusalem, but first I have to tell you about the River Jordan and the Dead Sea. Truly, good things are worth the wait. Let's go to the River Jordan. Throughout the journey, the tour guide gave us detailed information regarding the history of each location. We arrived at the river in the afternoon.

The spiritual significance of the Jordan was dramatic as we realized it was at this very spot that John the Baptist made that memorable announcement recorded in John 1:29.

A general prayer: Father, I thank You for Your unconditional love, that while we were yet sinners, You sent the Lamb of God, who sacrificed His life for us. He became a living sacrifice once and for all peoples. I praise You, in Jesus' name. Amen.

The water from the Jordan coursed its way down to the Dead Sea. Many from the party took off their shoes and waded in the water; another tour group close by was performing a baptismal ceremony. We also had a worship session there that was rather refreshing. We had two worship leaders on our team who made the trip exciting because both had their guitars.

The next day we traveled down to the Dead Sea. We had to drive through the Judean Desert. What a barren place! I was reflecting on David's encounter in that area.

> O God, You are my God; Early will I seek You; My soul thirsts for You; My flesh longs for You in a dry and thirsty land Where there is no water. So I have looked for You in the sanctuary, To see Your power and Your glory. Because Your lovingkindness is better than life, My lips shall praise You. Thus I will bless You while I live; I will lift up my hands in Your name. (Psalm 63:1–4)

Most definitely in that type of harsh and barren place, you would need to start your journey early, before sunrise. If not, the temperature rises rapidly to unbearable heat that would drain both energy and strength. Dehydration would set in. Before going on the tour, we were advised to drink lots of water and also carry water with us at all times. Thirst would torment the mind like a throbbing thumb being accidentally hit by a carpenter's hammer. All strength would be gone. Even worse would be the seemingly impossible task of making an uphill climb in the blazing heat. The call on God for strength becomes the heart's cry because weakness has set in. At that stage you are vulnerable to the attacks of the enemy. Do you remember, "If you are the Son of God, turn these stones into bread"? God becomes the source of your deliverance, your refuge, and your source in your moment of trouble. David turned to God. We should turn to God also by learning from Him. God will become our refuge who will bring us to rest.

It's an act of wisdom to seek God early. We should make it a daily lifestyle to avert defeat. David expected God to be as real to him there as he was in the sanctuary. The daunting challenges could dampen one's confidence in almighty God. If this setting in the Judean desert was where he was fleeing from Absalom, as a parent, the thought of one of his children causing him such serious emotional stress would make the longing for God more meaningful. We also need to give some thought to the fact that David was now well up in age—an old man. His fighting days were over. So the twin challenge of the barren Judean desert and being hunted by his son, Absalom, were of the same magnitude. It is like a distraught mother's uncontrollable moaning for her precious lost babies—like the crying that was in Ramah. Nothing could have comforted or given satisfaction to the soul apart from God alone.

As we continued through the Judean desert heading toward the Dead Sea, another thought entered my mind. I was reflecting on the Son of David in this same area and His encounter with Satan when the fast ended. Sometimes Satan attacked at the front end of the fast with fear, as we encountered when we began the fast for the Muslim nations, which I will discuss later. God revealed to us who was involved when He showed me the word *Diablo* when my eyes were closed.

I was making comparisons regarding the environments with Adam and Eve and Jesus. We need to look more thoughtfully at the magnitude of Jesus' victory over Satan in the wilderness. It was an irrevocable victory. Adam and Eve were in a garden of plenty when they were tempted and fell, while Jesus was in a desert of barrenness where He was tempted and defeated Satan; the strong man was bound. Glory, hallelujah! Thank You, Lord Jesus, my Conqueror over Satan, principalities, and powers. Amen.

He relied on the Holy Spirit, who gave Him victory. He was showing us that we can have victory over Satan also by relying on the Holy Spirit.

The profound realities of those two encounters meant David's kingdom remained intact, and Jesus provided access for us to reign with Him in His kingdom. The spiritual importance was playing in my mind as we made our way down to the Dead Sea.

Arriving at the Dead Sea Resort

We eventually arrived at the beautiful Dead Sea Hotel Resort. There were many different types of entertainment to keep everyone happy. I was fascinated to see some ladies having mud packs put on their faces! As it was my first time seeing this, I found it rather intriguing. There was much to see and do. After some time when the curiosity faded, we changed into swimming costumes and headed to the Dead Sea itself. I was amazed at the viscosity of the water. In the past, it was impossible to stay afloat at other resorts; I had to paddle with my hands. There at the Dead Sea I didn't need to paddle as I stayed afloat unaided. I enjoyed every moment in the water. I had one of the team members take pictures of me having that experience. It was a busy resort. We spent the rest of the day there before taking the long drive on the winding road through the Judean desert back to our hotel.

The Bible made more sense and came alive as the tour progressed. Previously, as I read my Bible about all this, I never grasped the fullest meaning until I saw the places in person. We visited many other places I cannot recall. However, the size of the river where God had Gideon test the thirty thousand men had dwindled to the size of a small pool of water. From there we journeyed on toward the place I wanted to talk to you about earlier—Jerusalem!

All of us were ecstatic when our team leader made the announcement—as if some awakening took hold of our subconscious mind and activated the memory that was long forgotten of a distant past. Awakening the spirit to remember God—what got triggered in my mind was the Muslim encounter that took place in 1994, ten years before the trip in November

2004. In Haifa I began to draft what took place during that first encounter. It caught the attention of some of the party, who suggested I should read what I was writing to all. Some insisted I should write a book due to its godly importance. I embraced what was said wholeheartedly because previously, though I was writing, it was sporadic.

It was a long journey to Jerusalem. The main purpose of why I was in Jerusalem never left my mind. Our destination drew closer by the hour. Dusk was approaching, and the excitement and anticipation was increasing for all of us to see Jerusalem. This was my first trip. I've read, spoken, and sung about Jerusalem. I also thought about Jesus saying He must go to Jerusalem.

The coach began to climb the hill toward the gates. My mind was racing; there was a moment of uncertainty minimizing the purpose like, "Maybe it's not that important." After that, an uneasy feeling crept in. At the time right there I took action, got bold, stood up, and announced to the tour leader what I would like to do. I could see the gates! My big moment had come! I said to her that I would like to sing Psalm 122 on entering the gates of Jerusalem. The short moment waiting for her response seemed like forever. As they had heard me sing before, she gave no opposition. "Merlin, go ahead!" was the response. I was overjoyed with gladness and excitement—my precious moment had come!

The moment to release the new song that began five months earlier in my room in Niagara Falls, New York, had arrived. I was singing to the entire team yet to an audience of one, my King Jesus, our Lord and Savior. I sang with all my heart. I felt humbled that our King Eternal received my offering: the melodious, glad and joyful Psalm of Ascents 122 in song. Praise the Lord! Glory to You, King Jesus!

It was easy for me to sing it without any difficulty because I had sung it numerous times since its inception. I also had it memorized to make it come forth with clarity, confidence, and gladness.

I wish I could find an easy way to convey the overwhelming gratitude I felt when it was actually happening right there, going through the gates of Jerusalem. In addition, to think that Jesus actually walked through the gates of Jerusalem when He was here on earth super-charged my emotions. A million thanks and praise to You, Lord Jesus! I love You with all my heart! Hallelujah!

As I am now writing about that wonderful encounter, all the memories are flooding my soul.

A Prayer from My Heart

> King Jesus, I am still captivated as if it was yesterday. Indeed, You are the Alpha and Omega—no beginning of days or ending of days, the same yesterday, today, and forever, my King Eternal. I worship You. I am glad that grace is poured on Your lips, and God has blessed You forever. You fill my heart with gratitude and joy. Thank You for showing me how much You love me by sacrificing Your life on the cross. Jesus, I give You thanks for allowing me to sing that

> Psalm of Ascents to You at the beautiful gates of Jerusalem. Thank You, Father God. Amen!

After that memorable encounter, we arrived at the beautiful King David Hotel. The warmth and cordial response of the service attendants impressed me. The feeling was transmitted, "We are happy to serve you." We had to get ourselves situated quickly as the Sabbath was setting in. It was understandable that everything stops on Sabbath, even the elevator. Walking was the high point for the day. It wasn't unusual for me to see folks walking everywhere. Having grown up in London, England, I was familiar with the Orthodox Jews walking on Sabbath to their respective synagogues. I am talking about entire families.

As a former Adventist, we never lit fires from sunset to sunset as a way of honoring the Sabbath. All meals were prepared on the Friday.

The hotel meals were excellent—an elaborate assortment of delicacies. Again, I could recall the feasts after synagogue service was finished. We entered a banquet room that was part of the synagogue facility and appreciated the goodness of God. There was time to socialize and make new acquaintances. Later on toward the evening, we were privileged to meet with ministry partners Daniel Juster and Asher Intrater, who were affiliated with IHOP Israel's Mandate. The meeting was in the King David Hotel Conference Hall. Their insight regarding Israel and the church is information those of us who were brought into the church through Jesus Christ need to know, just to reemphasize that the God of Abraham, Isaac, and Jacob has not cast away His people.

After Sabbath ended, we were able to see the beauty of the city at night. The following day we had an extensive tour of the temple ruins, including the Wailing Wall and Hezekiah's tunnel. Later on we had communion at the Garden Tomb, said to be the authentic burial site of Jesus. There were other teams taking communion also. During that sacred service, the presence of the Lord was so evident. Then we went to the Mount of Olives. I had this gnawing in my being for many days. It was in regard to how almighty God would heal the breach between Ishmael and Isaac. This is written by birth, but if by promise, it's Isaac and Ishmael.

In Jerusalem, one could easily observe the stark difference between the beauty of the Jewish quarter and the unattractive side of the Arab quarter. The disparity could be likened to light and darkness. While we were on the mount that overlooks the Temple Mount with the Dome of the Rock dominating the area, I asked the Lord how He was going to resolve the issues between the Jewish people and the Palestinian Arabs. He strongly impressed upon my heart that He would, "Cause the rain to fall on the just and unjust." That was the Lord's answer. With that response from the Lord, the gnawing immediately ceased, and I found relief in my soul.

After that answer from the Lord, we walked through the Arab section to see the difference in lifestyle; the light was very dim. I could identify with the Arab people because back in 1994 the Lord had switched my intercession from the Jews to the Arabs with fasting—a forty-day fast surrounding Ramadan of that year. I repeated another forty-day fast for all the Islamic nations the following year after my trip to Israel in 2005. The Bible says in the mouth of two witnesses a matter is established. As Christians, we need to ask Father God for mercy and grace and a heart of compassion to intercede for both the Jewish people and the Arab Muslims. Let us pray that they come to repentance, ask God's forgiveness, and accept His loving provision to salvation, accepting Jesus Christ as Lord and Savior, He who is the promised Seed and not through the seed of reasoning. Through revelation of Jesus, they would be able to turn to each other and forgive one another from the heart. This time it will be a love embrace far removed from that of Esau and Jacob after his night of wrestling with the angel at the Brook Jabbok.

I occupy the role of intercession on behalf of both brothers. Prayer was a major part in our trip to Israel. Therefore, we cannot stop praying but must increase it to day and night vigil. The tour ended three weeks later. We arrived back at the prayer room in Kansas City as exuberant saints because the trip was successful. I spent a week in the prayer room before taking my flight back to Niagara Falls. I anticipate returning to Israel soon.

Here's the promise for those who love Israel and pray according to Psalm 122—prosperity is the result. Following was another assignment I was given to do.

BLESSING THE MUSLIM NATIONS

Due to the significant time frame we are living in, I sense it is time to make known some of the things revealed regarding the Muslim nation, not only because of their importance but also due to the fact they have had beyond twenty years of maturing since the Lord began to speak these things to me. I believe these things will make sense to many but more specifically to the prophetic ones who read this book. We do not run because we can, but rather we run because we have a divine message. He said to run and told us where the finish line is: the glory.

Of the many revelations given over the past years, some were too terrifying to mention, so I chose not to write them down. Perhaps I should say they were way beyond me. However, I will mention six specific dates—three in days and three in years, the results of forty-day fasts.

- On September 26, 1993, after finishing the second forty-day fast earlier that month, the Spirit of the Lord said to start praying for the wealth of the wicked. I have been faithful ever since.

- On November 11, 1993, during a night dream, the airwaves were taken away from the Enemy. He came and asked for a six-month extension of time, which I refused. The result? I believe these are possible results—broadcasting of TBN and GODTV across Europe began.
- I had just returned from San Diego prior to starting the third forty-day fast. I was there to gather information that would assist me on this particular fast. The date was January 10, 1994. The Lord asked, "What did Moses' rod do to the Egyptians' rods?" I will discuss this later in this book.
- Please note the things God singled out in the first three dates: finances, communication, and people. In 1993 I was told that there would be three significant years of importance. They were 2005, 2007, and 2012. I have devoted much prayer concerning their importance. I watched and searched events, looking for clues regarding these dates. As a result, the following highlights unfolded. He led me to travel to the following countries: Northern Ireland, the United States (where I reside at this writing), the United Kingdom, Isle-of-Wight, India, and Israel. None of these locations were of my own choosing, but I went gladly in obedience as He opened the doors. In 2007 the Muslims' Ramadan and our ministry's forty-day fast converged. In 2012, a life of higher consciousness and awareness began where an old paradigm ended and a new one began. Also of significance, a witness came into my spirit that my missionary work in Niagara Falls, New York, would be ending.

Let's begin this journey of how God unfolded to me a tested strategy for reaching the Muslim nations. During the years between 1992 through 1995, God was moving rather dramatically in my life and no doubt in the lives of many others who also chose to set themselves apart to hear from Him. The results were a deluge of prophetic revelations. Although those were tough years on my physical body, they proved to be spiritually fulfilling.

Whenever God wanted me to take a special step of faith to fulfill a major assignment, I had to come to America. I was living in London, England, during that time. He would also provide the money when I thanked Him for it in faith—someone, somewhere always provided the funds needed with the statement, "God said."

Of late I have discovered through CBN's DVD[4] *God's Plan for America: How to Prepare for the Days Ahead* that when the original missionaries landed at Port Henry in Virginia, they established a covenant with almighty God. Because of this it made sense during one of our ministry's forty-day fasts that the Lord said to write, "Repent" on the American flag. I carried out the instruction. May God still bless America? Yes!

Just like one of the questions asked on the DVD, "Could a remnant get before God on behalf of the nation?" I said yes. For example, we knelt at a cenotaph in Northern Ireland in 1997 asking God's forgiveness. He did forgive, evidenced by the fact that two years later peace was established.

---

4 Pat Robertson, DVD: "God's Plan for America How to Prepare for the Days Ahead." Centerville Turnpike, Virginia Beach, Virginia 23463. The Christian Broadcasting Network, Inc, 2012.

We need to understand the extent to which the God of Israel values the mystery of intercession. The entertainment in the churches must end, and instead we must fervently seek the Lord of hosts! This is His invitation to us to be one with Him in advancing His kingdom. Ishmael and Esau are coming into one new man in Jesus. He said He would make Ishmael a great nation, but I am viewing this from a spiritual point (Genesis 17:20). When the Messiah is revealed to them, the glory will be seen in unprecedented proportion. We have glimpses of it in the Old Testament era in Numbers 16:19. Why did I mention that particular chapter? Because there was judgment also! God Almighty has opened up the airwaves. He will be providing the finances to fund His projects to expand His kingdom!

With what has been said, dear readers, please take your time to read the encounter below. The whole earth is about to shake. When the shaking comes, your only safety will be under the shadow of our Lord Jesus Christ, as mentioned in Psalm 91, for His Father has made Him King of all the earth!

A Man in a Dream

In August 1993 I had a strange dream. In the dream three fat white men were beating up a black man. Upon waking up I said to the Lord, "Why give me this dream when I don't know the man?" I interceded for him until I felt God had acknowledged the petition. Later on, I literally saw this black man from my dream at a bus stop at Manor House, near Finsbury Park, North London. I was waiting there at a bus stop to catch a ride to Mission in London. Standing at one of the bus stops was a pregnant white woman and her friend. The black man and his two friends, who were all drunk, approached the white couple. The one I had seen in the dream approached her. She was terrified. He stretched his hand to place it on her large stomach. I was praying in tongues (a prayer language), and he looked at me and withdrew his hand. He and his friends walked away.

Later on the day the revelation (Ramadan) came, I took the bus to my local church (Rainbow) that was on the other side of Finsbury Park, not far from where I lived. I went to collect information about the British Broadcasting Corporation (BBC) because the church I attend was praying for the BBC that week, and its motto is taken from Isaiah.

> Now it shall come to pass in the latter days that the mountain of the LORD's house shall be established on the top of the mountains, and shall be exalted above the hills; and all nations shall flow to it. Many people shall come and say, " Come, and let us go up to the mountain of the LORD, To the house of the God of Jacob; He will teach us His ways, and we shall walk in His paths." For out of Zion shall go forth the law, and the word of the LORD from Jerusalem. He shall judge between the nations, and rebuke many people; they shall beat their swords into plowshares, and their spears into pruning hooks; Nation shall not lift up sword against nation, neither shall they learn war anymore. (Isaiah 2:2–4)

A Horrifying Dilemma

On my journey home I had planned to take the bus when I heard, "Walk through the park." The bus stop is next to the main gate to the park (that area was noted for drunkenness, prostitution, and drugs). I was reluctant at first, but I obeyed. While walking through the park toward my home, there were a group of drunks, about fifteen males and females, some standing, some sitting and seemingly happy. Getting almost adjacent to them I heard, "That is the man." I turned my head to look and kept walking. The same words were repeated again but stronger, "That is the man." My heartbeat increased rapidly; I was terrified. I begged the Lord to let me go home and talk to him another time. I was in limbo. But I knew I couldn't go home yet. My time of confrontation had come.

I sat on a bench in the park not far from them, contemplating my horrifying dilemma of having to go in among them. Home wasn't my primary destination anymore; it was in among that drunken group! That's what my Sovereign Lord wanted. That bench became my seat of reckoning. Oh the horrors that passed through my mind as I surveyed that drunken group. I had no desire to be among them whatsoever. All sorts of agonizing thoughts entered my mind. I was like a bird caught in a snare. Finally, I decided I would go to them, as I had no other choice. They began to call to me, saying they knew me. As I got up and started heading toward them, something that felt like a soft sheet came over me and covered me from my head to my toe; His shield surrounded me. I call it a mantle of peace or His divine covering.

I Went In Among Them

My fears and horrors disappeared as boldness and confidence engulfed me. I went into their midst. I heard myself say, "I came to see this one," pointing in the direction where he was sitting on the bench. I walked toward him with boldness and crouched before him with confidence. Then I looked at him with assurance. I had a divine message for him. I said to him, "The Lord showed you to me in a dream in which you were beaten up by three white men, but I prayed for you." He got up off the bench where he sat and stood before me. I got up from my crouched position and stood facing him. I had no fear of any of them or anymore. He embraced me, kissed me three times on my face, and sat back down on the bench. From his action, I knew he was a Muslim. I went back to my stooping position looking at him, waiting for a response. Our eyes locked. I kept my eyes fixed on his. He looked at me quizzically with his red, drunken (evil) eyes as if studying me and what I had said to him earlier. That brief moment of waiting seemed like forever. He seemed to be searching in his alcohol-saturated memory for cohesive words that would make sense. Somehow he brought out a gem. He said, "You are a prophet. There is terrible evil in the atmosphere. Have you got a pen?"

I said, "Yes"

He said, "Write." The information was profound!

I then asked, "Are you a writer?"

He said, "Yes."

I responded, "I, too, am a writer." He also shared some other information regarding why he ended up drinking. The causes of his drinking were family problems that drive people to habits so common among humanity.

They continued their drinking, talking, and laughing. They all seemed to be rather happy. I took my pen, tapped his tin of lager three times, and asked him, "How about this?"

He said he would give it up in three weeks. I knew it was impossible because he was bound by the demon of alcohol. After talking with him for a while, I sensed it was time to leave. I was prompted by the Holy Spirit to give him my address, letting him know he could visit me anytime. I came out from among them, waving good-bye.

The victory had been won! There was no longer a need for me to rush home anymore. Praise the Lord! Instead, based on what he said to me about the three weeks, I stayed in the park in another location interceding for him by the leading of the Spirit. I prayed about what he said until release and victory were accomplished and I knew God had answered. I gave the Lord thanks and then went home with joy in my heart.

His Face Was Glowing

Time had now passed. One morning while coming out of the washroom, the Lord gave me an open vision concerning the man in the dream I met at the bus stop and finally in the park (let's call him Hassan). I saw Hassan in his room throwing up. I knew what was happening. The Lord was cleansing him from the years of drinking. I laughed out loud in happiness. The Lord said Hassan would be at my house in three days.

Three weeks later to the day we met, Hassan turned up at my home. That Sunday morning, I couldn't get out of my bed. I had forgotten about what I saw and heard. At about 6:15 a.m., a rap came on my window, and then I heard a voice that I recognized as Hassan's. Immediately I was set free. I got up, let him in, and saw his face was glowing. I blurted out, "Hassan, you have changed!" His countenance had changed to shining from the previously drained face with evil eyes. As he related what happened to him at his house, I sat him down and made him a warm tea. As he shared, I could smell the strong odor of the chemicals from his encounter. We talked for some time and I didn't know what else to do for him, so I called my mother in the Lord, who is also a state registered nurse (SRN).

I told her what had happened to him. She asked the color of what he was vomiting. I told her it was green. She said the green color meant he was being set free from the spirit of Islam. That morning, which was resurrection morning, he accepted Yeshua as his Lord and Savior! "What did Moses' rod do to the Egyptians' rods?"

The time was January 10, 1994—in San Diego the previous day, a Jewess came and told me that Yeshua (Jesus) came into her room and told her that He is the Messiah. I had just returned from the World Conference in San Diego, where I had met many of my intercessor friends from around the world. I arranged for them to pray with me, as I would start the third (in a series of five) forty-day fast in February of that year. Those five fasts were in relation to the five senses. "Why?" you may ask. Man stopped hearing. I arrived back in London, and upon entering my room, as I was about to put my traveling case down, I heard, "What did Moses' rod do to the Egyptians' rods?" Unsure of how to answer I responded, "Swallowed them up?"

> Then the LORD spoke to Moses and Aaron, saying, "When Pharaoh speaks to you, saying, 'Show a miracle for yourselves,' then you shall say to Aaron, 'Take your rod and cast it before Pharaoh, and let it become a serpent.'" So Moses and Aaron went in to Pharaoh, and they did so, just as the LORD commanded. And Aaron cast down his rod before Pharaoh and before his servants, and it became a serpent. But Pharaoh also called the wise men and the sorcerers; so the magicians of Egypt, they also did in like manner with their enchantments. For every man threw down his rod, and they became serpents. But Aaron's rod swallowed up their rods. (Exodus 7:8–12)

The command came back, "Do that to the Muslim nation." I was stunned as I involuntarily put my hand to my throat, thinking, *How could I do this impossible thing?* But He said, "Do it!" What also caught my attention was the sudden switch to the other brother. I was to petition God on their behalf in divine love. Oh how pleasant it is when brothers dwell together in unity! Both need a revelation of the Messiah.

"Ramadan" Was His Whisper—God's Infinite Love for the Muslim Nation

I pondered the command for many days and then began to pray to Him with the one request: "You said to pray for the Muslim nation, so how do I do it?" This went on for two to three weeks—I was desperate for an answer! Finally, one sunny afternoon I knelt down and asked God again. "Ramadan," His whisper came regarding God's infinite love for the Muslim nation. I knew that was the answer. I got up and called my Turkish friend. We exchanged pleasantries in her language and then asked the question, "When does Ramadan begin?" February 9, was her response… I sent letters out to my prayer partners to change the fasting date from March to February of that year. We started the fast (one meal a day) three days before Ramadan on February 6 and ended seven days after Ramadan on March 17. Although I cannot go into all the details of what I encountered, it is sufficient to say that what I did was God ordained, which was my security.

On the day we started this particular fast, we were on our knees asking for God's protection and guidance when the spirit of fear and darkness gripped us. This terror came up out of the floor where we knelt, and the word *Diablo* appeared before my closed eyes. I didn't know what the word meant at the time, but the evil associated with it caused me to take action immediately and bind the spirit of fear and loose faith in us in Yeshua's name. I commanded that we keep our minds on Yeshua. Later that day the darkness ceased. Much time was spent in prayer, worship, and the Word.

First Fruits

The first fruits of these encounters in 1993 and 1994 regarding the Muslims began to insistently come into my mind again on my trip to Israel in 2004. I spent time asking God the significance of that command (which I obeyed then), its relevance, and my purpose for being in Israel. How was He going to solve the problem when both Jews and Arabs were in Jerusalem? At the moment He gave the answer, the gnawing in my gut left! I began drafting in Haifa what took place back in 1994.

On my return from Israel I sought out when Ramadan would begin (November) and stumbled into the year 2005. I realized this was one of the years God mentioned at the beginning of this journey. I knew there were other important events in 2005, but this one stood out. I began rehearsing some dates in my mind and discovered that Ramadan would converge with the yearly fast of our ministry—Inner Circle Worship Ministries, Inc.

A Dream Documented in My Journal on February 5, 2005

I only came across this dream again while going over my journal on December 28, 2005, during a visit with my brother in Atlanta, Georgia.

I was in the midst of a large group of Arabs. The place seemed like Jerusalem. I had visited Israel in November 2004. An older Arab was encouraging the little ones to take off the heads of their enemies. One of the little Arabic children didn't want to do it, so the older Arab picked up a child, put him on his shoulder, and pretended to wring off his neck. In the next scene I could only see the body. Looking closer, I saw he had this garment made that covered the head of the child to give it a headless appearance. When the garment was removed, the complete child could be seen again. In the dream I picked up a little child and had him on my knees, rocking him. The older Arab who had been encouraging the children to do that ghastly thing came over to me and was talking to me. I heard what he was saying but never responded. He also commented upon the child on my knees as a good thing. He inquired about Jesus Christ, whether He was just for some people. I motioned with my left hand, making a circle that indicated Jesus was for the whole world, and he understood. The circle I drew shocked him. He then asked if it meant him too. I said that he could have Jesus as Savior immediately, if he wanted. As soon as I said that he could have Yeshua too, he began to cry. I told him to repeat the sinner's prayer after me if he was ready to accept Jesus Christ as his Lord and Savior. He said the prayer and was immediately transformed by the joy of salvation. Then the dream ended, and I woke up.

I got up and prayed that the spirits of rejection and murder would be removed from the entire nation and that love and acceptance would be released into the entire nation.

The Second Forty-Day Fast

In the process of time since the first forty-day fast, and almost nine years since the second forty-day fast for the Muslim nations, God honored my humble attempt to respond to His command.

By faith, our ministry started a forty-day fast for the Muslim nation surrounding the time of Ramadan that was in progress that month. We fasted from November 1 through December 10, 2005. We did the fast just as we had done back in 1994. Interestingly, we did this all by the Spirit's leading without my remembering the dream I had in February 2005 noted above. On December 8, 2005, the thirty-ninth day of the fast, I was at the very location in Finsbury Park, North London, UK, where the first fast had played out over eleven years earlier. Father is full of surprises!

Months later a newsletter was given to me written by a prophetess in Jerusalem, relating how many Muslims of all ages were receiving revelations of Yeshua (Jesus). As we heard these reports, we rejoiced, believing our fasting of 1994 and 2005 had contributed to this moving of God in the Muslim nation. Glory to His name!

A Heartfelt Prayer

Beseeching God's loving-kindness toward Ishmael and Esau in prayer.

> Father, because of Your loving-kindness and tender mercies, I humbly ask You to remember the children of Ishmael and Esau. Look at what they are doing around the world today! Remember what You said to Hagar and Abraham about making Ishmael a great nation and what Isaac promised Esau about the yoke being removed. We know Your words will not return to You void. Is

now this the set time for You to bring Your word to pass?

Because you are the same yesterday, today, and forever, honor Your word, Father God, and magnify Your name among the nations. Let the Father heart of God speak tenderly to Ishmael and Esau, that they will see You at last and behold Your Son, Jesus Christ, Yeshua. Speak to them in dreams and visions, signs, wonders, and miracles so they may know their rejection is reversed and they are accepted in the Beloved, forgiven by You; chosen through the promised Seed from the foundation of the world.

Thank You for all the wise servants who are participating in this end-time harvest. Provide us with all the special reaping tools we need (that includes more than enough finances) to cause thunderous rejoicing in heaven! Father, if any of Your reapers are in any debt, set them free today. Place Your shield about us: our families, ministries, and businesses in Yeshua's name.

Father, let Your kingdom come and Your will be done on earth as it is in heaven. Amen.

This prayer was first drafted in Haifa on November 8, 2004. Inner Circle Worship Ministries, Inc., completed this fast from November 1 through December 10, 2005.

Please join us in prayer for God to increase His kingdom with millions from the Muslim nations and other nations also. As one famous evangelist used to say, "Empty hell to populate heaven."

Will You Hear the Voice of the Martyrs?

My journey of sacrifice is one practiced by many others also, like what is happening with Voice of the Martyrs. I cannot encourage the saints enough to get involved in supporting their cause. It is part of my prayer for every church in this country to send missionaries overseas so they can understand what life is like for some Christians suffering for the cause of Christ. I believe it would remove the casual and complacent attitudes I see common here.

My heart is touched deeply as I read of how those Christians are suffering for their faith in Muslim-dominated countries. I woke up with the Scripture, "Blessed are those who are persecuted for my name's sake, for theirs is the kingdom of heaven" (Matthew 5:10).

The only meaningful thing to do is offer fervent prayer on behalf of the sisters and brothers in those countries where religious freedom is unreal. I wonder if it is possible for prayer warriors to gather with prayer and fasting to bind the strongman in those nations. I am only speaking from the fact of Jesus' admonition to bind the strongman in Luke.

> But when a stronger than he comes upon him and overcomes him, he takes from him all his armor in

> which he trusted, and divides his spoils. He who is not with Me is against Me, and he who does not gather with Me scatters. When an unclean spirit goes out of a man, he goes through dry places, seeking rest; and finding none, he says, 'I will return to my house from which I came. (Luke 11:22–24)

I grew up with many of those nationalities therefore I have some idea of how passionate they are in their beliefs. And to change to another is traumatic in itself and cause for much soul searching. In addition, it is showing us how violent the spirits influencing people today can be. Therefore, we cannot take these persecutions lightly. We must mobilize and get serious about our Christian walk by praying, and taking action in financing these projects to get the gospel moving forward to the fulfillment of the commission—go into all the world and make disciples of all nations.

It is with permission from The Voice of the Martyrs[5] I reprint these two testimonies to let you know or have some idea of what is actually taking place even in our present Internet, technological, and motorized society. Christians are being martyred for their faith by the hundreds of thousands! They are taken from ***The Voice of the Martyrs Magazine*****,** ***April 2013*****.**

---

5 Taken from *The Voice of the Martyrs Magazine*, April 2013 issue. Visit http://www.persecution.com Contact: The Voice of the Martyrs P. O. Box 443, Bartlesville, OK 74005-0443. Orders and contributions: 800-747-0085. Ministry information: 877-337-0302. E-mail: thevoice@vom-usa.org

Threat or Opportunity?

By P. Todd Nettleton

Mohammad is the kind of person who doesn't do anything half way. He pursues every endeavor with complete, pedal-to-the-metal abandon. When he was a drug addict, he abused every drug he could find. And after coming to know Christ, that same personality was used to further the gospel. Mohammad, who became a Christian four years ago, says he shares the gospel with everyone he meets and that more than one thousand people have knelt with him in prayer and committed their lives to Christ.

Such prolific sowing of the gospel seeds in Islamic Iran means you will face persecution. But God provides opportunities for planting more seeds even within persecution.

Mohammad was at the beach witnessing to people when the police arrested him. "When they arrested me… I just knew that God was sending me to a place to witness," he said. "So I didn't fight or [argue] so they would take me to jail."

"They took me to jail, and I saw two people who were bound because their crimes were very serious. When I came to those people I told them, 'God has sent me to save you.' By faith I believe that those who are around me God has sent for me to share the gospel. So I shared the gospel with them very briefly, just about fifteen minutes, and they received Christ!"

"I only had those fifteen minutes to share the gospel because immediately after I had shared the gospel the police came and said, 'You have been very good and you shouldn't be here. You were very kind to us, and we want to release you.' They opened the door and said I could go. When they opened the door to release me, I hugged those two criminals and they were crying and hugging me really hard. So the warden of the police said, 'You have only known these people for fifteen minutes and they act like you are family.'"

Mohammed understands the dangers, as there are more arrests and more persecution. But there is no fear or intimidation in him. Where many would see only danger and suffering, God has given Mohammed the eyes to see opportunity.

The Iranian government's pursuit of nuclear weapons and the unpredictable actions of the country's leaders cause many Western governments to view Iran as the world's greatest threat. But God helps people to see the truth even inside the world's greatest threat. The church in Iran is growing at an astounding rate. As you read this, the gospel is being presented somewhere in Iran, whether via satellite TV, an Internet chat room or through a newly converted young man sharing the gospel with his parents or younger sister. As Mohammed's story shows, our Iranian brothers and sisters are willing to answer Christ's call to preach the gospel to every creature (Mark 16:15).

"I am serving God now and I will serve God until the day I die," Mohammed said. "I have goals, but I feel I have reached my goals. I feel like I am fulfilled. I don't want anything from God, because I feel like I am paying Him back for what he has done for me. I know He has a great plan for me and He will take me step by step towards His plan for my life."

Shahnaz and Ebi—Beating Jesus

Instead of using threats and legal action to persuade his child to return to Islam, Shahnaz's father had a different plan—he'd use love.

When Shahnaz became a Christian more than two years ago, her father, Ebi, thought his daughter was simply going through another phase. Ebi, a devout man and Iranian government official, had watched her follow different Islamic prophets and Western pop stars. Surely this Jesus phase would pass just as the others had.

But the Jesus phase didn't pass and Shahnaz's faith grew stronger. She told others about Christ and began leading a small Bible study group.

Shahnaz's parents came up with a plan to lure their daughter back to Islam. Before Shahnaz began to follow Christ, she had been in love with a young man who lived nearby. At the time, Shahnaz's parents had refused to allow her to marry the young man, but now they thought he might make her forget her love for Jesus.

They invited the young man and his parents to their home to discuss the possibility of the two being married. After the families had talked for some time, Ebi took Shahnaz to a back room in their house and asked her what she thought of the potential marriage.

"I'm sorry, father, but I am a Christian now," she told him. "I cannot marry a Muslim man. My life has changed. My goals are different now. I have a goal to serve God." Then she again urged her father to accept Christ.

When the young man's parents realized Shahnaz had rejected their son, they left the house angrily. Shahnaz's parents were embarrassed. In a rage, Ebi took off his belt and began to beat his daughter.

"Do you realize," he screamed, "that I can kill you right now and it is legal? You are a Muslim who became a Christian. You are an apostate! My reputation is ruined because of you. I am going to keep beating you until you get on your knees and renounce Christianity and return to Islam."

"Lord," Shahnaz called out, "I don't want to deny my faith in You. Jesus, help me!" Suddenly the beating changed. Instead of beating his daughter, Ebi began to hit himself with his own belt. His voice changed.

"I am a bad person," he said. "I am so dirty. I am so stupid. I am fighting with God!" He began to call out for forgiveness from God, and finally he fell to the floor, apparently near passing out. At that moment Shahnaz's mother came into the room.

"What did you do to your father?" she screamed. "Did you kill him?"

"He was about to kill me," Shahnaz replied. "I don't know what happened." Shahnaz and her mother were about to call the ambulance, but Ebi told them he didn't need one. He wrapped his arms around his daughter and began to apologize. "Please, honey, forgive me," he said. "Ask your Jesus to forgive me. Now I realize who I am fighting against."

> Then Ebi told Shahnaz how God had opened his eyes to the truth. As he was beating her, he saw a vision of Jesus with his left arm wrapped around Shahnaz and his right arm motioning for Ebi to stop swinging the belt. "Don't beat her," Jesus told him. "She belongs to me." Ebi realized as he was swinging the belt, he was beating Jesus.
>
> Shahnaz forgave her father. "Even Jesus said, 'Forgive them for they know not what they do,'" she told him.
>
> Ebi became a Christian and today he hosts a church meeting in his home. He now encourages and supports his daughter as she pursues her Christian calling."

For information about Voice of the Martyrs and how to contact them, see the bibliography.

Who Spoke through the Edomites?

Over the years until the present, I have wondered at the significance of the reality of what took place in 1993 and 1994. During my trip to Israel in November 2004, what I saw and heard triggered the incident again and caused me to realize the significant strategy the Lord had given me in January 1994. I feel encouraged to pursue this now most wholeheartedly. There is no better time than the present day with the major threat from that part of the world fulfilling Daniel's interpretation of Nebuchadnezzar's dream in

Daniel 2:44–45. The end time thrust by this evil spirit hiding in Islam is the one I believe who spoke through the Edomites and said, "Raze it, raze it to its very foundation."

> Remember, O LORD, against the sons of Edom
> The day of Jerusalem, Who said, "Raze it, raze it,
> To its very foundation!" (Psalm 137:7)

> Thus says the LORD: "For three transgressions of Edom, and for four, I will not turn away its punishment, Because he pursued his brother with the sword, And cast off all pity; His anger tore perpetually, And he kept his wrath forever." (Amos 1:11)

I hear a people crying out for acceptance and not rejection. We must embrace Yeshua's command to love our enemies. This is tough but appropriate. We must adopt the love posture of prayer and fasting so God can take out from among them a people for His kingdom. *Love conquers hate, humility destroys pride, and good overcomes evil.*

Read the timely testimonials of these key personnel below. These three testimonies are used with permission from the [6]*Elijah List mail out on September 12, 2005.*

---

6 The Elijah List mail out September 12, 2005—website http://www.elijahlist.com

The Time has come for the Islamic Veil to be pierced!
—James W. Goll

With amazing insight, Faisal Malick lifts our perspective higher into God's purposes in his timely book *Here Comes Ishmael.* Revelation flows... Scriptures unfold... God's heart is revealed... as you partake of the pages in your hand. The Kairos time has come for the Islamic Veil to be pierced and a great end-time harvest of souls to be welcomed in. This book will help pave the way! *—James W. Goll,* Encounters Network.

I was incredibly blessed by Faisal Malick's book *Here Comes Ishmael.* Not only did it give me a clear understanding of the dynamics of Islam, but it also imparted a burden into my heart as well as a love for the Muslim people. I experienced a major paradigm shift in my view of this precious people... I now see them through the eyes of God's destiny for them! *—Jessica Miller,* Elijah List Assistant Manager.

Prior to Sunday, July 3, 1994 at 12:45 p.m., Faisal Malick was a devout Muslim. Born in Pakistan and opposed to the deity of Jesus Christ, he proclaimed nothing on this earth could ever make him confess that Jesus Christ was the Son of God. He was determined to win Christians, in particular, to Islam. All this changed in a sudden encounter with the living God. Engulfed in God's Holy Presence, Faisal was infused with this revelation—Jesus is the Son of God. Today, Faisal and his wife Sabina travel and minister across denominational barriers, speaking for the mysteries of the Gospel. As founders of Covenant of Life Ministries, they are strategically working with the Body of Christ to see the Glory of God revealed amongst the Muslim people.

Love Your Enemies through Prayer and Fasting

> You have heard that it was said, "You shall love your neighbor and hate your enemy." But I say to you, love your enemies, bless those who curse you, do good to those who hate you, and pray for those who spitefully use you and persecute you, that you may be sons of your Father in heaven; for He makes His sun rise on the evil and on the good, and sends rain on the just and on the unjust. For if you love those who love you, what reward have you? Do not even the tax collectors do the same? And if you greet your brethren only, what do you do more than others? Do not even the tax collectors do so? Therefore you shall be perfect, just as your Father in heaven is perfect. (Matthew 5:43–48)

I feel compelled to send out this invitation for your consideration and if you feel this could also be God's strategy for you, and there is a witness in your spirit, let us join together and cry to the Lord mightily on behalf of the Muslim nations.

Inner Circle Worship Ministries, Inc., intends to pursue this command to love, pray, and fast until He says, "Well done." That factual and proven encounter in the '90s took place over a nine-month period. We could well take this to another level. *No politician, president, or nation* can grant the kind of peace mankind needs. Peace cannot come without righteousness. Only Yeshua can bring peace as the Prince of Peace.

> Peace I leave with you, My peace I give to you; not as the world gives do I give to you. Let not your heart be troubled, neither let it be afraid. (John 14:27)

God Almighty will respond to the fast He ordains. Just imagine hundreds of millions from that region swept into the kingdom because of His sacrificial love and our willingness to fast and pray. Let's do it!

> For God so loved the world that He gave His only begotten Son, that whoever believes in Him should not perish but have everlasting life. For God did not send His Son into the world to condemn the world, but that the world through Him might be saved. (John 3:16–17)

Ah—it is so worth it!

Passionate Prayer

Father, Your mighty acts are innumerable, and Your hand is not short that You cannot deliver a people. Your grace that brings salvation has appeared to all men—the children of Adam. Therefore, expand Your kingdom and glorify Your name because You did say in Psalm 2 to ask for the nations as our inheritance. That we ask today, in Jesus' name. Amen.

A VISIT TO MY INTERCESSOR TEACHER

My intercessor teacher was a slim, mature Caucasian sister in the Lord of German descent. I can't recall how we met. Most likely we met at some world convention held by one of the big names in the evangelical movement.

It was a bright, sunny day. I was fasting, and the Lord said, "Go down to your intercessor's home."

I stopped what I was doing and went to my intercessor's home as directed. I took the bus to her home, which was located in another area in the city of London. The journey took about fifteen to twenty minutes. The walk from the bus stop to her home was about five minutes.

I had called to let her know I was coming and ask her permission to come. I finally arrived at her home and knocked on her door. She opened the door, and we said our greetings. I followed her to the sitting room. She sat in her usual chair, and I sat on a couch with my back toward the window.

I have a lot of admiration for her, as she was my prayer and intercession coach. She was purposeful, and it was like being trained in the army. Some of the things she taught me were how to reach those muscles in the abdomen while praying and going through the pain barrier to get into the Spirit. This activity takes much practice and determination. Being able to perform that function helps one to end up in the Spirit. As stern as she was, I treasured those moments. I finally understood about travailing prayer when the Holy Spirit locks you in. When that happens, those muscles are engaged and there's no release until the task is complete. Your garments become soaked in perspiration through the process. She also taught me about fasting and being in the Word.

It reminded me of the type of praying Elijah did as mentioned in James 5:16 or Paul's travailing prayer in Galatians 4:19. It takes much energy and prayer power to master these disciplines. His rewards are priceless as faith comes alive and miracles break forth through boldness and confidence. It brings to mind how Jesus was praying in Gethsemane on behalf of the children of Adam and Eve.

On that day I was sitting in her home, not knowing why the Lord told me to go there. She was quiet for a moment, and then she began to talk. She had mentioned some big-name ministries (they are still in operation presently) who had prayed for her but to no avail. I sat and listened to her intently without saying a word. She spoke continuously about numerous events. Her conversation lasted around three hours. In listening I got the answer about why I was sent.

A side note here—the Lord never gives all the information up front. We have to step out in obedience and faith. In the action of faith, He will then reveal the next stage. There are countless incidents like this in the Bible.

The reason for my visit was revealed as she mentioned she had cancer in her throat. When she said that, my spirit man rejoiced! I was learning or being trained by the Spirit to monitor a situation and have faith in God's leading. I knew in my heart that God would heal her when that spiritual connection was made. My heart was filled with excitement. When she concluded talking, I said, "Now I know why I was told by the Spirit to come to your house today. The reason is to free you from what is causing you concern." I had noticed previously that she was getting thin but did not give it much thought as she was a slim person and was strict about what she ate. After she mentioned the cancer, the loss of weight made sense.

It was my turn to speak, but I didn't say much, wanting to get to the point. Now I knew why I was there, and the Lord was going to heal her. I cannot recall whether I touched her throat or spoke the word, but Jesus healed her on the spot. Hallelujah!

My task was completed, so it was time for me to leave. She followed me to the door to let me out. She asked me, "How come you were able to heal me and others couldn't?"

The question was relevant because she was my intercessory prayer coach, and Father God decided to flow through her student. I wondered what lesson we were both to acknowledge. Perhaps it was that God uses whom He chooses and we should rejoice!

I sensed the source of the question, paused for thought, and glory to God, He answered by reminding me of the Bible verse that says, "The heart of the righteous studies how to answer," (Proverbs 15: 28a). I took that line and in a split second asked the Holy Spirit how to respond. I said to her, "It wasn't for them to do." I then said good-bye and went out the door, whispering thanks to almighty God. What followed next may be directly attributed to her my intercessor's mentoring.

OPEN VISION AT MY MOTHER-IN-THE-LORD'S HOME

Early one morning in December 1994, while I was at the home of my spiritual mother, I had an open vision. I was tightening screws in her household furniture to make it sturdier. While I was on my knees working, the thought came into my mind that what I was doing was like securing the body of Christ. Next a picture instantly appeared before my eyes. I was seeing in the Spirit.

I saw a corrugated circle, and inside the circle were all the members of the body of Christ moving away from the perimeter because they were in fear. They were being attacked by something outside the circle driving them toward the center. I was astonished at what I saw. My reaction was one of surprise as to why they were fearful. I knew it was the body of Christ because that was the impression that came to me while watching the vision.

I pondered the scene and made mention of it to my spiritual mother. I continued to tighten up the rest of the items until I was done. I pondered the meaning of this vision during the remainder of the day.

Open Vision at Convention in San Diego

As a regimen, I normally fast the last three days at the end of each year. The reason for the discipline is I usually attend a Christian evangelical conference every January of the following year. At those conferences, other intercessors from different countries in our group and I would meet. Most of the saints attending those meetings would have spent time fasting prior to the event, so the atmosphere would be electric and buzzing with excitement! Expectations would be high. It's a good venue to make new friends and in my case, new prayer partners as I wanted to build a global prayer base. My thought was this—some principalities would not be overpowered by a local prayer team but by a gathering of saints from different countries, fasting and praying simultaneously.

At those conferences, teaching is received that is not given in a local church setting. The saints would come away from those meetings with new insights, boldness, and courage. Our belief level would be extremely high so we could go back and make a difference in our local areas. The anointing would prevail to maintain the belief about two weeks beyond the end of the conference, and then it would wane. That type of anointing caused adverse reactions in the saints in the local church. I am speaking based on how the Holy Spirit would work through me. I credit the miracles based upon recognition of the difference in anointing level of local and conference gatherings and all-night prayer.

I decided to maintain the conference level in a local setting. This was not going to be easy like a casual walk in the park, but the benefit would be to God's glory. To see souls set free is totally rewarding. This includes living a fasted lifestyle, day and night prayer, and being a yielded vessel to maintain that level or a comparable level of anointing. I had a revelation of day and night prayer based on what Jesus said.

> And shall God not avenge His own elect who cry out day and night to Him, though He bears long with them? (Luke 18:7)

If I am giving the impression that night praying is easy, that's not the case. It is demanding and calls for determination. It takes much practice. You have read a passage somewhere where Jesus spoke about when men slept the enemy came and sowed tares. I don't think He was referring to sleeping in the daytime but rather in the night. It is during the night that most evil acts are performed, as highlighted by the earlier statement. I'm not saying everyone has the capacity to stay up in the night. Jesus did it, so I believe we can give it a try for the experience's sake. A lot of the new songs from the Spirit were birthed during those hours.

The above goes beyond the praying, forgiving, and fasting in the Beatitudes. It reinforces the need for keeping a vigil around the clock.

Below there's an "And when you…," "But if you…," and "Then they will" sequence I feel is worth mentioning. The reason for this is that some say there's no fasting mentioned in the gospels. Therefore I felt it was necessary to include these pointers. Again,

I trust I don't give the impression that fasting is easy. It's not. Bear with me. I like to think I am a journeyman when it comes to fasting, yet sometimes a little one-day fast gives me horrors, as if I haven't got a clue what is going on. I cry to the Lord for help. This is what I believe happens. Instead of one thousand coming at me, ten thousand are sent. Does that make sense? I'm not saying that is what actually happens, but the pressure of the one-day fast is so intense I have reason to believe that is what usually takes place.

So Jesus is talking about praying, forgiving, and fasting. Yes, fasting. He told His disciples specifically that when He left they would fast because the Bridegroom would be absent.

Jesus on prayer says,

> And when you pray, you shall not be like the hypocrites... But you, when you pray, go into your room, and when you have shut your door, pray to your Father who is in the secret place; and your Father who sees in secret will reward you openly. (Matthew 6:5–6)

Jesus on forgiveness says,

> For if you forgive men their trespasses, your heavenly Father will also forgive you. But if you do not forgive men their trespasses, neither will your Father forgive your trespasses." (Matthew 6:14–15)

Jesus on fasting says,

> Then the disciples of John came to Him, saying, "Why do we and the Pharisees fast often, but Your disciples do not fast?" And Jesus said to them, "Can the friends of the bridegroom mourn as long as the bridegroom is with them? But the days will come when the bridegroom will be taken away from them, and then they will fast." (Matthew 9:15)

Due to the rapid increase of secular programs geared toward making money through the media, it would be seriously worth considering the saints taking up the cause as Jesus mentioned in the above Scriptures. Instead, a social gospel is being preached without any power, just mere words. Christianity is being degraded so severely that it's almost impossible to tell the difference between the ungodly and the godly. It is far removed from the precedence stated in Mark where Jesus called, appointed, and sent out the twelve.

> And He went up on the mountain and called to Him those He Himself wanted. And they came to Him. Then He appointed twelve, that they might be with Him and that He might send them out to preach, and to have power to heal sicknesses and to cast out demons." (Mark 3:13–15)

I am amazed at the lack of desire in the hearts of most of the saints when it comes to prayer. There's shocking negligence also in praying for our government! It seems as if we do not realize the dire need to take responsibility to pray or we won't have godly governments. Neither does the reality seem to dawn in our consciousness that they are the ones passing laws against humanity. Do we not think that the governments of this earth will pass laws targeting Christians? Who do we think is causing the heads of states to decree those laws? God? No, it's Satan!

Continuing with the vision, the conference in Anaheim, California, in January 1995 had ended. The saints were returning to their various nations. On Sunday morning around 9:00 a.m., the Holy Spirit was prompting me to read the book of Acts. I was missing my intercessor friends. I finally responded around 3:00 p.m. Sitting in my hotel room alone, I started reading from chapter one. Then I read this:

> Repent therefore and be converted, that your sins may be blotted out, so that times of refreshing may come from the presence of the Lord, and that He may send Jesus Christ, who was preached to you before, whom heaven must receive until the times of restoration of all things, which God has spoken by the mouth of all His holy prophets since the world began. (Acts 3:19–21)

I entered into a spiritual location where time disappeared. My surroundings looked no different than the normal hotel room setting. What seemed like a moment lasted three hours! When the vision ended, I looked at the clock, which showed 6:00 p.m. There in the hotel room, in the vision, I saw the body of Christ together in harmonious prayer, praying fervently for King Jesus to return.

I was amazed after the scene! I also repented for not responding earlier by allowing my emotions to take precedence over the Spirit's promptings. After much contemplation, I continued reading the verses several times and noted what Peter was telling us. He was talking about repentance, times of refreshing, and how heaven must receive the restoration of all things, and then God would send Jesus Christ. I coined a little jingle to remember the five words beginning with the letter R: repent, refreshing, receive, restoration, and return. He's a King! I came to understand that almighty God does nothing here on earth unless someone prays. He will not change that mode of operation. Simeon and Anna saw the baby Jesus as the result of their prayers.

It only makes sense to talk with God before we do something of significance. I believe many answers are delayed because the thought doesn't come to us to pray about events. We tend to believe they will just happen. Saints, they stay dormant until we pray to Father God. He is the One who makes things happen for us and for all humanity. I cannot stress enough for the saints to realize that Father God intends us to fervently seek His face. I am finally realizing that the many things He has showed have been delayed because I thought they would just happen. Prayer is one of the key factors in my relationship with Him.

It has been more than nineteen years since this vision. We have talked much about it, written about it, and placed it on our ministry website, and I have recently been really seeking Father God about it. Since seeking Him, I am noticing a change in my actions in the sense of letting it be known that every member in our local church should pray. In other words, the greater majority of saints in churches across the nations do not pray, but this is changing.

The secular world appears to dominate their lives. I find myself making the call to pray, out of which a prayer movement has started—*houses of prayer from homes.* It is patterned after a little booklet placed in my hands of the same name many years ago. That ministry gets the credit for the inspiration. I will always give thanks to God, and may that ministry prosper continuously to glorify Father God.

The mission is to advance this prayer movement beyond the walls of our local churches. I pray that all the churches in our city will catch this vision and become involved. We must advance beyond our city of Niagara Falls and into our state of New York. From there we will advance into all the other states, this nation, and the nations of the earth where all other prayer movements merge into one huge ocean. I have purposed in my heart that wherever I go, I will make it known. Through the Internet it could travel more rapidly or even go viral. I am not referring to a onetime event but a continuous effort until Father God responds. In other words, a gradual awareness developing that what's to be done is not a casual undertaking. The demons of hell are not playing a game when they infect a child of Adam with cancer, arthritis, or Parkinson's disease. Their purpose is to destroy!

I believe as we continue to engage in the kind of crucial activities Jesus mentioned—praying, forgiving, fasting, and day and night prayer—we will see significant changes within the hearts of every member in the body of Christ toward Jesus. He will begin to, and eventually become, our magnificent obsession. There will develop a yearning in hearts wanting Him to return. He did say His return will be seen according to Mark 13:36.

What is our present relationship with Him? Is it like a terrified mouse seeing a cat? We must cast off our addictions to worldly desires, realizing an incorruptible Seed has been planted in the dead soil of our spirit, and it will be brought to life. It can take in the Word of God, and it *will* germinate! God had a purpose for us, before time began, not to live for ourselves. He has saved us and called us with a holy calling according to His own purpose.

> Who has saved us and called us with a holy calling, not according to our works, but according to His own purpose and grace which was given to us in Christ Jesus before time began, but has now been revealed by the appearing of our Savior Jesus Christ, who has abolished death and brought life and immortality to light through the gospel. (2 Timothy 1:9–10)

It's more than sitting in a church week after week being idle. Idleness causes spiritual implosion, like the fig tree without fruit. One day the Master was hungry, and He went to a fig tree. It was full of leaves but had no fruit. You may think His action was drastic in cursing the fig tree. However, it was not bearing fruit for eating; it was not fulfilling the purpose for which it was created. Maybe Peter at the time also thought Jesus' actions were drastic. He seems to have been noting everything Jesus said and did. What happened the following day? Who was the watchman? Yes, it was Peter who brought the matter to Jesus' attention. Would you want Jesus to say that in passing to your church? How's your church's fruit? Is your church fulfilling the purpose for which it came into being? We must take action now!

A Jewess in Anaheim Convention Center

Immediately after one of the 7:30 morning prayer meetings, I prayed what I termed a grumbling prayer to the Lord about losing everything and still not seeing one Jew saved yet. I then went to sit on one of the chairs in the prayer room. Instantly someone came and sat next to me on my right and began to speak. The first words I heard were, "I'm a Jew. Jesus came into my room and told me He is the Messiah. I'm on my way to Aruba immediately after the conference, and then I return to Holland, where I live. From here I'm going to the breakfast room."

While she was speaking, I never looked at her. However I heard what she said, processed the information, and felt I would never see her again, so I asked her for her address in Holland. She said she would give it to me after breakfast. I sensed it would not be possible to find her in that large crowd, so I said, "Why not do it now, seeing as you are present?" She agreed and gave me the information, and I have never seen her again up to the present. However, on returning to London, England, I began communicating with her by letter.

She wrote about her encounter with Jesus and her love for Him. It was really comforting for me to get that confirmation from a complete stranger in response to my prayer to almighty God. Because of it I saw His loving-kindness. He heard the cry of my heart and responded immediately. The pursuit of God cannot be achieved in our own strength. He is the one who creates the desire in our hearts. Echoing what Jesus said in John 15, apart from Him we can do nothing… indeed.

As time progressed, I gained many insights through her. Also the Lord would have her praying for me, strengthening me, and I prayed the same for her and her family.

I was progressing, growing in the Lord, and I would say rapidly, through much prayer and fasting, during that time period. I had also immigrated to America on missionary assignment.

One morning I decided I would go down to a location in the Niagara Falls area called the Devil's Hole. I had gone into that area previously, surveying the land after my research. Some call it spiritual mapping. Basically it is strategic to ascertain historical facts about a territory for which you intend to pray. Once the research direction is being pursued, there in the gathered information, you may see what you need to pray about. The gathering of information begins to empower the follow up of prayer. God may then give a vision or insight about why the location is in such spiritual decay. The prayer then, empowered by the Holy Spirit, rectifies or eliminates the barrier in that location. The attitudes of the inhabitants begin to change, and someone will cross your path to let you know. Someone will give some testimony, or you will find a messenger from God. It builds confidence in the praying vessel and gratitude to almighty God.

As I was saying earlier, that morning I was on my way to Devil's Hole here in Niagara Falls when the phone rang. I took the call, and it was my Jewish prayer partner from Holland. She said, "Merlin, God told me to call you and pray for you because of your assignment." I was overwhelmed with gratitude to almighty God for alerting her to call at that precise time and pray. The angels of the Lord encamp around those who fear Him, and He will deliver them. Praise the Lord, I was delivered! What was so amazing was I was just about to head through the door! Praise God from whom all blessings flow.

It's a good downward walk to get to this large stone. The idea was to anoint it with oil and pray over it, breaking every ritualistic purpose of the Enemy. The story goes that a sacrifice was performed on that rock. I must add at the time it seemed like an extremely scary place down there from an historical perspective. This little city had a dark and dismal appearance—one of hopelessness. Anyway, after the prayer I went and performed my redemptive work by the power and protection of the Holy Spirit.

A Dream over Northern Israel

In May of 1995, again in the season of those many long fasts, I had a dream, and the scene was over Northern Israel. The one dressed in white who was supervising what was taking place showed me a scene. It was a long and narrow volume of water stretching for miles. Its contour made a shape like the letter S. The water was rippling, and on the top of the water were millions of bubbles coming up from the bottom. As they came to the top, they would pop. As they popped, they released the most amazing musical notes. In the dream I was captivated by the sounds. During my observation, the tour guide asked me, "Do you know what that means?" I said, "No." He said to me, "That is the prayer of the Gentile nations ascending to God."

A little while after, another stretch of water identical to the first one rose up next to the first one, doing the same thing, making similar beautiful heavenly notes. He again asked the same question. I said no again. He said it was the prayers of Israel ascending to God. After that scene he brought me back to my original location and departed.

When I awoke, I gave thanks as usual. I pondered the scene. It was absolutely beautiful. I thought about the sheer beauty of the sounds made by both volumes of water symbolizing the prayers of both nations. My thoughts went to the prayers of the saints in Revelation 5—the harps and bowls setting.

FERVENT PRAYER RELEASES THE ANOINTING

The pursuit of understanding that fervent prayer releases the anointing began with a dream in May 1994. In the scene, I both saw and heard the person who spoke these words: "The ardent prayers of the saints the five angels ever receive in heaven." Although the phrase I heard was a bit broken, two words were imprinted on my mind—ardent and five.

A) Ardent: passionate, intense, fervent, diligent, burning

B) Five: grace, senses, ministry (both physical and spiritual—man and angels). This is figurative and represents the fivefold ministry of angels.

> Bless the LORD, you His angels, who excel in strength, who do His word, heeding the voice of His word. Bless the LORD, all you His hosts, you ministers of His, who do His pleasure. (Psalm 103:20–21)

Angels exists to serve God in five ways:

1. To bless the Lord in worship and service (Psalm 103:20a).
2. To do His work concerning activities on earth (Psalm 103:20b).
3. To heed the voice of God's Word as it is spoken through the saints on earth (Psalm 103:20c).
4. To minister on God's behalf (as said in Hebrews 1:14, "Are they not all ministering spirits sent forth to minister for those who will inherit salvation?") (Psalm 103:21a).
5. To do God's pleasure as His host and act at His direction (Psalm 103:21b).

How will all this come into reality? John gives the distinct answer.

> But you have an anointing from the Holy One,
> and you know all things. (1 John 2:20)

We will look at this statement later.

Unction could mean:

1. Anointing with oil for religious purposes.
2. That thing that comes on, in, and around you for service.
3. Fervent or sympathetic quality in words or tone, caused by or causing deep religious or other emotion; simulation of this: dark to light, despair to hope, hate to love. This change affects enthusiasm, bringing keen enjoyment to a situation or activity.

Other examples: A sad person who begins to laugh; becoming aware of acute refreshed breathing; lightness in atmosphere after breaking through resistance in warfare prayer. Take note of this:

> Launch out into the deep and let down your nets for a catch. (Luke 5:4)

It may also mean, in this regard, to change your prayer strategy from pleading to praise!

What Is the Anointing?

The anointing in relation to people was a religious procedure that would be followed in preparation of an individual who would enter into the priestly service of the Lord. Examples included Aaron and his sons being prepared for their priestly duties. Specially prepared oil was poured on their heads. This anointing began after Israel's redemption from Egypt and Moses receiving instructions from the Lord about how to build the tabernacle. Part of the instruction was on this particular procedure. Anyone who would hold an office representing the righteous God would be anointed, especially the priest, prophet, and king.

The anointing in relation to animals was an Eastern custom especially applicable to sheep. Because of their wool covering, they tended to pick up lots of foreign entities, like ticks, bugs, worms, burrs, and so on. Instead of pouring the solution on them, the owner would dig a hole in the ground and pour in the cleanser. He would then arrange the cleansing process in such a way that the sheep would have to jump across this opening into the solution called a sheep-dip. The sheep, in falling into the solution, would become totally immersed before coming out. In that way, all the parasites would be destroyed. This method is much easier than trying to pick off the parasites one at a time. In my and my brother's experience being shepherds to our grandfather's sheep, it was a slow process. Sometimes they had ticks in their ears. This parasite sucks blood, and is hard to remove. I'm going somewhere with this vivid explanation. In deliverance there are some demons that are hard to dispel also. That's why the anointing is of utmost importance. Therefore, in our time period, it is necessary to know how to produce the anointing oil, thus the title of this chapter, "Fervent Prayer Releases the Anointing." The process has been tried, and it works.

To continue, the Lord gave Moses the special compounds to use and the required quantity of each to produce the required anointing oil and aroma. The delegated perfumer would be skilled in its preparation to blend it the way the Lord specified. Everything related to the tabernacle, both human and articles, was to be anointed. The Greek word *charisma* spoke of the process, including the necessary cautions. See Exodus 30:22–30.

The specially prepared oil, charisma anointing oil, or holy oil is symbolic of the Holy Spirit who lives in us—the anointing, the Enabler to perform to advance His kingdom. Jesus promised us that "out of our bellies (heart) will flow rivers of living water" (John 7:37–38).

How to Produce the Holy Oil in Prayer

So how do we get this anointing to flow? As a side note, there arc many Christians (and some denominations) who believe that praying in tongues is from the Devil. I have no argument or criticisms for their stance on the subject. Neither would I say there's no counterfeit. Satan is the deceiver. All I know is this—praying in tongues is a dynamic and heavenly language. To engage in it demands an act of faith in trusting God. Therefore, if God only gives good gifts, and tongues is a gift from Him, maybe someone can help me understand how it's evil and from the Devil. One thing I do know is without faith it's impossible to please God. If you intend to stay in the war and endure to the end, I would suggest you consider believing God and step out in faith into that world of a hyper prayer life. Tongues prayer language must be developed. If you can, believe this—I've seen in the spirit demons fleeing when a type of this language is spoken. Also, when a person trusts God (stepping out on a limb), he or she isn't afraid to speak in tongues. What I also perceive is that some won't take the route of tongues for fear they may lose control, not knowing what they are saying. They appear to be bound in the realm of the soul. If that may be the case, then there's likely a spirit of control in operation.

The anointing can be produced faster, and one of the ways is through persistent and fervent prayer in the Spirit. This is not just praying in tongues, but it can also be in your known language. A crossover from the natural to the spiritual realm must be accomplished. Could you just stop for a moment and ponder how awesome was the praying power of Elijah the prophet? I've not come into contact with any records he had the gift of tongues!

In that domain you are under the influence of the Holy Spirit, where unlimited anointing is made available while being carried by the Spirit.

The Making of the Altar

The altar is where the Holy Spirit births intercession. It is not of the flesh or of the soul. Here Satan has no influence whatsoever over the individual. It is here where the fragrance of the spices ascends to the Father as a sweet aroma, symbolic of the life of Jesus Christ. God gave Moses the specifications on how to build the altar of incense.

> He made the incense altar of acacia wood. Its length was a cubit and its width a cubit—it was square—and two cubits was its height. Its horns were of one piece with it. And he overlaid it with pure gold: its top, its sides all around, and its horns. He also made for it a molding of gold all around it. He made two rings of gold for it under its molding, by its two corners on both sides, as holders for the poles with which to bear it. And he made the poles of acacia wood, and overlaid them with gold. (Exodus 37:25–28)

The altar was carried by the Levites, symbolizing being carried in the Spirit. The shittim wood (man) was overlaid with gold (Christ), gold purified seven times in the fire, which is being covered by Christ's righteousness. In other places we are told we are covered by Christ's righteousness, to put on the garment of praise, and to be clothed with humility. The incense burned on the altar was a sweet-smelling aroma. Sweet incense was to be burned every morning, pointing to us praying, evening, morning, at all times, perpetually throughout all generations, and it should be even more so today.

Pray without Ceasing

Time seems to be condensing, and as saints we cannot afford to be part-time prayer people. The more we procrastinate, the faster Satan escalates his wicked agenda. There is more ungodliness appearing daily. There is credence to the command to pray without ceasing. It has been more than two thousand years since Jesus said it. Somehow we must catch on. We must not wait for another devastating tragedy before we act. Oh, how blessed it would be if we could reduce our programs and decide to have a prayer fest! I give honor to IHOP and other ministries who believe God and have an undeniable love for Jesus. It is evident on entering the prayer room there is harmony with their fasting lifestyle. Again, Jesus said that men ought always to pray and not faint. He is praying right now. Paul also reminded us to pray always.

> Praying always with all prayer and supplication in the Spirit, being watchful to this end with all perseverance and supplication for all the saints—and for me, that utterance may be given to me, that I may open my mouth boldly to make known the mystery of the gospel. (Ephesians 6:18–19)

Prayer should be a normal habit to us and continuous, as is symbolically shown in Aaron's duties: the lighting of the lamps and keeping the fire on the altar. Since we are priests and kings, this type of spiritual and governmental lifestyle should be automatic in our thinking. That's my opinion. I wish the local churches would make prayer a priority and really get to know what is happening in the lives of their congregation.

God gave Moses instructions regarding Aaron's duties. One of them was to burn sweet incense when he tended the lamps in the morning and at twilight. Do you believe there was a purpose in those duties that still have relevance today? He is the same yesterday, today, and forever.

> Aaron shall burn on it sweet incense every morning; when he tends the lamps, he shall burn incense on it. And when Aaron lights the lamps at twilight, he shall burn incense on it, a perpetual incense before the LORD throughout your generations. (Exodus 30:7–8)

Atonement or forgiveness is a component of prayer.

> And Aaron shall make atonement upon its horns once a year with the blood of the sin offering of atonement; once a year he shall make atonement upon it throughout your generations. (Exodus 30:10a)

The altar is a holy thing, and most holy to the Lord—and so are we.

The Holy Anointing Oil

Quantities of unequal amounts were mixed together for anointing of the tabernacle. It was no small task looking at the various quantities.

1. Liquid myrrh: five hundred shekels
2. Cinnamon: two hundred and fifty shekels
3. Calamus: two hundred and fifty shekels
4. Cassia: five hundred shekels
5. Olive oil: a hin (six quarts)

> Moreover the LORD spoke to Moses, saying: "Also take for yourself quality spices—five hundred shekels of liquid myrrh, half as much sweet-smelling cinnamon (two hundred and fifty shekels), two hundred and fifty shekels of sweet-smelling cane, five hundred shekels of cassia, according to the shekel of the sanctuary, and a hin of olive oil. And you shall make from these a holy anointing oil, an ointment compounded according to the art of the perfumer. It shall be a holy anointing oil. (Exodus 30:22–25)

The Incense Compounded

The making of this compound was to produce the fragrance when placed on the altar of incense. Special skill was required in its preparation.

> And the LORD said to Moses: "Take sweet spices, stacte and onycha and galbanum, and pure frankincense with these sweet spices; there shall be equal amounts of each. You shall make of these an incense, a compound according to the art of the perfumer, salted, pure, and holy. And you shall beat some of it very fine, and put some of it before the Testimony in the tabernacle of meeting where I will meet with you. It shall be most holy to you. But as for the incense which you shall make, you shall not make any for yourselves, according to its composition. It shall be to you holy for the LORD." (Exodus 30:34–37)

The ingredients of sweet spices were of equal amounts. It means God gets your best!

1. Stacte is a resin from the storax tree.
2. Onycha is a dark brown resin.
3. Galbanum originally comes out of the plant as a milky substance that changes to gum.
4. Pure frankincense is an aromatic gum resin.
5. Salt—the amount is measured by the perfumer. The sweetness is dependent on how much one yields the will to the Spirit.

The Role of the Perfumer

The perfumer adds the required quantity of salt to make the incense pure and holy. Some of the mixture was beaten very finely (our offering of worship) and put before the ark of testimony. This meant persistently praying in tongues or your known language way beyond breakthrough. Then and only then could we enter into the Holy of Holies. How was this mixture compounded? After the materials were carefully selected, they were washed, placed in a mortar, and repeatedly crushed with a pestle to produce the right texture, blend, and aroma. A portion of the compound was crushed more finely (signifying contriteness of heart) before being offered to the Lord.

Golden bowls were full of incense, which are the prayers of the saints as we are told in Revelation 5:8b. In Revelation 8:1–4 we see the angel having the golden censer, and he was given incense and the prayers of all the saints.

> Then another angel, having a golden censer, came and stood at the altar. He was given much incense, that he should offer it with the prayers of all the saints upon the golden altar which was before the throne. And the smoke of the incense, with the prayers of the saints, ascended before God from the angel's hand. (Revelation 8:3–4)

The Pestle and Mortar Process

It is this process of producing the sweet aroma we are interested in today. If we take the literal processing as a guideline, then we could expect the spiritual counterpart would be no different. As the pestle repeatedly crushed the compound in the mortar to produce the aroma, so we see all kinds of prayer in the spirit till way beyond breakthrough. The constant pounding or crushing (*shachaq*) produces the sweet aroma of Exodus 30:36. So the effectual fervent praying in the spirit produces the anointing.

You have to pay the price

We have heard constantly, "You have to pay the price." Pay what price? What are they talking about? How is it done? No one is explaining. Yet we know this anointing is of the utmost importance because Jesus told the five hundred to tarry in Jerusalem for the promise of the Father in Luke 24:49. James wrote about effectual praying after Pentecost. He was also with the 120 in the upper room! He did not say how to do it either! He used the prophet Elijah as an example. What was Elijah's technique? Was his face between his knees (1 Kings 18:42)?

What of John the Baptist? Jesus mentioned something started from John's days until now in Matthew 11:12. Jesus Himself did much strong praying with loud crying! We know loud praying is part of the pattern. We also know from an earlier statement that this anointing is within the body of the born-again believer, and this anointing gives the ability to know all things (1 John 2:20). John went on to say in 1 John 2:27 that the anointing abides in us and teaches us all things. What is John talking here about? In John 14 Jesus gave us the facts about the teacher, the Holy Spirit. We must acknowledge these words in the red writing seriously because it's our King and Lord who spoke. Whatever King Jesus said is correct! No questioning, it must be accepted as truth and life, and therefore we must adhere to the instructions or commands. The Father points us to Jesus Christ. When we accept salvation, a deposit of the Spirit is given to us. With the

Spirit comes the ability to know all things. Glory be to God! Selah—pause and think of that.

Jesus also said, "And you shall know the truth, and the truth shall make you free" (John 8:32). When that truth becomes a revelation to you, then it is the truth. The reality of this is borne out in seeking prayer that is desirous to know. In that case, who do we pattern ourselves after and why? Jesus is the pattern Son, and it is His instructions we should follow, guiding us to follow the Holy Spirit. We need the spirit of revelation to advance the kingdom by setting men free. The Spirit of Truth and the teacher is the Holy Spirit. He will guide us into all truth (written and operational), and through the Holy Spirit we will come to know the Truth—Jesus Christ. The Holy Spirit will anoint us to tap into His gifts, that is:

1. The gift of the word of wisdom
2. The gift of the word of knowledge
3. The gift of faith
4. The gift of healing
5. The working of miracles
6. The gift of prophecy
7. The discerning of spirits
8. Kinds of tongues
9. The interpretation of tongues

The Holy Spirit's Anointing

It is the Holy Spirit who anoints us to understand the Scriptures and helps us to pray the Father's will—what He intends. He is the one who reveals and directs in different prayer patterns and in this case, fervent prayer releases the anointing, which I now make known to you for quicker and more effective results to produce the power. Remember, the yokes or bondages break due to the anointing the Holy Spirit gives, and not man's intellectual knowledge, charisma, or monetary wealth.

> It shall come to pass in that day That his burden will be taken away from your shoulder, And his yoke from your neck, And the yoke will be destroyed because of the anointing oil. (Isaiah 10:17)

As I stated earlier, seeing no one was telling me how to pay the price and I desperately wanted this anointing, recognizing its importance, I thought the best person to ask was the one (Jesus) who said that the Holy Spirit would guide us into all truth. Now what was revealed I would like to impart to whosoever desires to know. One thing is right, though; you must be willing to pay the price. Simply pray, "Father, please give me the will to be willing, and Holy Spirit, please take me through in Jesus name, amen." There are pain barriers you must be willing to go through by faith. With persistence you will eventually cross over into that realm of unlimited power, tapping into the source (the anointing), "and out of his belly will flow rivers of living water," as it is written. The time it takes to enter into the spirit will vary for each individual. For some it may be after a few minutes, but for some it may take half an hour and beyond. One thing is certain: if you persist, with practice you will begin to notice a change in speech and behavior.

The Technique

The technique is so simple that it almost sounds strange! Start by taking a deep breath, step out in faith, and then pray in tongues until all the air is exhaled from the lungs. Then, go a little further, expelling what extra air you can. At that point you have gone beyond yourself. You are virtually gasping for air. At that point you are dependent on almighty God. Now inhale and note the grasping of air rushing into your lungs (gusto). Continue this technique, and in the process of time, change will come. Again, nothing new comes easily like a small feather floating on a still breeze. Prayer is work. I must tell you the truth. However, when the desired place is reached, work ceases and you enter into rest. The Spirit takes over. Some call it the second wind.

You will soon begin to notice changes in your physical body. You will notice you are becoming stronger, confident, and more aware of others and their needs. Your words are becoming weightier and more meaningful. The anointing is starting to flow—His manna from heaven. The anointing is necessary to do the Lord's work.

> And Jesus came and spoke to them, saying, "All authority has been given to Me in heaven and on earth. Go therefore and make disciples of all the nations, baptizing them in the name of the Father and of the Son and of the Holy Spirit, teaching them to observe all things that I have commanded you; and lo, I am with you always, even to the end of the age." (Matthew 28:18–20)

It also helps to protect us from the attacks of the Enemy, whether in the home or anywhere else, as is written in Isaiah 54:17.

Out of this anointing comes gratitude and a desire to worship God and to love His Son Jesus Christ through the love and power of the Holy Spirit. As Christians, we need this anointing to keep the parasites (demons and all other ungodly entities) out of our lives. The anointing breaks the yoke; the blood cleanses sin and purges our conscience.

Spiritual Application

None of the Old Testament witnesses had this anointing in them. They had it poured on them out of a horn. The prophet Samuel anointed Saul as king and later anointed David to be king as Saul's replacement. The Spirit came upon them: Samson, Elijah, Elisha, David, and others. The power began with Jesus.

Verification of the Wilderness Encounter

Jesus was led into the wilderness after His baptism. He engaged Satan in an epic spiritual battle and won. After this encounter He returned with power of the Spirit, hallelujah. Satan tempted Jesus.

> Then Jesus was led up by the Spirit into the wilderness to be tempted by the devil. And when He had fasted forty days and forty nights, afterward He was hungry. Now when the tempter came to Him, he said, "If You are the Son of God,

> command that these stones become bread." But He answered and said, "It is written, 'Man shall not live by bread alone, but by every word that proceeds from the mouth of God.'" Then the devil took Him up into the holy city, set Him on the pinnacle of the temple, and said to Him, "If You are the Son of God, throw Yourself down. For it is written: 'He shall give His angels charge over you,' and, 'In their hands they shall bear you up, Lest you dash your foot against a stone.'" Jesus said to him, "It is written again, 'You shall not tempt the LORD your God.'" Again, the devil took Him up on an exceedingly high mountain, and showed Him all the kingdoms of the world and their glory. And he said to Him, "All these things I will give You if You will fall down and worship me." Then Jesus said to him, "Away with you, Satan! For it is written, 'You shall worship the LORD your God, and Him only you shall serve.'" Then the devil left Him, and behold, angels came and ministered to Him. (Matthew 4:1–11)

The Beginning of Jesus' Anointed Ministry

Sometime after His return, on a particular day, He entered a synagogue. He was given the scroll and purposely read,

> The Spirit of the Lord GOD is upon me; because the LORD hath anointed me to preach good tidings unto the meek; he hath sent me to bind

> up the brokenhearted, to proclaim liberty to the captives, and the opening of the prison to them that are bound; To proclaim the acceptable year of the LORD. (Isaiah 61:1–2a)

Before His baptism, there's no evidence this anointing was on Him.

a. The Spirit came on Him like a dove.
b. He was filled with the Spirit.
c. He was led by the Spirit.
d. He returned with power.
e. He made the announcement.
f. He later declared the Father in Him was doing the works.

It was after His death that resurrection life entered His body. Like His mighty power, which He exerted in Christ when he raised Him from the dead—resurrection power, glory to God. That power is in us! Therefore the Holy Spirit can enter us, because in the mind of God, we are dead in Christ, a new creation. We are the people of which the Psalmist spoke:

> He shall regard the prayer of the destitute, And shall not despise their prayer. This will be written for the generation to come, That a people yet to be created may praise the LORD. (Psalm 102:17–18)

Folks, that corn of wheat fell into the ground. We are the result of His suffering. The glory is to Jehovah God, our Covenant Keeper!

Conclusion

The purpose of endeavoring to produce this anointing is that the body of Christ must become like the Head—the same likeness (1 John 3:1–3). The Scriptures must be fulfilled, as Jesus Himself said in John 14:12.

If you are willing, we could work together diligently to produce this anointing, which will cause the manifestation of the glory of God to change our lives, families, churches, communities, cities, country, and nations. Therefore, if you give yourself to this type of prayer, you also will experience that fervent prayer releases the anointing. Your life would change radically.

Contemporary Exponents of the Art

Contemporary exponents of the art of this loud, strong type of prayer were: Gordon Lindsey, Charles Finney, Smith Wigglesworth, and others. It is said of Charles Finney that he used to roll on the ground in the woods with loud crying and groaning, fervently producing the anointing because of his compassion for the lost!

Here's a paradigm shift. In a later chapter I will lay out a pathway I believe Jesus wants His church to follow right now. We have been meandering all over the place with various ideas of how to pray, worship, and enter the presence of the covenant keeping God—the God of Abraham, Isaac, and Jacob. The Spirit of revelation is needed for us to follow Jesus and His way of doing things. Have you ever thought on, "My Father hears me always," in John 11:42? I have. Have you ever wondered why it is possible when we ourselves wondered if God even heard some of our prayers? Do you want to know? I did, so I asked the Holy Spirit numerous times, until He finally relented. Twenty-one years have passed since hearing one Sunday morning February 16, 1992, "Go, beyond the flesh." It took ten months of prayer to arrive at this Scripture:

> It is the Spirit who gives life; the flesh profits nothing. The words that I speak to you are spirit, and they are life. (John 6:63)

All I have written could be categorized as bronze and silver in relation to the chapter I will term as gold entitled, "Heaven Came down to You through the Son."

Twenty-one years of searching the Scriptures, praying, and fasting was worth the toil to arrive at this revelation year by year, little by little it unfolded, and then it blossomed in the year 2012. Just as the Spirit had mentioned to me almost twenty years earlier that it would be a significant year, so it was as the revelation unfolded! To God be the glory. I am truly thankful to almighty God for unfolding this truth, so now I present it. The anointing is on every word as I sit down writing this book from the secret place of that revelation. For now, allow me to continue with other ministering led by the Lord. All these progressive revelations were necessary operations to get to the gold that's coming up later. Hallelujah!

In my wilderness journeys, something new was being offered to me—meditation into stillness.

MEDITATION INTO STILLNESS

It seems the best time to make an offer is when a person is hungry, thirsty, or in the wilderness when sand is everywhere and he or she is apt to see a mirage. I could say I was on the wilderness timeline of my life. I considered myself lost and desperately needed direction to get out of the sand dunes where the prince of darkness held me captive. There was no way I could find my way out, though all directions were open before me. The problem was, I didn't know which way to go. I spent most of my time thinking the same thought: *How are you going to get out?* Yet I just stayed where I was in my open prison.

As time passed by, I cried out to the Lord for help, and God answered. This was around December 6, 1992. That was the day I wrote down what was being revealed on "Meditation into Stillness." It is necessary to go over what's being said and also written to get a better understanding. Though much of what was said in the writings made sense at that time, the real impact occurred much later. Not only that, but as we grow in spiritual maturity, so increases the message in the writings. This brings to mind a Scripture in Proverbs verifying this truth.

> My fruit is better than gold, yes, than fine gold, And my revenue than choice silver. (Proverbs 8:19)

The word never fades; it just increases our spiritual awareness. It brings us to the place where we begin to meditate on it, finding a quiet moment like this Scripture is telling us, when the Word becomes a delight.

> But his delight is in the law of the Lord, And in His law he meditates day and night. He shall be like a tree Planted by the rivers of water, That brings forth its fruit in its season, Whose leaf also shall not wither; And whatever he does shall prosper. (Psalm 1:2–3)

To meditate is to engage in contemplation or reflection, to dwell on thoughtfully, to mutter quietly.

I grasped the understanding from my earlier past time as a shepherd. One of my brothers and I were tending our grandfather's sheep. That was something I did enjoy. When we brought the sheep home and put them in their pen, they would lie down. A little while after that, like an object moving on a conveyor belt, up from their stomach and moving along their long necks to their mouths, would appear this little round ball. I could see it bulging in the neck on its way up. Then they would begin to chew. I observed all the sheep lying down were doing the same thing.

As a young boy, I was fascinated. I wanted to know what was happening, so I watched them. Eventually I found out they were regurgitating the grass they had eaten earlier to chew on it more. During this quiet time, while they were in their pen lying down, they refined and digested the grass. It's called chewing the cud. I have never seen them chew their cud while standing up, eating, or playing—only when lying down. Even out in the pasture when they were lying down they didn't do it. Those experiences gave me some insight into the art of meditation. It is like chewing the cud.

On certain occasions we sit in quietness some time or other but do not deliberately plan to meditate or do what we ended up doing. Maybe some past transient thought already stored in the memory was activated to dominate your attention at that particular moment. You voluntarily stopped what you were doing and automatically went and sat down. Usually we sit with the head bowed or tilted sideways, looking down at some imaginary object at an angle of about forty-five degrees, or straight ahead into the infinite but never upward. During that time period, a million thoughts are processed out of which one then magnetizes your attention and becomes the focal point. It takes you away in spirit by such deep concentration of thinking that even when someone calls you, it takes longer than normal before you can respond.

In that moment, your natural surroundings are nonexistent and so unreal that the world entered is the real world. While you were there, you probably found a solution to a problem or things didn't seem difficult anymore. However, when you return from that thought world and come back to your familiar world, reconnected, what you saw seems to be an illusion because your natural sight and surroundings blocked out what you saw. Well, you participated in thoughtful meditation without realizing it, dwelling on one thought. My brilliance as a telecommunications technician was due to this phenomena. Numerous troubleshooting solutions were solved by this method. I would tell my technician friends to sit down and think instead of running around and take the stress off their hearts.

Meditation also involves muttering a word, phrase, or sentence verbatim. The eventual outcome should be some revelation or epiphany, added insight about some situation to benefit the object of the purpose. In that early stage of the journey, it became of utmost importance to go through the Scriptures. Many times we do things and we do not realize why; we have no answer to offer when questioned at that time. But sometimes, at a much later date when the answer comes, we spontaneously say, "Oh, so that's what I was doing!"

Understanding was not present at the time, but it followed well after the action. Look at this Scripture of God's righteous judgments relating to the Gentiles without the law.

> For when Gentiles, who do not have the law, by nature do the things in the law, these, although not having the law, are a law to themselves, who show the work of the law written in their hearts, their conscience also bearing witness, and between themselves their thoughts accusing or else excusing them. (Romans 2:14–15)

Since we already have an idea of thoughtful meditation, we will place more emphasis or bring it to the awareness of our conscience or activate it as a daily activity. We could also say ponder, dwell on, learning to spend longer time on a particular word, verse, or sentence, or even taking a chapter verse by verse. Add to that, as a youth, I have observed honeybees entering flowers to collect pollen. If you have ever taken the time to observe their meticulous dedication and workmanship, they take ages before they emerge from the flower. When they do, their pollen baskets are coated with the pollen from that flower. Jeanne Guyon[7] also spoke about approaching the Scripture like the action of the honeybee.

It is of great importance to take note of certain words that are spoken by the speaker that caught your attention. Jot them down immediately. He or she may belabor the point to heighten awareness. If you can catch these words and meditate on them, you would bring forth a higher yield. "Let those who have ears to hear..." Sound familiar? If we heed the alert to follow the instruction, the objective would be realized through an enriched lifestyle. This increase in knowledge and understanding, when passed on to others, would extend untold joy and happiness. Normally, thankfulness is returned with gratitude.

In stating the above, my mind took a thought transfer (in the twinkle of an eye) to Joshua 1:1–9. After reading these verses several times, I began to think about what God was emphasizing to Joshua. It must have had special meaning, and the benefits must have been supernaturally beneficial. He told Joshua not to forget to read the Word night and day. He went to a higher alert to impact Joshua with an image that was still vivid in Joshua's

---

7 Recommended Book by Jeanne Guyon, *Experiencing the Depths of Jesus Christ.* Sowers of Seeds, Inc, 1981.

mind in His opening command. God said to Joshua, "Moses my servant is dead." Even still, death arrests our attention! I have some idea of how that statement would have impacted Joshua's mind and emotions.

In November of 2005, I distinctly remember how I felt when I received the call from my mother to let me know my father had died. At that time I was in a forty-day fast for the Muslim nations. I believe being in the fasting mode shielded me from the impact of the shock. Like a roaring male lion, I blurted out one prolonged, spontaneous word over the phone, "Wow!" In a flash of thought, I remembered asking my father not to leave his homeland, as we planned to carry out evangelistic work there the following year. I made arrangements to get to United Kingdom to attend the funeral.

I thanked God for His miraculous intervention at that time, allowing the immigration authorities to grant me access into UK because my passport had expired. I loved my father. On my return to the United States from the UK, the Lord comforted me with a beautiful song from the Spirit, "Prince of Peace Sweet Shalom." After all these years, it still feels strange knowing my father is not alive in this physical realm.

Moses was no ordinary leader. He was phenomenal! All Israel mourned for him for thirty days. My imagination is alive to imagine that all Israel was possibly encountering a traumatic mind-set. God in His mercy came and encouraged Israel's new leader. After that God continued with promises, reassurance, confidence, companionship, territory, and courage. God then commanded Joshua not just to read the Word but also to read and meditate on it day and night! In other words, he needed to give thoughtful attention to it; go over it time after time again until it became alive in his subconscious—until the Word became spirit. Following God's command, the Word would create involuntary actions emerging from Joshua like the blinking of the eye. That's how the Word would take effect in us today if we would heed God's command. Success in every endeavor would be accomplished. Involuntary actions of evil are not normal. If an individual finds him or herself in such a situation, he or she should seek deliverance. Also, an understanding of *Curses to Blessings* should be of great benefit and could found in the book by [8]Derek Prince.

We know that lack of knowledge causes destruction.

> My people are destroyed for lack of knowledge. Because you have rejected knowledge, I also will reject you from being priest for Me; Because you have forgotten the law of your God, I also will forget your children. (Hosea 4:6)

This has been evident throughout the ages and is still common today. It's amazing how factual this statement is, even though the Scripture confirms knowledge will increase specifically as the time of the end as revealed.

> But you, Daniel, shut up the words, and seal the book until the time of the end; many shall run to

---

8 Recommended Book or Video by Derek Prince, *Blessing or Curse: You Can Choose.* P.O. Box 6287, Grand Rapids, MI 49516, Chosen Books, 1990. http://www.derekprince.com.

> and fro, and knowledge shall increase. (Daniel 12:4)

I'm still amazed that most of us do not know the Bible for ourselves. We are still existing on "I think," "maybe," and "I'm not sure" when with certainty we should purposefully say like Jesus, "Have you never read?" (Matthew 21: 42), or "It is written" (Luke 4: 4). We should strive to be like Jesus since He left us instructions in the red writing. Studying the Scriptures daily should be our priority. In doing that we would develop confidence, knowing we have supernatural assistance at our disposal through the Holy Spirit. Jesus sent the Holy Spirit to help us understand the Word and to guide us into all truth. Jesus asked the Father to send us help! Have a look at this beautiful Scripture of confirmation.

> But as it is written: "Eye has not seen, nor ear heard, Nor have entered into the heart of man The things which God has prepared for those who love Him." But God has revealed them to us through His Spirit. For the Spirit searches all things, yes, the deep things of God. (1 Corinthians 2:9–10)

Please ask the Holy Spirit for assistance to make the Scriptures easy to understand. None of us can get the honey out of the Word without the Holy Spirit. It is He who creates the desire in us to love the Word and thirst after, hunger after, and yearn after it. Like the deer at the water brook, only the water can satisfy. Likewise, He said, "If any man thirst let him come and drink of the Living Water, Who is Jesus." Nothing else can quench our thirst. The Samaritan woman said, "Give me this water."

Oftentimes we forget that accepting Jesus Christ as our Savior quickened our spirit and that we have been translated from the kingdom of darkness into the kingdom of light—from a physical to a spiritual kingdom. See John 15:19 and Colossians 3:2–3. What I am saying is this: Our present method of building God's kingdom without revelation knowledge is useless. It's like marching around the walls of Jericho without shouting. In other words, we must develop the loving dedication of the honeybee, contemplating or meditating on the Word. Instead, it seems as if we are always in hurry and adamantly sticking to our programs and deceitfully believing we're doing what Jesus asks of us when He calls us to abide in Him. We are far from it.

The practice of meditation should be performed often. It takes time and patience. Because we're so used to noise, we don't know what to do with silence. We need to slow down and learn to dwell in His presence. The Holy Spirit would get the opportunity to quicken our understanding during that period. Was that the reason why Joshua was so successful in leading Israel? He had learned to linger in the tabernacle even after Moses left. We need to adopt his method if that was the case. Here is some scriptural evidence on meditation.

- Isaac in the field—Genesis 24:63; see also Psalm 77:12, 143:5
- God's instruction to Joshua—Joshua 1:8; see also Psalm 1:2, 119:97
- in the night watches—Psalm 63:6, 1:2
- on His precepts—Psalm 119:15, 27, 78
- on His decrees—Psalm 119:23,48
- on God's promises—Psalm 119:148

- David asking God to consider—Psalm 5:1
- asking acceptance—Psalm 19:14, 119:99

The understanding that is unfolding is this—meditation provides the energy or power to illuminate the Scriptures. The reader will get the truth directly from the Holy Spirit as that Scripture is studied, and finally, whenever the Scripture is repeated to the listener, faith and anointing cause revelation knowledge to arise. This then qualifies you, and the truth you know will make you free as John 8:32 says.

Jesus spent a lot of time with the Father, and every time He went among the crowd, something miraculous occurred according to the Scriptures. See Luke 4:42, 6:12, 9:28. I believe for Christians, this should be normal. This knowledge and understanding would enhance our spiritual progress. The body of Christ is entering into an exciting season, so let's look attentively at the next chapter.

GO BEYOND THE FLESH

God is able to change abject despair into assured hope. I was in the midst of that kind of despair when I had heard this word one Sunday morning on February 16, 1992. Every so often it would come to the forefront of my thinking. The instruction that was impressed upon my heart like a sword cut through the other discouraging words I was hearing.

On that specific Sunday morning, there were four beautiful children (one boy and three girls, ages from four to thirteen) in a family of six. I was driving a red van traveling from Stoke Newington to Lower Clapton. I cannot recall what triggered the high-level, one-sided discussion, but in the mix, twice I heard—"Go beyond the flesh."

The words overpowered my hearing, shut out the outside world, and magnetized me into giving them audience. They were powerful words, just like how the Scriptures describe them.

> For the word of God is living and powerful, and sharper than any two-edged sword, piercing even to the division of soul and spirit, and of joints

> and marrow, and is a discerner of the thoughts and intents of the heart. And there is no creature hidden from His sight, but all things are naked and open to the eyes of Him to whom we must give account. (Hebrews 4:12–13)

I was having a God encounter to rescue me from the unnecessary violation of my emotions because He knows there is good in every situation. No matter how bad your so-called enemy feels, he or she knows that no person ever does bad or evil all the time. It is pride that prevents us from acknowledging this fact, preventing us from speaking the truth. Hence, God breaks in every so often to steer us from disaster as we go out into the world where a triune evil threat awaits us: self, the world, and Satan. He beckons us into the secret place where He dwells in righteousness, peace, and joy in the Holy Spirit.

Dear reader, it is in that domain, beyond the flesh, beyond the inhibitions of this life, beyond the lure of humanity's mortal enemy, that your Creator God awaits you. After all is gone, you may hear yourself say a beautiful prayer: "God, it's just You and me now."

Your pure and powerful words of prayer send a message. Another child of Adam is ready to come home. Your heavenly Father was awaiting your call, the cry of your spirit. Your journey back to your home has just begun. Somehow you knew He heard you because it was a spirit-to-Spirit communication. The plan is activated through a process of learning and doing to bring recovery and restoration to get you home. Praise the Lord! You then responded because He answered you. Then you said to Him, "What do I do now!"

He may say, as in my case, "Go and pray."

So I went off to pray in what I thought prayer meant, without any fear or intimidation whatsoever. You see, dear reader, there's no fear in that secret place, only tranquility. The place where the soul and flesh inhabit is a world of numerous fears. What happens from that moment on is your actions are performed void of fear. Only the voice of your Shepherd you will now hear and follow.

> I am the good shepherd. The good shepherd gives His life for the sheep.… I am the good shepherd; and I know My sheep, and am known by My own. As the Father knows Me, even so I know the Father; and I lay down My life for the sheep. And other sheep I have which are not of this fold; them also I must bring, and they will hear My voice; and there will be one flock and one shepherd.… My sheep hear My voice, and I know them, and they follow Me. And I give them eternal life, and they shall never perish; neither shall anyone snatch them out of My hand. (John 10:11, 14–16, 27–28)

So I began to pray. Then realized I didn't know exactly what He meant or even how to pray. So I went back and said, "Father, You said to pray, but I'm sorry, I never thought of asking You how to pray." His answer was one word: "Intercede."

I didn't know what intercession meant, and I didn't feel like asking Him what it meant. I knew I could look it up in a dictionary, so I did. I found the definition of what it meant—praying for someone else or standing in the gap. Again, after some time it dawned on me again that I didn't really know exactly how He meant it. So I went back again to ask Him how He meant it.

My words to God were, "Father, You did say to pray. When I realized I wasn't sure what You meant, I came back and asked You. You then said to me—intercede. I went and looked it up in a dictionary and was doing what it said. I then realized I didn't really know how You mean it. I'm sorry. Could you please explain to me what You mean?" Glory is to God.

He laid out for me James 5:7, step by step impressing it upon my heart. It went like this.

> Therefore be patient, brethren, until the coming of the Lord. See how the farmer waits for the precious fruit of the earth, waiting patiently for it until it receives the early and latter rain. (James 5:7)

God said, "You know how a farmer sees a plot of land full of trees? He then goes and cuts down all the trees and takes out all the stumps. He then plows up the land, making rows. He then goes and plants his seeds because he saw a harvest."

I spoke aloud, "I got it!" That moment, intercession became a revelation.

There are many models of intercession in the Bible where a servant stood in the gap on behalf of the people. For this example I will use Pethahiah, a Levite's intercessory model, in Nehemiah 9:5–38. Pethahiah took the role to make the supplication on behalf of his people. His prominent role of importance is written in Nehemiah 10:24.

> It was in the seventh month on the 27th day, the entire assembly of 42,360 most likely the number mentioned in 7: 66, was fasting in sackcloth, and with dust on their heads. They had inter-married with the people of the land; they read from the book of the law for a quarter of the day, and confessed their sins and the iniquities of their fathers. Another fourth of the day they confessed and worshiped.... and Pethahiah, said: Stand up and bless the LORD your God Forever and ever!" (Nehemiah 9:5–38)
>
> Blessed be Your glorious name, Which is exalted above all blessing and praise! You alone are the LORD; You have made heaven, The heaven of heavens, with all their host, The earth and everything on it, The seas and all that is in them, And You preserve them all. The host of heaven worships You. (Nehemiah 9:5)

Pethahiah's prayer ended at verse 38 and is worth reading in its context to see the similarities in their content. Their prayers were influenced by the position they held in the community and government during that time, even though they were in captivity in Babylon.

Jesus is our High Priest, and every saint should take the role like the Levites and learn to do what they did, as in the above model.

In a little book called *The Secret of Intercession*, by [9]Andrew Murray, he made some valid statements regarding God, intercession, and the church. See bibliography and note page 16, "God Seeks Intercessors." "Of what infinite importance is the place the intercessor holds in the kingdom of God! Is it not indeed a matter of wonder that God give men such power?"

I am a dedicated follower of Andrew Murray and own many of his books. I also believe every saint who has not read his book *Humility* should do so immediately.

To continue, the process of going to God the Father was developing a relationship of communication where He came to me at my Holy Spirit training lodge in North London, UK, and explained through an illustration that He has ears and He can hear me. That sacred intimacy created confidence in me so that I do not pray in the usual religious norm. I talk to Him. He is my heavenly Father who loves me and always hears me, whether He responds outside my expectations or not.

---

9 Andrew Murray, *The Secret of Intercession*. 30 Hunt Valley Circle, New Kensington, PA 15068: Whitaker, 1995, (Page 16).

> And I know that You always hear Me, but because of the people who are standing by I said this, that they may believe that You sent Me. (John 11:42)

I understand what Jesus is saying. There's an intimacy that exists beyond mere words. Total trust is developed in purity, spirit, and truth. Ceaseless, steadfast love in motion exists between Father and Son. I was moving in that direction.

Later that year, on the night of August 31, I understood what it meant not to oppose another's will that is determinedly set on doing what he or she wants to do. From that moment that night my quest for almighty God was born. It took ten months of persistently seeking God to understand what "go beyond the flesh" meant. I had to know.

My persistent prayer to Father God was, "I believe You gave me those words because they didn't match what was being said, and neither were they audible. They captivated my mind. I believe You were telling me where the answer resides."

During the time of this persistent praying, God had instructed me to sell the business for fifty thousand pounds. Later on I moved to a new location—my Holy Spirit Training Lodge. It was there on December 27, 1992, I began to write what I understood "go beyond the flesh" meant from what I discovered in John 6:63 about what Jesus said in that Scripture of truth.

God was revealing Himself in a marvelous way even in the midst of the chaos and confusion. What a wonderful God we serve. His love, faithfulness, and companionship are amazing. He was guiding me through a series of writings since the day I heard, "Go beyond the flesh." What I discovered is this: He gave the practical demonstration of Himself, which I'm now realizing led up to that unforgettable day in Bible college of Him wanting me to know His glory; He wants all of us to know His glory.

Lord, I'm ready to receive and to make Your glory known globally. Help me, Holy Spirit. I believe the time is right. We *must* go beyond the flesh. Amen!

A DEEP SPIRITUAL WOUND

The writing penned on December 27, 1992, began like this: "These words, 'Go beyond the flesh,' were heard internally on February 16, 1992, while I was in intense, indescribable pain—pain beyond the description of the dictionary—and I am now receiving the explanation as I write. The pain was due to a deep spiritual wound. My emotions felt the effects, but it was beyond intellectual understanding, hence no description of the pain." (See Romans 8:26.)

From that Sunday morning, I sought the meaning of that revelation, which was my second step to freedom. I prayed about it, went over it again and again and time after time. I knew it was of great importance. Otherwise it would not have been spoken to me, and it was relevant at the point of my need. It was the cure for my situation. I began to grasp the meaning. To overcome the present situation or what we are actually experiencing, God is saying, "Get to higher ground." That is, let your thoughts rise above the carnal mind to spiritual thinking, enabling us to deal with the flesh. Carnal pictures in Scripture include Esau and

Egypt. From that day a learning process began where I saturated my mind with the Word of God even though I was not fully aware of what I was doing then. I saw the ungodly bombard their minds with pop music, so I thought, *I will bombard my mind with godly music night and day, at every opportunity, because I am a Christian.*

The pain did not go away until mid-April, but during that time, my understanding was increasing day by day in the area beyond the flesh. We know that words, which are spoken and heard, are invisible yet effective, just like the wind. This led me into the Scriptures searching for the meaning or understanding of, "Go beyond the flesh," which I found Jesus explaining to the crowd and His disciples. He said, "It is the Spirit who gives life; the flesh profits nothing. The words that I speak to you are spirit, and they are life." (See John 6:63, 1 Corinthians 15:50, Philippians 3:2–3, Romans 8:6–8, John 4:22–24.)

From these Scriptures I began to see the problem from another plane where we have to look at the literal problem as a byproduct of deviation from the truth through Adam and Eve, hence the suffering. One must return to the true path irrespective of how painful the process may be. It is vitally important for us to take heed to the words of Jesus and remain in Him as stated in John 15:7–8. It is very sad that crisis seems to be the only way to force us back to seeking the true way, and that way can only be attained through true repentance and forgiveness. Let us read about David's experience when he realized his separation from God. (See Psalm 51:11–17, Acts 2:38.) Humility is the only way that will allow God to accept us back because He opposes the proud (James 4:6).

Furthermore, the arm of flesh will fail us if we are trying to achieve God's requirements by our standards or in our own strength. To escape prolonged agony and anguish, it would be best for us to be obedient by simply submitting and saying, "Father, increase Your grace in me to overcome and trust You." You will begin to sense that getting through the painful process can only be done through faith because self is exhausted and has given up. You are now in no man's land between turning back and going forward. Tears are of no comfort. You are in the land of "all alone." Friends cannot help you, and God, it seems, has abandoned you. You can only wait to be rescued; the days seem to get longer, and the nights are tormenting.

However, when you begin to sink into discouragement, God supplies the lifeline through the Scriptures to lift the gloom with hope.

> For I know the plans I have for you, declares the Lord, plans to prosper you and not to harm you, plans to give you hope and a future. Then you will call upon me and come and pray to me, and I will listen to you. I will be found by you, declares the Lord, and bring you back from captivity. (Jeremiah 29:11–14)

See also Isaiah 26:3, Proverbs 3:3–6, Psalm 91:14–16, Isaiah 40:31, 43:2–4, and Hebrews 12:5–12

There is no game or pretending in this matter. It's a life-or-death situation. Truth you know becomes a reality, and you realize you are in a real-life drama you have no control over and will be lost forever if God does not respond! The commitment stage then begins where you have no choice but to surrender all by placing your life on the altar of sacrifice and utter the irretrievable promise, "Yes, Father, I am willing to pay the price; forward or death, because going back is erased from my memory. I submit and yield completely to You, and from today I will obey You totally by grace. Help me…" Finally… deliverance! Glory to God! What joy and freedom!

The Scriptures then begin to pulsate with new life; it's springtime again.

> When the LORD brought back the captivity of Zion, We were like those who dream. Then our mouth was filled with laughter, And our tongue with singing. Then they said among the nations, "The LORD has done great things for them." The LORD has done great things for us, And we are glad. (Psalm 126:1–3)

> Our soul has escaped as a bird from the snare of the fowlers; The snare is broken, and we have escaped. Our help is in the name of the LORD, Who made heaven and earth. (Psalm 124:7–8)

A new lifestyle begins where everything is done according to His will. The confidence and assurance come that God will answer when you call. Read Jeremiah 33:3, 1 John 5:14–15, Psalm 27:1, and Isaiah 51:11–17. Praise His holy name.

From that month forward, inspirational writings began and are still ongoing. After the opening of this portal, new songs began to flow from the Spirit. As I stated earlier, I cannot write lyrics, and neither am I a composer. However, when I pick up the guitar and begin to play, the words and music begin to flow. In the early days of God breaking in, I didn't understand what was happening, and many songs were lost. I began to notice the beauty in the songs and eventually got a little tape recorder to capture more when they came. I began to notice that they would come during my nightly prayer and worship sessions. I literally used to do what the Bible said. The Psalmist used to rise at midnight to give God thanks because of His righteous judgments, so I got up at midnight and did the same. The strange thing was that during some of those midnight encounters, around midnight I would start playing, sometimes with my eyes closed, and I could see what looked like people sitting on the floor around me. They would get up and leave, and then another group would come and sit in the same area. It was then I began to notice a harmonizing of singing and playing. There would be a shift in my singing and playing from ordinary to extraordinary. Songs like "Know Your Spiritual Position," "Heaven Came down to You through the Son," "Who's Going to See Me through," "Last Call, Last Call," "Take Me Beyond the Veil," "Prince of Peace," "Sweet Shalom," "I Cried to the Lord," "At the Stirring of the Waters," "A Higher Place in You," "Psalm 122," and many more came forth. These songs were created from the foundation of a fasted life with prayer and worship.

Some of the above songs are extremely long, and some are extremely heartrending, where much weeping and moaning in intercession was offered due to what I saw. I poured out my heart in intercession for the nations, asking Father God to forgive them, for they did not know what they were doing. I prayed God would stretch forth His hand of mercy and save the people, even those who had rejected salvation because they refused to forgive. The angel took me to a cave and showed me where they were inside, weeping and wailing. I recognized some of the people inside the cave. While leaving the cave he said, "Last Call, Last Call." Below are the words to that song. I taped it and memorized the words and melody.

Last Call, Last Call

Last call, last call
That day will be the last call
When the word goes forth
You will know in your heart
That the message is final
You will know it's your last call, last call

I saw the nations: black, white, yellow, and brown
Huddled together, weeping, and mourning!
The Spirit who showed the scene
Said they rejected salvation
Because of unforgiveness
His words on leaving the scene
Were last call, last call

I woke up with tears running down my face
As the words sank deep into my heart
I fell to my knees before the Father

Heart rent, torn apart, weeping!
Wailing and mourning, interceding
I poured out my heart for the nations
Praying, Father God, forgive them
For they know not what they do
Stretch forth Your hand of mercy
And save the people.

You will know on that day
When the words are spoken
That precise moment you will hear,
Come to Jesus now, open up to the Lord
There will be no more time
That will be your last call, last call.
Remember what Jesus said,
That in the last days it will be
Like when Noah was here on the earth.

We're now living in the days
Where pleasure is the norm
Ungodliness, lawlessness, and selfishness:
The spirit of the world
Has captivated the hearts of men, women, and children
But hear the words of the Spirit,
It's last call, last call.

Come to Jesus now
He is the truth and the way
No man can enter in, only through Jesus
He paid the price on Calvary
For you and for me, and the nations, no distinction

It is written, for the grace of God
That brings salvation hath appeared to all men

It is said that He died for the sins of the whole world
That means you've been included.
Reject unforgiveness, take the bitterness
From your heart so there will be
No mourning, weeping, or wailing.
This is last call

This will be the last call kairos,
God's appointed time
For you to be saved in His kingdom
You will know in your heart
That it will be your last call, last call.

You will know you will know
They will pierce your heart
Unforgiveness will have to leave
Because the anointing will be there
To give you salvation, because it will be
Your last call, last call, last call

Contact by Tel (716) 381-2871 E-mail tidal2009@live.com

On February 13, 1993, was the next writing. I kept them over the years, believing one day they might become useful to someone.

THROUGH THE GLASS CLEARLY

I penned this life-changing writing on February 13, 1993. I spent Friday evening and most of Saturday in a contemplative spirit, mostly looking inward in quietness, observing, imagining, and noticing many different scenes. Psalm 1 captivated my thoughts. What was unfolding was the tree bringing forth its fruit in its season and leaves that do not whither.

It was interesting to note the fruit grew from the nourishment or substance drawn in from the earth. "Let the earth bring forth her abundance…" we know was spoken in Genesis, and fruit appeared. So the tree that brings forth fruit is the effect of the Creator, who is the sustenance and source from which the trees are manifesting: the cedars of Lebanon, fruitful vines, olive trees, oaks of righteousness, and so on. This brings to mind that we are part of the process of thought and the effect of thought; that is, God's thought, which means we can bring forth in abundance by following the principle.

We are all different yet all one because we all draw from the same source of infinite supply, who is God. It is not man or any other source but God. He is the Giver and the Gift. But the supply will not flow as it should or could without realization. Realization only comes through dying to self—that is, casting off the flesh and taking on the Spirit. Or better still, a seed sown into soil dies and through death brings forth new life. The Ultimate Seed is Jesus Christ.

So through realization, anything can be manifested through the infinite supply of our Father Creator, which Jesus confirmed.

> Do not fear, little flock, for it is your Father's good pleasure to give you the kingdom. (Luke 12:32)
>
> Son, you are always with me, and all that I have is yours. (Luke 15:31)
>
> He who did not spare His own Son, but delivered Him up for us all, how shall He not with Him also freely give us all things? (Romans 8:32)

The abundance, whatever form it may take when received, must be shared and not hoarded. How is it achieved?

- Step 1: Believe.
- Step 2: Have faith.
- Step 3: Persevere with steady faith until manifestation of the Word becomes flesh or reality—tangible.

Always ask for abundance so you will always have enough to give.

> For the administration of this service not only supplies the needs of the saints, but also is abounding through many thanksgivings to God, while, through the proof of this ministry, they glorify God for the obedience of your confession to the gospel of Christ, and for your liberal sharing with them and all men. (2 Corinthians 9:12–13)

Because infinite supply is complete, He gave us all when He gave us Jesus Christ. Note carefully here that God gave first; also notice He specifically mentioned the seed already provided.

> Then God said, "Let the earth bring forth grass, the herb that yields seed, and the fruit tree that yields fruit according to its kind, whose seed is in itself, on the earth"; and it was so. And the earth brought forth grass, the herb that yields seed according to its kind, and the tree that yields fruit, whose seed is in itself according to its kind. And God saw that it was good. (Genesis 1:11–12)

Therefore, whatever you give is termed a seed. The principle of spiritual law is to give and give cheerfully.

> So let each one give as he purposes in his heart, not grudgingly or of necessity; for God loves a cheerful giver. (2 Corinthians 9:7)

The question is, why are we so distant from reality or what we term reality? Reality is seeing the same thing we previously saw from degenerated man but now from a spiritual point of view, or as

God sees it. Previously what we saw as true was false because the thoughts were those of fallen men who deviated from the truth. Hence the wrong concept—death bound instead of toward life. Once the illumination comes, the spiritual viewpoint takes over, which is real, and again we see as He sees, and the Spirit gives confirmation or correctness, and wonderings cease. Previously we were viewing from a point of hallucination because we were born into, and part of, a big dream that has the whole world mesmerized.

All of us are in that dream, and we call it being human. When things go wrong we say, "I am only human" when there's no explanation. But there is an explanation. The human catchphrase is the dream term and will continue if we do not come to the point of realizing that the dream is a deviation from the truth, and our so-called life in that state is a false concept. It is not of the truth, hence the difficulty of breaking out. How do we break out? By lifting our consciousness above the flesh, which is a trap in its dream state of fallenness.

Once the thought is lifted above the flesh or the kingdom of this world, and understand through revelation, the flesh, Esau, and Egypt will be seen differently. We then realize how useless the flesh is without illumination by the Holy Spirit. Get up to the higher mountains, you gates, lift up your heads on high, and I will lift up my eyes unto the hills, which is a state of higher consciousness. Spirit-inspired prayer is the answer. This will give insight into why Jesus said,

> I will no longer talk much with you, for the ruler of this world is coming, and he has nothing in Me. (John 14:30)
>
> If you were of the world, the world would love its own. Yet because you are not of the world, but I chose you out of the world, therefore the world hates you. (John 15:19)

Therefore, we are no more of the fallen world because we have taken on His likeness. We must ask the Holy Spirit to help us set our minds (the mind of Christ in us) on things above (Colossians 3:1–3, Ephesians 2:1–10). Daily reading of the Word with prayer and fasting are essential for spiritual growth and understanding.

Praise is to our glorious Father! This was a season of revelations pouring forth. Let's move to the next revelation: "For God's Sake Reverse It."

FOR GOD'S SAKE REVERSE IT

I specifically recall writing this on February 25, 1993. I was preparing for an exam while attending London Electronic College, Earls Court. That day the Lord just broke in. I had learned to stop what I was doing and give wholehearted attention when He did this. In the earlier days before moving from the business, in my ignorance, I asked if He could wait while I attended to my son! Oh, Gentile mind—I still acknowledge this truth.

The second-most-powerful prayer in all the earth is family prayer: husband, wife, and children together. It is so powerful that the enemy buffets the family incessantly, and the evidence of his success is an escalating madness of a statistical divorce rate that is mushrooming out of proportion. It has catastrophic repercussions upon all involved, both Christians and non-Christians alike.

I could understand the fate of the non-Christian, but for the Christian it was a puzzle until the answer came in this form: "I saw Satan fall like lightning from heaven." Then I understood the

Christian fall from spirituality to carnality through deception by thinking our own thoughts and neglecting prayer.

He has been so successful with the same old trick, yet we deem it normal. But it's not normal! The reason why he has been successful is because he knows we do not know the power and control we would have over him if we'd pray. He capitalizes on our ignorance and then laughs at us Christians as the biggest joke on earth. He has contaminated things with his venom of pride until there seems no way of recovery. Then I cried out, "Oh God, from where comes love, tenderness, affection, compassion, unity, and faithfulness in marriage!"

This response was impressed on me: "They all come from Me, my son. I put them all in as part of My creation. You have nothing, son, nothing. All individual beings are manifesting me, and any two can come together who I have drawn to my Son. If they have any problem, which is in the flesh, and they come to me, I will put it right. I know the thoughts I think toward them."

The Enemy now knows that I know, and right at this moment, he is in a state of limbo, not knowing what the outcome will be. He knows that one decision will defeat him or give him victory. It is that crucial. One decision could signal victory or defeat for him. I want him defeated again and again.

Satan hasn't changed his plan from the garden of tempting us through our five senses. It's always the same, and his timing is to come in just before God's intention is to do something big in Adam and Eve's lives. This is the basic pattern throughout the Scriptures and still in our lives. He short-circuited the process through fleshly stimulation, and they fell flat. Today it's still the same. But look what has happened, which was true in the garden of Gethsemane before sin: "Father, that they be one in us." This was Jesus' prayer of redemption for us.

Adam and Eve fell into a spiritual sleep, out of which about 95 percent of the world's population is desperately trying to escape. When someone does us wrong, we need to find a way to break out of the emotional state without being hurt and without harboring bitterness of any kind. Was I part of it? Yes! Did I escape? Yes! How? I'm delighted you asked the question, and rightly so.

Well, there was no way I could have escaped on my own. I was beyond recovery. I termed my state "beyond insanity." First, I needed deliverance. Next, I had a revelation, which I will now share, that came in a spectacular way from deep within but clear as crystal: "Go beyond the flesh." That is, beyond the five senses. But there is a much quicker and more effective way to restoration than the arduous and stumbling route of forward and backward, up and down that I took.

First of all, as the thought comes that you want a better life than the one you have, or that you want to rise above the gloom, instead of waiting for the warm air currents rising from the valley to take you up, as that thought comes of wanting a better life, latch onto it. It's not based on how you feel; the feeling will betray the action that would lead to deliverance. Rather, it's based on action and speaking the word. You would get victory just doing it, whether you feel like it or not. Just repeat, "Father, I forgive everyone who has hurt me, and I forgive myself as well." You may not feel any release at that moment, but know that words are spiritual. By speaking those activating words, you have done what is necessary to initiate change. Your action of faith enabled your Father God who sits on the throne to set you and the others free.

This is what happens. A process takes place in the spirit realm where the decree went forth to the satanic kingdom to remove his demons from everyone who was held captive and kept in gloom and doom by the unforgiving spirits. Result? All become free. Forgiveness of others is necessary for mental peace and radiant health. Forgiveness is love manifesting. Love for everyone is restored. You no longer see them as enemies; rather, you see them as God sees them.

Finally, forgiveness is a covenant. Hence, God is fighting on your behalf as you call. The prayer to quicker release comes as I seek only the grace of God. "I seek only the word that comes from You, Father of spirits. The word You give is truth. Therefore, I will wait in silence and be still. Speak, Lord, for Your servant desires to listen. Holy Spirit, teach me how to listen. Thank You for the answer. I glorify Your name, Jesus. Amen."

Do this often. The best time is before you go to sleep. Pray until peace and harmony come and your thinking ability climbs to another level, to that of transcending consciousness.

TRANSCENDING CONSCIOUSNESS

There was a lot of personal turmoil taking place in my life, and in the midst of it all, the Spirit of God was guiding me because I wanted a better life in God. He heard my heart's cry and came to my rescue. I had lots of help from the cell group in our church. Praise God, they were my invaluable helpers. "Father God, I ask You to continually bless them, wherever they are. Be a shield about them even now. Love of the spirit we all must give, from deep within our hearts. Let it flow." This writing came into existence on March 19, 1993. After this writing, my relationship with the Lord improved.

After the area meeting at Andover on Thursday, March 18, 1993, one of our church members came and spoke with me. She was inquiring as to the progress of my fasting. She was the one who stirred my mind about the work of the spirits behind divorce and to enter into fasting immediately. Her instruction was on March 11, 1993. It made sense what she said, and I entered into fasting the following day, March 12, 1993.

I have learned to listen to others but respond only when my spirit witnesses how I should respond—yes or no. I believe the meeting was no accident but was planned by Father God for us to meet at that particular time, at that particular place, for the particular words she had to be spoken. That is spiritual timing. We as Christians need to know that we must be in God's timing. If we are in God's timing, we will always be in the right place, at the right time, and doing the right things according to His divine plan for our lives.

Since that time, this became part of my daily prayer. "Holy Father, please let me be in the right place at the right time, doing the right thing, according to Your divine plan for my life today." With that you should never be out of your spiritual position because your steps are ordered of the Lord. Here is God's guidance for the young through Solomon in Proverbs 3:5–6. By the way, all of us qualify because we are all children of the King.

On the eighth day of the fast, God answered as the true warrior He is and saw me through. That night, March 20, 1993, I put on my spiritual armor according to Ephesians 6:10–18. That night on entering my room, I went into battle. I took the sword from its sheath and went into battle, led by the Captain of the Hosts. While praying, I bound them one by one in the name of Jesus, namely spirits of divorce, resentment, unforgiveness, deception, unbelief, pride, division, separation, spirit of the world, and feminism. Then I loosed the spirits of marriage, love, acceptance, unity, faith, and truth. I felt the victory that night. Praise seemed to be the agenda for the remainder of the forty-day fast.

Since then, daily, I put my spiritual armor on like a soldier would dress for battle. They use physical weapons, and we use spiritual weapons. Our words of faith, through delegated power and authority, demolish strongholds.

Later that night I had a dream. I woke up and gave thanks to God for the dream. I was taken up to a point above the earth and shown the state of the human race. They were struggling to overcome being mesmerized by evil but without any success. I saw the success we desired is dependent upon God intervening through His chosen servants.

Those who don't believe there is anything else for which to live spend their time purely for the flesh. They do not know that the gratification or the vice-like grip is part of the international mesmerism. They refuse to believe in anything else except what they see.

Then there are the intellectuals trying to satisfy their inquiring minds, trying to reason God out of existence so they are relied upon as truth bearers through scientific reasoning.

Finally, there are the spiritual men and women, the selected light bearers chosen by God to guide man out of the mesmerism. However, it seems like they do not really know what they've been given. They have been blessed with the Spirit of God to pray, battling with entities in the spirit realm to bring change on the earth. Winning this war would lift man from the deviated thoughts that have incarcerated him in the penitentiary called mesmerism.

I pondered the scene and saw why there are so many wars, murders, rapes, robberies, divorces, adulteries, denominations, divisions, family breakups, self-gratifications, carelessness, and the like. It was then I understood the state of descending consciousness that permits only depravity. It typifies the man in a drunken stupor who still tries to lift his glass for another drink. I don't think that dismal picture was the intended outcome—far from it. It's a somber state that's very distant from the original image his Creator intended.

> So God created man in His own image; in the image of God He created him; male and female He created them. (Genesis 1:27)

It is a spiritual war where the illuminated ones have been called to engage and win because of their transcending consciousness—journeying ever upward till we can say like Jesus, with a deep knowing.

> I and My Father are one. (John 10:30)

Without illumined consciousness or reaching the gold lampstand, we will not complete the task of reaching the entire world. Instead, the nations are confronted with the twin curses of lying and stealing.

I saw the dream from the dimension of the spirit realm. So we then understand that the discord is in the carnal realm of finite states of consciousness where the spirit of the world rules. His rule leads to chaos, destruction, and death. Let us quickly thank God for faith that will get us back into His kingdom through the only access possible, and that is through Jesus Christ our victorious Lord, the Son of the living God.

Therefore, how do we accomplish this honorary task? It can be accomplished by the only way possible, and that is total submission of our wills to Jesus Christ, just as He totally submitted His will to His Father, who gave Him total victory over Satan on the cross. That kind of obedience to Christ Jesus would give us the victory also. These Scriptures inform us of the validity of His presence, delegated authority, and partnering with us.

> Behold, I give you the authority to trample on serpents and scorpions, and over all the power of the enemy, and nothing shall by any means hurt you. (Luke 10:19)

Even though our knowledge and understanding are making leaps and bounds, we have come to know that apart from Jesus, we can do nothing.

APART FROM ME YOU CAN DO NOTHING

I distinctly remembered when the Spirit of the Lord came to my Holy Spirit Boot Camp and said He wanted me to do a series of fasts. He didn't say anything like, "Hail, mighty man of valor" or, "You are greatly beloved." I was scared, and I voiced my fears. A promise was made, which gave me reassurance. Somehow I knew to pray before starting each fast. The first fast began in August of 1993. Thereafter came the revelation, "Apart from Me you can do nothing," which was written on September 1, 1993. I understood the significance of this, and in reality, I acknowledged the fact it was true. Without that understanding, I couldn't have completed the series of fasts that ended in 1995. Throughout the journey His guidance and protection assured victory. The red writing tells us Jesus Christ was sent into the world. He said He came down from heaven not to do His own will but to do the will of Him who sent Him (John 4:34) and to finish the work. His purpose—the Son of Man came to save that which was lost (Matthew 18:11). Mankind was lost—because of original sin through Eve and Adam's disobedience.

I want to utilize the word *juxtapose* in relation to love and obedience, leaning one against the other. My opinion is this. In the inner core or heart of love rests the word *obedience*, and in the inner core or heart of obedience rests the word *love*. In other words, they are inseparable and interchangeable. Jesus' statement, "Apart from me you can do nothing" holds true because He is the only person who was sinless. Therefore, He qualifies to be Savior, Son of Man, Perfect Man, and King of kings. He said, "Ask in My name" because the Father qualified Him as the beloved Son in whom He is well pleased, and we should hear Him (Matthew 17:5b).

We must pray for a revelation of who lives within us and to know that it is the Spirit of Jesus Christ who does the good works in us. He is our hope of glory (Colossians 1:27). The fullness of the Godhead also dwells in Him, and therefore in us, bodily (Colossians 2:9–10). Such Scriptures need much meditation to comprehend their spiritual significance and enable each saint to live an overcoming life.

Our conditions (strongholds) before being saved must be dismantled or pulled down to enable us to align our thoughts with Christ's thoughts through the Holy Spirit (1 John 2:15–17, Colossians 2:8, Ephesians 4:17–32, 2 Corinthians 10:4–6). In the latter Scripture notice verse 6 regarding obedience. In my estimation we often say we love Jesus, but obedience is a word we do not understand in the context of spiritual matters. Had it been so, I believe the power and fire of God would be burning in every nation today.

Fasting sharpens our spiritual awareness, and with that, one must be careful not to become judgmental. The horrors of sin become grotesque and bring on the condition of wanting to hide. Isaiah thought he was righteous until that holy encounter exposed him for what he really was, that which he confessed, a man of unclean lips in relation to God's holiness. God's grace then takes on new meaning to sustain us through the unveiling of the despicable state of the human mind. We need Jesus, who sanctified Himself for us. Indeed, apart from Him we can do nothing—at least nothing holy that would be accepted by a holy God. He is the gate of righteousness through which we can enter into the holy of holies.

We are seated with Christ in heavenly places as we read in Colossians 3:1–3. What does it really mean? We could have the best explanation by our most learned theological scholars, but do we really understand, and are we implementing it? I don't think so. Why do I make such a tacit statement? Is it because of the increasing selfishness on the increase in the church? Unbelief is rampantly dominated by a worldly lifestyle. For us to embrace what Jesus has said, we must take time out to meditate on that truth. I do not have the answer, only a belief about why things are the way they are. The majority of Christians are struggling to make ends meet on a daily basis, and only a few are living a fruitful life in God. Over the past years, many people who came into the church with substantial wealth have ended up in poverty. What happened? Is it because they abandoned the promises of God concerning fruitfulness and have been adhering only to the person of Jesus Christ? Or is it that we are separating two parts of a whole and our wealth is as sons and daughters of inheritance? Our Father has made both His person and His inheritance ours.

We Are to Perform Good Works of Service

We are created to perform good works of service, as Ephesians 2:10 shows us. Whatever we are doing, God must be involved in it for it to work and to be productive. For instance, as Christians we need to understand that investing is not a bad thing. We are still here on the earth, and the principles Jesus taught can be applied to increase wealth. Riches are a facet of the glory of God. My belief is this: there shouldn't be one poor Christian on this earth, bearing in mind the principles Jesus taught regarding money. His riches are tried in the fire according to Revelation 3:18, so we need Him to guide us toward their attainment. Neither do I believe we should have to approach a bank to borrow money to start a godly project. Please remember, I am only sharing my opinion.

Paul said, "I can do all things through Christ who strengthens me" (Philippians 4:13). May God strengthen us with divine might in our inner man by His Spirit (Ephesians 3:16). May He also give us the wisdom to get wealth to live well and also finance the end-time harvest.

Let's see how the Holy Spirit Boot Camp Training played out in a real drama in the following chapter. We must see beyond the people and discern the spirits involved in initiating action.

GOD'S PURPOSE FOR MARRIAGE

I knew the information from the Lord was of great importance due to His presence that accompanied the writings. Six months later, in September 25, 1993, this message came from the Lord on time to bring about a reversal in a court decision that was happening during the writing of, "For God's Sake Reverse it." Its relevance became evident in a courthouse in Edmonton, North London, on October 7, 1993. He did speak through the prophet Isaiah that His word would not return void (Isaiah 55:11). I have seen it proven over and over. Also, His word is forever settled in heaven (Psalm 119:89). Peter said we have a more sure word of prophecy (2 Peter 1:19).

Oftentimes we hear a certain word mentioned, and not knowing what it really means, or sensing that the description given does not sound quite right, sometimes we still don't think to search out the word for ourselves. This can cause uncertainty if we do not know the thought that comes to us should be searched out, especially if it is a good thought.

In this brief I will put some light on God's purpose for marriage according to His Word. First we will commence with God's command before the flood.

> Then God blessed them, and God said to them, "Be fruitful and multiply; fill the earth and subdue it; have dominion over the fish of the sea, over the birds of the air, and over every living thing that moves on the earth." (Genesis 1:28)

Also consider His blessing to Noah and his sons after the flood,

> So God blessed Noah and his sons, and said to them: "Be fruitful and multiply, and fill the earth." (Genesis 9:1)

From these two Scriptures, we see the command given by God is not to shorten life but to extend it. God had the unique thought of family in His mind, hence the bringing of the woman to the man in the original setting.

> Then the rib which the LORD God had taken from man He made into a woman, and He brought her to the man. (Genesis 2:22)

Also take note of the revelation given to the apostle Paul.

> Submitting to one another in the fear of God. Wives, submit to your own husbands, as to the Lord. For the husband is head of the wife, as also

> Christ is head of the church; and He is the Savior of the body. (Ephesians 5:21–23)

The children they bear are God's, as understood by the Psalmist, who said,

> Behold, children are a heritage from the Lord,
> The fruit of the womb is a reward. (Psalm 127:3)

But in the book of Malachi, He's more specific, directly telling us He does everything through covenants. Child bearing should come as the result of participation in the covenant of marriage. He placed the conscious awareness of this in the heart of every child of Adam. God wants godly offspring, born within covenant.

> And this is the second thing you do: You cover the altar of the Lord with tears, With weeping and crying; So He does not regard the offering anymore, Nor receive it with goodwill from your hands. Yet you say, "For what reason?" Because the Lord has been witness Between you and the wife of your youth, With whom you have dealt treacherously; Yet she is your companion And your wife by covenant. But did He not make them one, Having a remnant of the Spirit? And why one? He seeks godly offspring. Therefore take heed to your spirit, And let none deal treacherously with the wife of his youth. (Malachi 2:13–15)

We need to understand that, though society acknowledges infidelity as if it is normal, it hasn't changed what God has created and decreed. The truth stands valid today, just as when He first spoke the word. Just because He spoke it thousands of years ago doesn't invalidate its truth today. We will each give account for our actions whether we follow ungodly or godly trends.

Going back into the distant past, let's look at God's instruction to Moses for the children of Israel that still stand today. This instruction was about how the children must be taught and how often:

> Hear, O Israel: The Lord our God, the Lord is one! You shall love the Lord your God with all your heart, with all your soul, and with all your strength. And these words which I command you today shall be in your heart. You shall teach them diligently to your children, and shall talk of them when you sit in your house, when you walk by the way, when you lie down, and when you rise up. You shall bind them as a sign on your hand, and they shall be as frontlets between your eyes. You shall write them on the doorposts of your house and on your gates. (Deuteronomy 6:4–9)

As relating to the above Scripture, sometime before this writing, I was making excuses for my past actions, declaring my innocence. The Holy Spirit came and took me back in time; it was a spiritual encounter. He was telling me to go back, and my spirit man knew what to do. I went through some of the books of the New Testament. We crossed over to the Old Testament, going through the books in a reverse order. We went all the way back to Leviticus.

Still going backward through these last books on my discovery, we went through Deuteronomy and Numbers, and when we got to Leviticus, He changed His instructions to chapter by chapter, still saying, "Go back," until I got to Leviticus 5. Then He stopped speaking. I figured out that there must be something in this chapter He wanted me to see without telling me. I had to read and find it for myself.

I began reading from the first verse of chapter 5, slowly so I didn't miss anything—though I didn't know what it was I was looking to find. However, when I got to verse 17, the last part of the Scripture pierced my heart like a sword.

> If a person sins, and commits any of these things which are forbidden to be done by the commandments of the Lord, though he does not know it, yet he is guilty and shall bear his iniquity. (Leviticus 5:17)

Oftentimes we confess to ignorance or claim innocence as if it is a way of escape. We tell ourselves (and sometimes others) that we should not be held responsible. But the Holy Spirit let me know that day I was responsible. I came to know that day there is a sin called ignorance. In it, I saw the love of God delivering me from its grip, from the darkness and the snare of the Devil. I repented and asked for forgiveness, and better understanding began to come on how to direct my life going forward. Since that encounter, I have never made another excuse for my sin. I saw my vulnerabilities in past mistakes and set about putting them right through repentance and the grace of God. In other words, I took responsibility for those actions and their consequences. Had I known there was a correct way at the time I chose some of those actions and decisions, it would have been different. As it was, when I was willing to take responsibility before God and repent. He helped me to make things right wherever I could.

In our present society, I have come to note that no one wants to take responsibility for his or her actions, and it is a scourge of weakness. It put the minds of men into passivity, where they lose the power to be strong and stand up for good morals, ethical values, and maintaining of godly standards. If the character is not strong, the weight of ungodliness causes us to yield to the mental pressure. God expects us to be victorious. Understanding that God never breaks covenant, there is no better place to stand strong and speak out than on behalf of the union of marriage. If men would stand for godliness, serving in the role of priest in the home and being the keepers of covenant with their wives and marriage partners, how different might things be today?

I believe we are aware that God never intended for any child to be born outside the marriage covenant. The intentional lack of teaching through the institutional system has programmed society into an ungodly lifestyle where chaos and confusion reign. It seems we are unaware of the trauma experienced by children born out of wedlock. Broken hearts, shattered identities, crises of morality… the list goes on.

These statistics taken from a recent [10]*Electronic News Letter, May2013 by Juster* tell a shocking story. Used by permission.

---

[10] Electronic News Letter by Daniel Juster—Tel Aviv, Gay Rights and the Boy Scouts - http://www.tikkunministries.org/newsletters/dj-may13.php.

Then, sexual relationships were delayed until marriage; now, most young people and young adults have sexual relationships before marriage. They often have many partners. They live together before wedlock or reject marriage altogether. Contrary to commonly held opinion, statistics show that those who engage in these behaviors are much more likely to divorce.

Now, forty percent of children are born out of wedlock; seventy percent of black children are born out of wedlock. This is devastating to the character and prosperity of the generation being raised. Long term bonding is missing! Recently, news reports stated that the greatest predictor of prosperity is being born to and raised in an intact family with a father and mother. 98% of young people so raised do not end in poverty.

Now, the number of children killed through abortions each year is astronomical. In 1956 it was illegal and rare indeed.

So what has caused all this social regression? A culture switch from a Biblically based worldview and ethic to a secular worldview and ethic (or should I say "anti-ethic") has been a primary cause. This is well catalogued in the great book by the late jurist Robert Bork, *Slouching toward Gomorrah.*

We're doing our best to make it acceptable when deep in our hearts we know it causes heartache, shame, and loss of dignity. We must begin to take thoughts of those pleasures where selfishness is the norm and acknowledge that eventually they lead to disappointment and irretrievable pain for someone else. We need to reflect and ask, "What if the role was reversed and I was the one feeling the eventual outcome?" I wonder if we would continue. I know I wouldn't. I don't think a moment of pleasure is worth a lifetime of suffering. What do you think?

Marriage is a godly institution and should not be treated lightly but rather with reverence. The thing to bear in mind is this: both parties enter into covenant where God is a witness to the agreement. It is then eternally sealed. Children are the fruit of this union. There is a purpose to every one of God's plans, and *all* His plans for us are for good!

Our lack of the fear of the Lord causes us to violate the commands through ignorance and disobedience and unavoidably suffer the consequences. Sadly, we blame God instead of humbling ourselves and asking forgiveness of one another. God is merciful. He will forgive. Instead of taking His example, too often we harden our hearts toward each other and pull away instead of listening to the Holy Spirit and entering into prayer. We refuse to accept our guilt and would rather blame everyone else, unaware of the selfish spirit Satan sent to attack that individual's mind.

In those undesired outcomes, we tend not to consider Satan as the destroyer of the relationship. Instead, we end up attacking the other person or the covenant itself.

Our minds become blurred. The Enemy then takes our wills captive and assists us from there on until we decide to separate—victory for him in another broken covenant. I must add that each party gets instructions from the Holy Spirit on the right thing to do. We allow pride to dominate our thinking, blaming the other party and eventually separating. I speak from experience. This is done by digging our heels into our horse called pride. Thereafter follow the twin terrors of destruction and a haughty spirit. Even at this point, there is still hope for reconciliation after separation. God is saying His desire for us is to keep the marriage vow. Note this compassionate response through Paul:

> Now to the married I command, yet not I but the Lord: A wife is not to depart from her husband. But even if she does depart, let her remain unmarried or be reconciled to her husband. And a husband is not to divorce his wife. (1 Corinthians 7:10–11)

This instruction was a revelation. If there were any children, the outgoing party should leave alone. The children should stay with the parent who decided to obey the Lord. Where two Christians are involved, they must realize that the issues are not against flesh and blood but rather a war against principalities and powers that would rather see our marriages ripped apart than succeed in love. They must grasp quickly that there's a spiritual war in motion and recognize it as such. Learn to be obedient in pulling down strongholds as stated here:

> For though we walk in the flesh, we do not war according to the flesh. For the weapons of

> our warfare are not carnal but mighty in God for pulling down strongholds, casting down arguments and every high thing that exalts itself against the knowledge of God, bringing every thought into captivity to the obedience of Christ, and being ready to punish all disobedience when your obedience is fulfilled. (2 Corinthians 10:3–6)

In other words, learn to be obedient by asking the Holy Spirit to lead each other into a more fulfilling life with Him. Ask to be taught how to use the spiritual weapons that are part of the covenant. These weapons have divine power to demolish strongholds and arguments that rise up against the knowledge of God. They help bring every thought captive to the obedience of the Lord Jesus Christ. If practiced, victory will become real and harmony at home maintained. Instead, we allow self-will to lead us into eventual destruction. After all that has been said, it may not seem there's any hope. But with our God, *all* things are possible! We must believe Him and trust His power at work in us. Here is another portion from the article which I also believe will happen.

Juster asked in the same electronic newsletter, *So How Can I Be Optimistic?*

> I am optimistic because those who are now the cultural elite will lead our Western nations to bankruptcy - both economically and morally and this will prepare the way for a great revival. I believe this will happen because millions of people are in prayer throughout the world. Never have so many

> people been involved in 24/7 prayer movements! The leaders of these prayer groups are unlike the leaders of the Jesus Movement. They have a different theology. They are dedicated to culture formation. In addition, most are committed to the salvation of the Jewish people. When today's secular elite is revealed to be bankrupt and revival floods the earth, the present culture formation elite can be swept aside and replaced. Let us prepare for the young people who will be part of this. The effect will be massive internationally and also in Israel. (Taken from Electronic News Letter, *May 2013, Tel Aviv, Gay Rights And The Boy Scouts*, by Juster. Used by permission. For information see bibliography.)

My question is, have the local churches fallen short in teaching about spiritual warfare? Before I give what I consider the reason for the lack, what I will say at this moment is this: it's failure to just preach about what the red writing in the gospels says. Instead, we must do what is written if we love Him as we say. Let me repeat. The conflict is not against a person. Our conflict is only with the enemy of our souls, so the Captain of the Hosts was sent to show us the way. Praise God!

Let's move into some **c**elebration by demonstrating our unconditional love through the ultimate—singing to Jesus the King!

TO JESUS MY KING I WILL SING

Is singing the defining act of love? There are numerous reasons why people sing. Sometimes it is due to some incident that brought on sadness, and singing is a way of recounting the situation. During the reflection of singing, further insight may come, and you find a rekindling of joy and happiness. Some people enjoy the act of singing. It may be a natural talent for some who sing like angels. I remember being at South Bank in London at the home of the London Philharmonic Orchestra listening to a female opera singer. I took a seat close to the stage so I could absorb every word and movement. I was absolutely fascinated with the range of her voice through years of training. I knew she enjoyed what she was performing because of the vibrations resonating from her and the orchestra playing in harmony. Moments like those are unforgettable. When I close my eyes, I can recapture the vivid scene instantly, including all the sounds.

I attended the opera during a period when I was experiencing transformation in my life in a religious way, and gratitude surfaced effortlessly when I listened to the music. Life took a turn for the better, and spontaneously, I began to sing. I've heard that it's a sign danger has passed in nature when the birds begin to sing again. I am of a similar nature. I heard myself singing. The date was actually October 1, 1993. As I caught myself singing, I thought, *Why not? Yes, to Jesus my King I will sing!* From that moment until now, new songs still flow from the Spirit.

I had always loved singing but never incorporated the idea of taking singing lessons. However, let me tell you how dedicated I became at embracing my passion for singing. I had recently moved to North London and was looking for a new church home. I was informed of a church in Holloway, North London that had a male voice choir. My interest was piqued, so I went to check out the church and find out about the choir. In addition to that thought, I had accepted Jesus as my Lord and Savior, and I had this burning hunger to know Jesus Christ in a deeper way. Eventually I was introduced to the choir leader, told him my desire of becoming part of the choir, and asked what I needed to do. Many things were mentioned, including punctuality, reliability, and training. I saw no problem in fulfilling each of the stipulations because my desire was to be part of the choir. Having listened to them during rehearsals, I was impressed with his leadership skills and the choir's response—they were in oneness of harmony. I could see that the leader was well respected by the entire choir. He was warm and gentle and drew the best out of the men.

As time progressed I became absorbed in wanting to perform at my best each session. Part of the training was performing breathing exercises of various kinds, adopting the ability to keep the stomach muscles from trembling, being able to maintain long notes on a single breath, and the like. For that regimen my personal discipline was to adopt running exercises to expand the lungs. I would get up early in the morning and head to the park to practice. Singing at my peak was my goal; therefore taking on the discipline of running was to glorify my King Jesus. There were other training exercises, like vowel recitation for diction to make sure the words were pronounced properly. I looked forward to the training and practice sessions because, in my mind, I saw myself preparing each time to sing to my King. I had to be at my best, so I became totally involved.

It was at those trainings I learned to read sheet music until I could be given any sheet of music and sing the song on sight. The choir had four parts: first and second tenor and first and second bass. I was part of the first bass group or alto. During the church service, the choir would sing two songs. Those moments were marvelous. Holloway Male Voice Choir was well known throughout London. To be part of that choir was like a dream come true. To be part of such a prestigious group was an honor I didn't take it lightly.

The other thing that made me appreciate the choir even more was the charitable singing we performed after each church service. On Saturday afternoons we would go to the elderly homes that were scattered around London and sing for the elderly folks. I saw how those elderly folks embraced us with genuine, heartfelt appreciation. Wherever we went is was the same result, even outside of London. During my time with the choir, we eventually recorded an album at a recording studio in Edgware Road, London. I still remember one particular song penned by the leader about Jesus' return. For me it brings to mind Zephaniah 1:15. Much will unfold on that day. In my case, years later, God brought me through much darkness so I had reason to sing.

I sing to my King because I am thankful and I know He loves singing. I also had the training to give Him my best. It brought to mind when the Lord was questioning Job out of the whirlwind. One of the questions was, "Where was Job when the morning stars sang together and all the sons of God shouted for joy?" It reminded me of a time in June 2005. After I ministered the salvation message to an individual, I returned home and immediately got my guitar. A song came from the Spirit I entitled, "Creation's First Day." The spontaneous and harmonious words and music were based on Genesis 1:1–5. Part of the lyrics was Job 38:7, culminating with hallelujah and glory to God.

Jesus said God is Spirit and His worshipers must worship in spirit and in truth. Therefore, I would say singing is an integral part of the essence of true worship. It should be exciting because of Who we are singing to—the best in the whole universe, our God and heavenly Father.

Here are some of the definitions of the word[11] *sing:* "To utter words or sounds in succession with musical modulations of the voice; to perform a song or voice composition; to produce melodious sounds"

Let us take the penultimate phrase, "to perform a song or voice composition," and in this context direct our thoughts to the Creator of music—almighty God. As we come to know Him more and more, there will come a time when singing will automatically come forth from our hearts because of joy and gladness with

---

11 Definition of song: Dictonary.com http://www.ditionary.reference.com/browse/sing

thanksgiving. Singing to Him will become an unconscious expression as the reality of the price of salvation dawns in our consciousness. Being miraculously delivered from an impossible situation because God is good is another reason for joyous song.

Paul spoke of singing with his understanding and singing in the spirit. Singing in the spirit is the ultimate because it bypasses our understanding, at least initially. Singing in our known language is beautiful, but when we can get beyond our soul and transition into singing in the spirit in the heavenly language, glory to God, there's nothing to compare; it's ineffable. I believe heaven gets involved. There are numerous Scriptures throughout the Bible where there are causes to sing to the Lord because of His goodness, mercy, and grace.

All Israel sang after the parting of the Red Sea. They had cause to sing because of the predicament they were in with Pharaoh's army bearing down upon them and being obstructed by the Red Sea. Only the outstretched hand of God could save them, and that He did. Yes, they had great cause to sing to the Lord (Exodus 15:1–10)!

You also will sing of God being good to you just like the Psalmist, singing to God among the peoples (Psalm 57: 9). How about singing unto the Lord all your life (Psalm 144:33)?

Is it possible to walk in wisdom and make melody in our hearts continually to God? I personally think so. It's simply a matter of choice. The apostle Paul believed it and admonished the Ephesians to be wise, understanding what the will of the Lord is—to be being filled with the Spirit, speaking to one another in psalms and hymns and spiritual songs, singing and making melody in their hearts to the Lord, and to give thanks.

> Therefore do not be unwise, but understand what the will of the Lord is. And do not be drunk with wine, in which is dissipation; but be filled with the Spirit, speaking to one another in psalms and hymns and spiritual songs, singing and making melody in your heart to the Lord, giving thanks always for all things to God the Father in the name of our Lord Jesus Christ, submitting to one another in the fear of God. (Ephesians 5:17–21)

Jesus and His disciples sang during the Passover at a certain man's house when ratifying the covenant of forgiveness (Matthew 26:26–30, Luke 23:34).

The Psalmist said to sing to the Lord a new song Psalm 149:1, and in Revelation 5:6–14 a new song was sung to the Lamb that was slain. His blood purchased us for God (1 Corinthians 6:19-20).

Finally, the secret to increase the anointing in your life is to build on a solid foundation of intercessory prayer. This will perfect the special gift God has given you (1 Timothy 2:1–6, Ephesians 6:9), and singing is a great boost in the Spirit for prayer. Intercessory prayer is going to flood the nations.

May we continue to sing to the King, giving glory to His name forever and forever. Sing because of His lovingkindness and tender mercies. Sing because He's given you glory to be one with Him. Sing because you are redeemed. Sing because your beautiful

Bridegroom King is coming again with power and great glory. Sing because you will be with Him forever. As we learn to sing in the Spirit, the glory of God will appear.

At creation the Bible says the morning stars sang. In the new heaven and earth, I believe there will be tumultuous singing. Those who have victory over the beast, image, mark, and number of his name sing the song of Moses and the Lamb in Revelation 15: 3–5, saying,

> Great and marvelous are Your works, Lord God Almighty! Just and true are Your ways, O King of the saints! Who shall not fear You, O Lord, and glorify Your name? For You alone are holy. For all nations shall come and worship before You, For Your judgments have been manifested.

Praise the Lord! Let us sing of His love forever! Hallelujah!

Let us go to the next chapter rejoicing because heaven came down to you through the Son.

HEAVEN CAME DOWN TO YOU THROUGH THE SON

Out of heaven, proceeds eternal unconditional love. "Love of the Spirit we all must give, from deep within our hearts let it flow, to give God the glory forever more." I am extremely happy! These three lines are from one of my songs from the Spirit entitled "I Cried to the Lord." The morning He gave this song I had spent the remaining hours of the night in prayer and worship because of a deep wound in my heart. When I felt victory was accomplished, I believe the Holy Spirit prompted me to raise my head to see the clock indicated 6:00 a.m. With a beaming smile, spontaneous worship broke forth to God's glory. Hallelujah! I got up off my knees and picked up my guitar, and the song and melody poured out. In the song from the Spirit, you can feel what I experienced during that night prayer time—the wrestling, travailing, and ultimate victory until the clock struck six. I was overwhelmed with gratitude. An intercessor must wrestle in the spirit for his or her brothers and sisters, governments, and nations. Intercession is love on the knees.

There are many kinds of love. However, to focus our attention on what I'm about to share, let's agree and guide our minds' eye to the love of the Spirit. It is in His love we find the sustaining joy we seek. You and I know it's not in our homes, communities, cities, states, and nations. Neither is it in our favorite meal, holiday resort, or even workplaces among our work associates even though we encounter some semblance of joy in these things. Truly, the joy in these is not lasting! Like a magnet, we are drawn back into worry, stress, frustration, and disappointment. We try our best to live around the problems that make cycles in our minds. Every so often certain transient thoughts like joy enter our minds. We wonder if it would be possible to have joy for a whole week, a month, or even forever.

Let's agree we do not fully understand the glory, splendor, and majesty of the Lord Jesus Christ just now. Saints, a greater knowing of Him is coming. Let us be encouraged to desire and find Him out now because this fullness of joy we seek is in His presence, and at His right hand are pleasures forevermore. Is there a way to live daily whereby we can increasingly discover this all-encompassing joy for which we were made? I believe there is! Let me share a story…

Lavender Discovers the Pathway of Righteousness

It wasn't the first time the transient thought of joy had entered the thinking processes of Jasmine's mind. In fact, this was the third time the thought had crossed her mind, diverting her attention. On this occasion she stopped what she was doing and allowed it to dominate her mind. She thought on some incidents from her past that she saw stacked up in her memory with a sign that said PENDING. Joy stayed prominently in view from this stack. She yielded her will and become engaged in thinking about joy. Joy began to create pictures in her mind that stimulated her five senses—sight, smell, taste, touch, and hearing. She was so absorbed in the possibilities of this joy that when the phone rang, it barely registered. In slow motion Jasmine reached for the phone. She spoke to the caller, but it was impossible to give her full attention because the thought of joy was playing in the background of her mind. Of all the activities in which she participated that day, her thoughts of joy dominated every one.

The following morning, after waking from sleep, the first thought to enter her mind was joy. She decided she would find out more about whether the attainment of such joy was possible and if it could last forever. She perused dictionaries, magazines, and other articles. She found nothing that could match what she imagined and believed could exist. Jasmine seemed passionately compelled from within to search out this joy she sensed existed. It dominated her mind and became her quest.

Morning, noon, and night she was consumed by it until it came to the point that something had to give. There had to be breakthrough. The thought that such joy could be possible brought her added happiness. She fully believed she was on to something. Nothing like this had ever consumed her thoughts with such intensity! She noticed she was not worrying about her everyday life as before. One day she heard herself say, "I *must* have this joy!" She felt she needed and deserved it. For her, on that day desire was born. The same night she had a dream.

Jasmine's dream came in fragments, and all she remembered was it had something to do with fruit and spirit and someone repeating the word joy. She woke up and had no idea what it meant. What did joy have to do with fruit and spirit? Jasmine was so busy trying to figure out her dream that she didn't realize she was running late for work. She ended up rushing out the door and arrived five minutes late. During the morning break in the cafeteria with her coworkers, one of her friends, Lavender, said to her, "In the five and a half years you've been working here, I don't ever remember you being late. Are you all right? What happened?"

Jasmine said, "It's true, I always try to be on time for work, but I had a weird dream last night. It had something to do with some fruit and the spirit and someone talking about joy. I can't seem to remember details, and I can't seem to forget about it either."

Lavender was shocked because she believed she knew exactly what the dream meant. She responded, "Oh my God!"

All the others who were sitting with them in unison said, "What!"

In all the years Lavender had worked there, she had never made it known to any of them that she was a Christian, and she had never witnessed to any of them about Jesus. She was shocked that Jasmine had had such a vivid dream about God speaking to her about joy, a fruit of His Spirit. This was a real wake-up call for Lavender and brought deep conviction to her soul. She hadn't been expecting God to rush into her life at work from left field. The impact of the dream put her in such a tailspin that she became slightly disoriented.

Jasmine looked worried about Lavender's reaction.

"Why did you say, 'Oh my God'? What is it? I hope it isn't scary."

"I'll tell you later, Jasmine," Lavender said.

They all looked at each other, mystified by Lavender's turmoil. It was unusual. For the first time since they had known each other, they all went back to their desks in silence. Jasmine went back to her desk, anxious and concerned about what Lavender might tell her later. She decided lunchtime would be the earliest and best time to find out.

Lunchtime seemed as if it would never come. Jasmine could hardly believe a few hours could seem to take so long. As soon as 12:20 p.m. came, Jasmine bolted from her desk to find Lavender. Arriving at Lavender's desk, Jasmine found it was empty! Now what! She found the supervisor and was told that Lavender had gone home sick. Jasmine was distraught. The answers she wanted were now locked up in Lavender, and she had gone home!

Jasmine was distressed. She began to reflect on all that had been happening since the day these thoughts of joy had begun to arrest her attention. Jasmine began to assess the events of her life since then: persisting thoughts of a joy that is deep and lasting, a dream she could hardly remember but seemed important, being late for work thinking about her dream, telling the dream to her friends, Lavender acting surprised and now being sick… *Why is this happening to me? What did I do? Is something wrong with me?*

Five days passed with these thoughts swirling around in Jasmine's mind, and Lavender still hadn't returned to work. Jasmine felt she was in a state of limbo with Lavender's, "I will tell you later" running through her head. Why was this dream still bothering her? She decided to console herself with waiting as patiently as possible. She was so fixated on getting the answer from Lavender that she never thought to ask anyone else. The girls had shared many secrets together over the past few years. Theirs was a trust bond that had developed during those years, and Jasmine felt that seeking advice from someone else was like betraying that trust. So she waited.

Jasmine remembered it was time for her monthly checkup with her family doctor. She rummaged through her bag to the little pocket where she kept her datebook, unzipped the pocket, took it out, and confirmed she did, in fact, have an appointment with her doctor for 6:30 p.m. that same day. She decided to leave right from work at 5:00 p.m. and get to the waiting room early, before it got crowded. As she sat on the bus, her thoughts wandered again to Lavender. She fidgeted anxiously, wondering when she was going to be able to find out what Lavender seemed to know about her dream.

Jasmine wasn't in the waiting room more than five minutes when the door opened, and to her astonishment and disbelief, in walked Lavender with scratches on the right side of her face and a bandage on her right arm. Jasmine thought to herself, *What are the chances? I haven't seen her for five days and now, here she is, at the exact time as me!* It seemed very odd indeed!

Lavender didn't see Jasmine as she entered. "Lavender, what happened?" Jasmine blurted out, so Lavender turned to see Jasmine and walked across the room to where she was sitting.

"Lavender, what happened? Do you want to talk?" Jasmine said with a concerned and hushed voice, touching her friend's knee. She waited patiently for Lavender to respond.

Lavender stopped in front of Jasmine. She looked into Jasmine's concerned eyes, took a deep breath, exhaled slowly, and then sat next to her friend. Jasmine patiently waited because she saw something new in Lavender's eyes and sensed it was more than physical pain Lavender was experiencing. It took a while before Lavender began to speak in a whispered tone. "Jasmine, I'm so sorry that I hurt you."

Jasmine heard what Lavender said but was quite uncertain as to what Lavender meant, "What do you mean? How did you hurt me? You are the one hurting just now."

"I have hurt you and many others by keeping to myself, almost as a secret, the life I enjoy every day."

Jasmine began to search her memory as to what Lavender could mean. As far as she could recall, since they had become friends, they had told each other everything. That was more than five years ago, and that was also when she had joined the company and noticed something different about Lavender.

Jasmine was about to ask Lavender another question when suddenly Lavender continued. "Jasmine, in all the years of us working together, I've never known you to be late, so I had to find out what happened. When you told me about your dream, it almost caused my heart to stop beating. It convicted me to such a degree that I became confused and a bit disoriented. When I went home sick, I fell getting off the bus and hurt my face and arm. Jasmine, it surprised and scared me that I knew what your dream meant. I also knew who gave it to you and for what purpose it was given to you. I didn't know what to do with all of that in that moment."

Jasmine was silent for a minute before replying, "Come to think of it, you startled me by the look on your face, and hastily blurting out, 'I'll tell you later.' It seemed to me you knew something, and I was afraid it was bad news when you ran away so quickly. It has made me anxious for days!"

Lavender went on, "All you see that has happened to me is the result of not doing what I should have done a long time ago. It shocked me that God would give you that dream. All I can say is that He loves you very much and wants you to know Him! Most of us who have been following Him for some time have not really paid close enough attention to what He shared with you in your dream. I realized I have become far too complacent in my love for Him, but He wants you to know about His joy. This joy is one of the fruit of His Spirit."

"What are you talking about, Lavender?" Jasmine asked, sensing a strange stirring inside her.

"Do you remember you said something about fruit and joy?"

"Yes."

"Did you ever have a strong desire of really wanting real joy?" Lavender asked.

"Why, yes! Awhile before the dream, this thought of having joy that would last forever kept popping up in my mind. It would never leave me. I eventually decided to give it my full attention, and after really thinking about it, I decided I really wanted that kind of joy. Then I had this dream. What are you saying, Lavender? Do you have this kind of joy?"

"Well, Jasmine," Lavender said, "this kind of joy you won't get at our favorite store, your best night spot, with your boyfriend, or at our best vacation spot. You're already aware how those things feel, and they never satisfy you for more than a few days, right?"

Jasmine replied thoughtfully, "That's true. Most of the time I wished being happy from those things would last longer, but they never did." She continued with a sad tone to her voice, "Especially the relationship with my boyfriend that I thought would last because I felt so much joy when I was with him. Lavender, whenever I thought the relationship was growing, it was like a plug would get pulled and we'd settle back into a dissatisfying normal. Eventually he began to make excuses that he had to work out of town, and well, you know the rest of the story. He broke my heart, Lavender. If that was love, it certainly did not bring any joy that lasted. I am so glad I have you as my friend."

"Thanks, Jazz," Lavender said. "I'm glad I have you as my friend, too. It's good we met up today. I don't think it was an accident.

I didn't know what I was going to say to you when I returned to work. I knew we needed some time to talk, more than we might have at work, but I didn't really know what to say to you. I was still a bit in shock about your dream. Over the past few days, I have had some time to be quiet, think and pray; now I am ready. Do you understand?

Jasmine thought for a few moments. "I think so. Can we talk about the dream right now?"

"Absolutely!" Lavender exclaimed. "Let's get right to it because you have an appointment soon, right?"

"Right," Jasmine said.

Lavender hadn't witnessed to anyone even though she had been a Christian for most of her life. She knew she needed to tell Jasmine about the dream: what it meant, and what she needed to do to have the joy for which she yearned. Somehow, she just couldn't get the words together. Jasmine's appointment time was approaching quickly, and Lavender began to feel flustered. She sensed she must tell Jasmine that to have the joy she longed for, she first needed to ask Jesus Christ into her life as Savior and Lord. Lavender decided to say a silent prayer in her heart to God that moment, asking for Him to send the Holy Spirit to help her. They were just staring at each other, both in different dimensional locations.

"What!" Jasmine said.

Lavender, with a beautiful smile on her face, gently reached over and touched Jasmine's right hand. Jasmine felt a sudden rush of warmth from Lavender's hand. The warm sensation went through her all the way to her heart. Jasmine said, "Wow! I've never felt anything like this before! What did you do? What it this heat I'm feeling?"

With that warm smile still on her face, Lavender said, "Jasmine, God loves you very much, and I didn't know what to say to you about the dream. While we were looking at each other, I said a silent prayer in my heart asking God to help me share His love with you. Because you truly, from your heart, wanted the joy that you sensed would last, He gave you the dream. Do you remember the dream about the fruit and someone talking about joy?"

"Yes."

"Well, what you were hearing was God telling you about His joy, a fruit of His Spirit, which God gives to those He invites for salvation. Because He knows you desire this joy, He is offering it to you freely as a gift that comes through the salvation that He provided through His Son, Jesus Christ. I know I didn't tell you I was a Christian, but somehow you knew and gravitated toward me. You also noticed I always defended you, and you never heard me join in gossiping. Neither have you ever heard me speak a swear word, right?"

"That's true! Some things are now beginning to make sense! Please go on."

"Jasmine, God knows the heart of every one of us and what we need most. You know you need joy, I know you need joy, and He knows you need joy. I knew I needed help to tell you, so I asked

Him to send His Holy Spirit to help me tell you about Jesus. Jesus is the best gift mankind will ever have because all of us have told some lie, cursed someone, said bad things about others, and so on. These are all classed as sin. Sin separates us from God's love and prevents us from being filled with His joy, peace, love, and all the other fruit of His Spirit. Our sin will eventually lead us to death. Have you ever thought one day you will die?"

"Yes, I have," Jasmine said.

"Imagine if you died with all those sins locked up in your heart without ever having the chance to repent or be cleaned on the inside. What do you believe would happen?"

"Lavender, I really don't know, but it doesn't feel good to think about that happening."

"Jasmine, my friend, I believe our meeting here today was God's arrangement. I believe it was ordained by my heavenly Father God to talk with you so that He might become your Father also. When I was where you are right now, I didn't know God was my heavenly Father, and I felt a void in my heart just like you do now. That space just wouldn't be filled with anything else."

Jasmine broke in. "That's how I just felt when you mentioned Father—a longing engulfed me, Lavender. What can I do? I don't want to have that feeling ever again!"

"To have God as your Father means He sent His Son, Jesus, to die for all our sins so that we can be free from sin forever. We can live in God's goodness. Jasmine, in the Bible, John 3:16, Jesus said, 'For God so loved the world that He gave His only begotten Son, that whoever believes in Him should not perish but have everlasting life.' Accepting Jesus as our Lord and Savior is called being born again—heaven came down to you through the Son."

Jasmine was listening attentively to what Lavender was saying. She quickly asked Lavender to repeat the last sentence, which she did. Jasmine closed her eyes while quietly whispering, "Heaven came down to you through the Son." Then she made it personal. "Heaven came down to me through Jesus." Lavender was listening to her friend and then heard no more words. She only saw Jasmine's lips moving. She remembered Hannah's prayer. Jasmine stopped moving her lips, opened her eyes, looked at her friend Lavender, and asked, "Lavender, what do I need to do?"

"Jasmine, I just have to mention a little more. God sent Jesus from heaven according to what the Scriptures say. He died on a cross, was buried, and God raised Him from the dead because of Jesus' unfailing love for and total obedience to His Father. He showed Himself first to Mary, then to His disciples. After that He was taken up into heaven, where He is sitting at the right hand of Father God *right now*! He is still praying for us. He will be your Savior today if you want Him! That's not all. He said He will be coming back with power and great glory to be with us forever. So, my friend, do you believe in your heart what I just said?"

"Yes, Lavender! I feel like I have been waiting for this moment *all my life!* It seems my heart is just going to burst out of my chest. Yes, I truly believe in my heart what you've said and how it was said. I can feel the love of the one you talked about who sent His Son."

As Lavender watched Jasmine, she saw there was a change coming over her. Jasmine was whispering, "Father." She said it three times, then turned to Lavender and said, "I'm ready to accept His Son as my Lord and Savior."

"Oh, Jazz, I am truly happy for you! Let's pray together. Repeat after me, 'God, I acknowledge that I am a sinner. I didn't know my sins separated me from You. I'm truly sorry. I'm asking You to forgive me of my sins. I turn from them this day and forever. I accept the salvation You provided through Your Son, Jesus Christ. I accept Him as my personal Savior. Thank You, Father, that I'm born again and accepted into Your kingdom. Hallelujah! Thank You, Father God, thank You. Thank You I can call You Father, and Your Son, Jesus, is my Lord and Savior. Thank You, thank You, thank You! Amen."

While the prayer was in motion, Lavender watched the expression of sheer joy on Jasmine's face. Jasmine had her eyes closed, and Lavender had to contain herself to finish the prayer of salvation. As soon as the prayer was completed, they looked at each other with beaming smiles of ecstasy. Jasmine tried to hug Lavender the best she could. She had to hug her to express the joy she was experiencing. All their problems and concerns vanished in that moment as another one of Adam's children found the doorway to the Father's house. The angels of heaven rejoiced as another sinner repented. Oh what exuberant joy!

Lavender said to her best friend, "Jasmine, my heart is at rest. Now we are together in our Father's kingdom. Another time I will show you a Scripture about the fullness of joy in His presence and the pleasures at His right hand forevermore. By the way, remember the Scripture says Jesus is at the Father's right hand. My Jesus, your Jesus, our Jesus!

They both realized time had rushed by and Jasmine's appointment was there. They parted with the biggest smiles of happiness and joy on their faces. With a parting wave of love, Lavender's left hand touched Jasmine's right hand. Lavender told Jasmine she had more to share with her later and also encouraged Jasmine, "Hey, why don't you share with Violet next time you see her at work? Tell her you accepted Jesus as your Savior and Lord."

Jasmine, full of exuberant joy, replied, "Okay," and disappeared into the doctor's office. As she started her appointment, Jasmine meditated on what Lavender told her Jesus said in John 6:44, "No one can come to Me unless the Father who sent Me draws him; and I will raise him up at the last day." Jasmine had confirmation of how precious she was to her heavenly Father that he would pull on her heart until she accepted Jesus Christ as her Lord and Savior. She felt loved to the very core of her being for the first time in her life!

Amazingly, Lavender and Jasmine had been so deeply engrossed in that eternal moment that intersected their timelines of life where Jasmine's spiritual birth occurred that they were oblivious to the patients filtering into the waiting room. Those patients had been surprise witnesses to Jasmine's spiritual birth.

The waiting room, which was usually quiet and filled with an eerie silence unless some child's playful voice was heard, was buzzing with life and excited comments. They had picked up genuine love flowing between the two friends. Their heads moved in both directions—toward Jasmine's glowing face as she entered the doctor's office and toward Lavender with a huge smile of satisfaction on her face as she headed toward the exit and home.

Lavender's Prayer of Thanks

The first thing Lavender did upon arriving home was to offer God a prayer of thanksgiving. "Father, I am so excited that You have accepted Jasmine into Your kingdom and have also given me a new infusion of life. I am eternally grateful to You for reviving Your life inside of me too. I now need a further revelation of what to share with Jasmine so she can advance into Your presence from the salvation she has just received as a new babe in Christ. I thank You, by faith, for answering my prayer. Amen."

Knowing she needed an answer for the coming Monday, she began to read her Bible. She believed there was a specific pathway into God's presence that anyone could follow to encounter Him. He said He could be found if we search for Him with all our hearts.

> And you will seek Me and find Me, when you search for Me with all your heart. (Jeremiah 29:13)

> I love those who love me, And those who seek me diligently will find me. (Proverbs 8:17)

She also believed if we did precisely as He said, it would work because He had demonstrated His infinite love for Jasmine less than an hour earlier. Lavender was looking for answers. She recalled reading Deuteronomy 6:5, which said,

> You shall love the Lord your God with all your heart, with all your soul, and with all your strength.

And Jesus' response to the lawyer's question in Mark 12:29–31:

> Jesus answered him, "The first of all the commandments is: 'Hear, O Israel, the Lord our God, the Lord is one. And you shall love the Lord your God with all your heart, with all your soul, with all your mind, and with all your strength.' This is the first commandment. And the second, like it, is this: 'You shall love your neighbor as yourself.' There is no other commandment greater than these."

Lavender began to take note of what was happening to her. She was developing a new hunger for the Scriptures since her best friend accepted Jesus as her Lord and Savior. She began to jot down the Scriptures. Other Scriptures were entering her mind. She remembered the story of Jesus and the Samaritan woman and their conversation about worship—that God is seeking those who worship Him in spirit and in truth. She decided to read the full story in John 4. She started reading and was looking for key verses. She got to verse 23 and stopped, then read on to verse 24. Two words of Jesus were lingering in her mind—spirit and truth. She began to repeat them verbatim. She became engrossed in the recital, not knowing that two hours had elapsed. She recalled hearing those texts spoken without clear interpretation as to their meaning or whether God had found the worshipers He seeks—she couldn't recall anyone volunteering. That night, Lavender desired to be one of the worshipers God seeks. She heard herself whispering a prayer to God that she would love to offer the type of worship to Him that Jesus mentioned to the Samaritan woman. She was so deep in thought her cell phone's ringer startled her! It rang several times before she was able to answer. The voice on the other end was so loud she had to move the phone away from her ear.

With raised voice the caller said, "Lavender! I had this strong impression to call you right now. Is everything all right?"

Lavender, trying to regain her composure, paused before she answered.

In the silence the caller hastily asked once more, "Lavender, are you there? Say something, anything! Please answer me!"

Finally she responded, "Mister Philippe Prentice, upbeat as ever. Yes, I'm all right. What makes you ask?"

"What's happening? Why did it take you so long to answer, Miss Lavender?"

Lavender laughed aloud. "Long? Philippe it wasn't even a minute!"

He replied, "It seemed like forever! Not only did your phone ring many times, but you took so long to answer. That raised a red flag for me."

"Nothing is wrong. I was just in deep thought."

Philippe laughed loudly and replied, "Deep in thought? I'll try to catch the mood." He lowered his voice and asked, "What piece of incriminating evidence were you looking at, Miss Detective?"

"Stop it, Philippe!" she said, laughing. "You're too funny. As a matter of fact, I was looking at something when you called."

He replied, "I knew it! I knew it had to be something important. Now you've heightened my interest. What was it?"

"I'm really glad you called because I'm trying to get some Scriptures together for Jasmine. Philippe, she just gave her heart to the Lord Jesus Christ earlier today!"

Philippe blurted out on the phone, counting his words, "Lavender… you… are… lying!"

She responded, "Philippe, ever since we've known each other, have I ever lied to you?"

He said, "No, but are you serious, Lavender? Tell me, tell me what happened."

"Philippe, I'm really, really happy. It all seems so unreal in a way. My friend, Jasmine, accepted Jesus Christ as her Lord and Savior today! I led her to the Lord."

Philippe broke in, "I'm shocked! You? I never knew you had it in you as you've never said much, just doing most of the listening!"

"That's okay, Philippe, it's true I have not shared Jesus much. That's why I am so thankful that Jasmine is now our sister in the Lord. What was so amazing, Philippe, was the change that came over her when I told her God would be her Father. Her entire demeanor changed. She just lit up! After seeing that, I knew she was ready. She asked what she needed to do."

He responded, "Lavender, that was marvelous and wonderful! I feel overwhelmed with gratitude. Praise the Lord! Is there anything I can do to help our brand new sister?

"Really?"

"Yes, I am serious. Heaven came down to her through the Son."

She said, "Well, okay, yes—wait a minute! Earlier today I said something similar to Jasmine."

Philippe said, "What do you mean, Lavender?"

"I told her what you just said—heaven came down to her through the Son. I said almost the same thing to her and was wondering where it came from because it was such a beautiful truth."

"Yes, I heard it somewhere, but right now I can't recall where I heard it."

"I'd sure like to find out. Anyway, as I was saying, the idea came to me to build a pathway for her from salvation to joy in Father's presence to the place where she can worship God in spirit and truth like Jesus said in John 4."

"I don't think I've heard of such a pathway mentioned before," he replied. "Let me think, let me think." After a pause he said, "Salvation to spirit and truth—I got it!"

"Got what?"

Philippe said it again, "Lavender, I got it!"

"Philippe… got what?" Lavender responded as if she was agitated. "Listen, Philippe, if you say, 'I got it' one more time, I'll call Poirot to examine your brain, you hear me?"

He laughed out loud at her humor and said, "I know who might be able to help with what you just mentioned."

"Who is it?" she asked.

"Remember I was telling you about this new friend of mine who always said, 'It's in the red writing'?" Philippe suddenly remembered where he heard, "Heaven came down to you through the Son" and blurted out, "I got it! Sorry."

"Philippe, I'll let you off this once." She paused. "Okay, go ahead."

He continued, "Lavender I know from where it came—my new friend! In our conversations you most likely heard me mention it. Well, one evening he invited me to his house. He showed me around. Lavender, the presence of God was everywhere. I mean *everywhere*! He asked if I would like a drink. I said yes but thought to myself, *He doesn't look like someone who drinks.* I thought to myself, *Oh well.* He went toward the kitchen and came back with a tray in his hand. On the tray were two tiny glasses with grape juice and two pieces of crackers! I couldn't contain myself, so I burst out laughing. While walking toward me, he asked me what had ignited such exuberant laughter. Such good medicine laughter, that is. Did it mean I didn't want the drink anymore? I put my right hand up, indicating for him to give me a minute. He placed the tray on the table and then sat down on a chair near to where he placed the tray.

"I managed to control myself, and said to him. 'When you asked if I wanted a drink, I thought, *You don't look the type to drink.* So when you brought out the communion elements, I saw the humorous side, hence the laughter.' He said, 'Really, Philippe? If I had the same amount as what's in one of those glasses, you would have to scrape me off the floor.'"

"Okay, so what else happened?" she inquired.

Philippe replied, "He asked if I would like to watch the Matrix movies. He had the full set. He asked if I had ever seen it. When I told him no, he was shocked! He thought I could not be serious. 'Every Christian should watch them at least twice,' he said. He went on to say that there's so much information about the Bible in them and about what's actually happening in the earth today. He was about to pop the DVD in the player but stopped suddenly. I asked him what was going on. He said he was just reminded of a Scripture he had been researching for twenty-one years. I said, 'Twenty-one years?' He said, 'Yes, twenty-one years.'"

Lavender asked, "Are you serious? I've never heard anyone say that before."

Philippe replied, "Me too. I got curious, wanting to know which Scripture."

Lavender interrupted, "I want to know which one too. Did you ask him?"

Philippe said instead, "Lavender, I am beginning to feel this is the reason I suddenly called you, because what he said to me after that captivated my mind. When he finished, I wanted to hear more. He left me with such hunger to know Jesus Christ. It seems as if that's all he talks about!"

"Philippe, what did he say to you? Are you going to keep me in suspense?"

"Yes, I mean no!" he replied. "Lavender, come to think of it, what he shared with me is what I believe you are looking for to give to Jasmine. Go get a pen and some paper."

Lavender asked, "Did you write down what he told you?"

"No. It branded my mind and is still very clear. He also mentioned many new songs he received from the Spirit: 'I Cried to the Lord,' 'Fill Me with Your Spirit,' 'Creation's First Day,' 'Prince of Peace Sweet Shalom,' and many others. Lavender, when he spoke about 'Heaven Came down to You through the Son,' he reacted like when a mother first sees her newborn baby. He also said he could hear violins playing whenever he thinks or talks about that song, and muttered something about wanting it performed by the London Philharmonic Orchestra.

"My friend, I can give you the information step-by-step. I also believe Jasmine will get it just like that too. I will say this—since hearing what he said that night, Jesus is definitely the way, the truth, and the life. Furthermore, He did show His disciples how to worship God in spirit and truth. We don't go through the physical movements anymore, but we need to know the movement of the high priest through the tabernacle as our reference when we minister unto the Lord daily."

Lavender said, "Philippe, I am so ready."

The Way, the Truth, and the Life

Jesus, answering Thomas's question, said to His disciples in John 14:4–6, "I am the Way, the Truth, and the Life."

Philippe was about to pass on to Lavender a clear path from salvation to living a life in the Spirit to being a true worshiper of a loving God. Jesus said the Father is looking for worshipers.

Philippe said, "Lavender, I truly believe that if this way of which my friend told me is followed, the glory of God will sweep this earth in no time flat. Okay, here we go! First, my friend and I asked the Holy Spirit to come and inspire us and cause the pathway to be branded in our memories, never to be forgotten.

"He said his journey began on February 16, 1992. On that Sunday morning, he and his family were on their way to Lower Clapton from their business in Stoke Newington. As they were on the way in conversation, the Lord broke in twice. He said the instruction to him was very clear to 'Go beyond the flesh.' He said he knew it was from the Lord because the other things that were being spoken to him were of an entirely different nature—divisive. He burst out laughing!

"The command stuck in his mind, and after some time he began to pray about it, seeking a fuller meaning. It took until December 26 of that year until the understanding came through Scripture in John 6:63, which he had found in the Bible a few months earlier.

"He said he spent three days in silence in his room until the understanding came, and he began writing. He said the impression was so strong that he left the location where he was and went home to wait on the Lord. Early that Sunday morning, he heard the command to write. He put pen to paper and an explanation on, 'Go beyond the flesh' came forth. Many writings, new songs, and other insights came also.

"Later on he looked at John 14:6, which is in the red writing, and noted what Jesus said and asked the Holy Spirit to explain verbatim what Jesus meant. Next he looked at John 4:23–24 to what Jesus said to the Samaritan woman about worship and that God is a Spirit and those who would worship Him must worship Him in Spirit and in truth. He concluded that fleshly and soulish worship is inappropriate for our God. Only worship spirit to Spirit is true and pure."

Lavender interrupted, "Philippe, stop a moment. My God! That's exactly what I was doing when you phoned me. That's why I took so long to answer the phone. I was locked in John 4:23–24. I need to read it again. 'But the hour is coming, and now is, when the true worshipers will worship the Father in spirit and truth; for the Father is seeking such to worship Him. God is Spirit, and those who worship Him must worship in spirit and truth.'"

Philippe said, "Are you serious?"

"Yes, go on."

Philippe continued, "After seeing the Scripture, he prayed and asked to be one of the worshipers whom the Father seeks—those who worship in spirit and in truth. Since then he has been used of God to perform many miracles. He kept on seeking and asking and another new song came forth called, 'Take up Your Cross and Follow Me'—a beautiful song. Then another titled, 'I'm on a Pathway That Leads to Life.' He then asked to be shown the pathway, and often he was shown the tabernacle. Eventually he began to read about the tabernacle in the book of Exodus. He said he lived a fasted lifestyle and had fasted for forty-day sessions more than ten times since he'd been saved. He believed that was why many gifts were coming from the Spirit of God into his life. In a dream in 1995 he was told that silence is the highest form of prayer. In a dream in 1996 he heard, 'Fervent prayer releases the anointing' and in another dream to, 'Work out the jigsaw puzzle.' Slowly all the phrases began to fit together. He said he prayed about everything that entered his mind.

Lavender asked Philippe, "Has he written a book? I would definitely want a copy; I'd want the song too. I'll pray for God to strengthen him so he can write it. I won't take any chances just thinking my own wishes.

"Philippe, in the salvation message to Jasmine, when I said to her, 'Heaven came down through the Son,' there was a change in the atmosphere. Go on."

Philippe continued. "He said when he was in Israel in November 2004 some of the team suggested he should write a book. He is working on it now. We might be able to get one soon."

"Good!"

He went on, "After he wrote out those revelatory messages, studying the movements of the crowd going through the gate and of the priests moving through the tabernacle, he began to see a pattern. He also referenced Psalm 16:11.

"After some time he felt inspired to combine John 6:63 and John 14: 6 where the seven movements through the tabernacle are described. In John 4:23–24, Psalm 46:10, and Psalm 16:11 these delights he found: the path of life, fullness of joy in His presence, and pleasures forevermore at His right hand. He noted this is only his personal pattern of piecing the Scriptures together to make the pathway into God's presence. He also said in a new song from the Spirit one of the lines says, 'The path is lit by righteousness.'

"He continued saying that years ago the Lord had told him that that for which he was seeking already is (exists), so he knew it would only be a matter of time until he found it if he would seek with all his heart, soul, mind, and strength. He then said, with glistening eyes, he found the path from salvation to dwelling in the presence of a holy God was fullness of joy and pleasures forevermore at His right hand."

Lavender broke in. "Philippe, that's similar to what Jasmine said about the dream she had and her great desire for joy that would last forever! Philippe, it's possible for her to find it! She can go after this joy. Please go on, and don't stop! Don't leave anything out. I'm taking notes. Praise the Lord! I mean really praise the Lord! Go on…"

"Okay! Here we go. Philippe prayed, "Holy Spirit, I need Your help to pass on this information. Thank You, in Jesus' name."

The Pathway Lit by Righteousness

"Both sides of the pathway from salvation to dwelling in God's holy presence are lit by righteousness, like the railing you hold onto for security. There's purpose in the statement, 'Stick to the basics.' Like Jesus said, no man can come to Him unless the Father draws him. The Holy Spirit will then come and bring conviction or an awareness of sin. We agree with Him and repent and go through the salvation process of Romans 10:17. My friend said that after salvation, water baptism should follow immediately. It does not need to be a long and drawn-out session. Then ask Jesus to baptize the candidate with the Holy Spirit and fire as John the Baptist said Jesus would do.

"The Holy Spirit then seals the candidate to the praise of His glory as stated in Ephesians 1:13–14. So what should be said to a new believer? Only go to church, read your Bible, stay in fellowship with other believers, and sin no longer… or is there more? What about the journey that began at salvation of getting to know Jesus their Savior in His fullness? Do we want to grow in the grace and knowledge of our Lord Jesus Christ? My friend found there are seven offices or revelations God helped him to understand that were based on the priestly walk through the tabernacle. He called it the highway of holiness. Lavender, his eyes were dancing with excitement.

"He said the seven revelations of our Lord Jesus Christ start first at the gate. There are four offices. The majority of us only know Jesus' office of Savior, period. Well, we need to know Him in the other three offices before we can move forward step by step on this righteous pathway. Are you with me?" Philippe asked.

"Yes, keep going," Lavender said.

The First Revelation of Jesus Christ—the Gate

Exodus 27:16, John 10:9, Psalm 100:4

Philippe continued, "The first revelation of Jesus and the four offices in that revelation are: King, Perfect Man, Savior, and Son of Man. In Bible college he was taught the offices represent the four gospels: Matthew, Mark, Luke, and John. We will try and keep the dialog in that sequence throughout. Your first introduction to Jesus in these offices is that of Savior. There are other symbolic representations of Him throughout Scripture, but let's stick to the basics for sound footing. For a moment, let's take an imaginary plane ride to the tabernacle in the wilderness. They knew you were coming, so they made a temporary runway close by. The plane, lands within walking distance from your terminal—the tabernacle. You get off and are so glad you brought the broad-brimmed hat and remembered to ask for a bottle of water on the plane. Phew! It's hot out here. How did Israel manage the extremes of heat in the day and cold in the night? You hear, 'A cloud by day and a pillar of fire by night.' Ah yes!

"You remember to hold your documents in your hand as you walk toward the gate or door. In John 10:9 Jesus mentioned that He Himself is the door. While walking you thank God for the short walk in the burning heat. Reaching the gate, you observe passing through that it was made of four materials of fine needlework—fine woven linen and threads of purple, scarlet, and blue. You don't allow your knowledge of the sequence of the original text to trouble you. Instead you admire the skillful work. You walk on, smiling, and that's not all. When you go inside the gate, you spontaneously begin to say, 'Praises to God! Praise God, it's cool and peaceful in here!'

"You say to the tour guide next to you, 'Wait a minute! I suddenly realized what I just did. I was acting out Psalm 100:4.' You are compelled to pull out your pocket Bible and check that you were giving thanks and praise. On discovering this fact, you say, 'That's what I just did! This is marvelous! You had me do it without even thinking about the Scripture, Lord. I am going to enjoy myself. Come on, where do we go next?'

"Our guide says, 'Well, according to the map the next revelation takes us to the altar of burnt Offering. Let's go and look at it.'"

The Second Revelation of Jesus Christ— the Altar of Burnt Offering (the Cross)

Exodus 27:1–8, Exodus 38:1–7, Psalm 118:27

"We are now in the courtyard and walking toward the altar of burnt offering. You may wonder why it is so huge, and someone from another tour party hears and shouts, 'So you don't miss it!'

"Okay, putting that witty remark aside, you notice it *is* really large. You're correct. God made it that way so we don't bypass it and try to progress by our own methods. He designed it that way so that to go forward, a sacrifice must be offered. Hundreds of thousands of animals were sacrificed here annually to remove the sins of the people of Israel. In other words, the blood of an animal had to be shed for a person's sins to be forgiven.

"Here, only the priests could perform the sacrifice. Notice they also go up on ramp walkways from any of four approaches. The altar is made of one piece, including all four horns down to its base, and covered in bronze to represent suffering. Let's personalize this experience. What if you were the one being brought here to be the burned sacrifice? I'm sure you would prefer to be dead before getting here. Those animals came here according to God's detailed specifications… and alive. I did say imagine. I will stop now because your countenance is taking a down turn. I will leave the gory details for another time, but suffice it to say those animals were without blemishes of any kind. This is the hallowed ground where worship begins—the ground of sacrifice. See those four horns way up there? They are sacred. The blood of the sacrifice was sprinkled on all of them.

"God told Moses to build everything exactly as he was shown. In other words, if God says to do something a certain way, we must do it that certain way. Usually He has purpose in doing things a certain way. For example, the four horns on the altar represent four specific things.

1. We offer our bodies daily as a living sacrifice (Romans 12:1–2).
2. We are justified through His blood (Romans 5:9).
3. Our old man was crucified with Him, which means we are dead to sin (Romans 6:6).
4. He became sin so that we might be made righteous (2 Corinthians 5:21).

"Here is where we learn to die to self by taking note of what Jesus said to His disciples in Mark 8:34. We notice it's a matter of choice to cultivate the desire for God, and we are asked to do three things: deny ourselves, take up our cross, and follow Him. These are choices you make when you are in your right mind and everything is going well. You consider fully the cost and make a conscious decision that it's the best choice to make. The Bible says Jesus destroyed principalities and powers, which included Satan. Jesus is at the right hand of God now, and that's good enough for me. Here's a clue to success: do what you do because you love Jesus and for the sake of the gospel and the kingdom. Ask for Holy Spirit's power to live in the red writing of Jesus' words.

"So here is where revelation finds a portal. The blood is of utmost importance because it is here where sanctification by His blood begins and is necessary to move to the next stage of revelation. I usually pray something like this: 'Father, I'm asking You to purge my conscience with the precious blood of Your Son, Jesus Christ, and to cleanse me thoroughly from all unrighteousness.' Here is where we are redeemed, cleansed by the blood, forgiven, and justified as if we had never sinned. Now that deserves all kinds of gratitude! 'Thank You, Father. I'm truly grateful.' One more thing before we move on. You came through the gate as one in the crowd. This is as far as you could go in the old covenant. You could only see into, not enter, the tabernacle. From this point forward, only the priests could offer the sacrifices and were able to make use of the laver and beyond. As we progress, you're *really* going to thank God for the new covenant sealed in Jesus' blood!"

The Third Revelation of Jesus Christ— the Bronze Laver

Exodus 30:17–21, Ephesians 5:26–27, John 17:17–19, Psalm 119:105

"This item was made from brass and polished to become like a mirror. It was filled with water for the priests to wash their hands and feet before they entered the holy place or approached the altar of burnt offering. If they failed to wash, they would die. Dreadful! It was some serious business. I tell you, our conversation and worship of Jesus should be all consuming because of His redemptive work. 'Lord, make me of such.'

"Jesus prayed that we be sanctified by the Word, which is truth. Paul said we are sanctified and cleansed by the washing of the water of the Word. To live, we also need God's Word daily, as Deuteronomy 8:3 and John 6:51 states. Jesus also spoke about searching the Scriptures in John 5:39, and Paul spoke about dividing the Word of truth in 2 Timothy 3:15. As we linger in the Word, it will begin to change from a Word we read to sinking into our spirit. That is, read the Word and stay with it until you sense change. This is how the Word becomes spirit as 2 Corinthians 3:6 said. All these Scriptures are telling us not to ignore the Word, even for one day. Ask the Holy Spirit to help you develop good habits and a desire for the Word of God. Hide it in your hearts. On that note, we continue to move onward."

The Fourth Revelation of Jesus Christ—the Table of Showbread

Exodus 25:23–30, Leviticus 24:7

"Twelve loaves of bread were baked and placed on the table in two rows of six. The tops of the loaves were coated with pure frankincense. You may have noticed that the previous two items, the altar of burnt offering and the laver, were overlaid with bronze. This represents suffering. This table is made of gold, but the bread is coated with frankincense. We come to know that the Word of God is sometimes called bread. We need to note here that often, when we serve the Word of God to others with godly intentions, as they digest the Word, they may oppose us unknowingly. This might be one reason we're told that the sweet-smelling frankincense eventually turns bitter—an exquisite aroma but a bitter taste. Look at these Scriptures as examples—Mark 4:18, Revelation 1:9, 10:10–11.

"For the benefits of this bread, see 2 Corinthians 3:6 and John 6:63. Here at the table of showbread (also called satisfaction), the Word becomes spirit due to a yielded will to the Word of God, and our minds are being renewed by the Word of God according to Ephesians 4:23. At this table the Word becomes spirit. Remember the flesh was sacrificed at the altar of burnt offering? Now our souls are going through the process of submission or being yielded to God's will. Transformation is taking place, which is the progression from life in the flesh to life in the Spirit. Next we approach the gold lampstand, where the word is given life, which is the fullness of life in the Spirit by illumination."

The Fifth Revelation of Jesus Christ—the Golden Lampstand

Exodus 25:31–40

"Here at the lampstand, illumination takes place. Sin, the world, and the Devil are brought into captivity to the obedience of the Lord Jesus Christ as we see in 2 Corinthians 10:3–6.

"Here at the lampstand, representative of the Holy Spirit, the soul comes into total submission and yieldedness to the control and influence of the Holy Spirit. Here is where the spirit man gets released from the bondage of the soul and unredeemed flesh. David, in Psalm 63, tells us how his soul follows hard after God and how his soul and his flesh cry out for the living God. Here is where intercession is birthed or given life. This means being led by the Spirit. Jesus, in John 6:63, alluded to the holy place and why every word He spoke was with authority and power—why all the miracles, signs, and wonders He did were successful. Satan's defeat was sealed. If the body of Christ would live in the Spirit, then Satan's defeat would be enforced. By faith, that's where we are heading… thank You, Jesus!

"We're also told the word is living and active and sharper than any two-edged sword. Therefore, getting to the lampstand calls for being yielded to the Holy Spirit through a sanctified lifestyle, which leads to holiness. Paul talks of walking in, being led by, and living in the Spirit. This is the place. The Holy Spirit births intercession here. Shall we move forward? I'm ready to engage in a Spirit-led prayer and on into night and day vigils."

The Sixth Revelation of Jesus Christ—the Altar of Incense

Exodus 30:1–10, Psalm 141:2

"Here, only your spirit man ministers. He is now liberated from unredeemed flesh through death to self, resulting in a yielded soul. These quietly observe. He is on the way to approaching the ark of testimony to commune with His Father-Creator between the wings of the cherubim. Here, at the altar of incense, you will find yourself going automatically into praying and ministering to the Lord. This type of prayer is effortless, whether it may be interceding on behalf of individuals or a nation. This is what Paul is referring to when speaking about 'all kinds of prayer for all saints' in Ephesians 6:18. Worship becomes a sweet aroma unto the Lord. Much earlier David refers to it in Psalms 141:2, saying, 'Let his prayers rise as the evening sacrifice,' and John, in the Spirit on the Lord's day, mentions it in Revelation 1:9. There are many more scriptural examples. However, here is where we should progress through the revelations of Jesus Christ to offer our prayers, our travail, and making prophetic utterances in the Spirit.

"Jesus' church is built in this domain, not in either of the other two domains of the unredeemed soul and flesh. Here you also find four horns covered with gold. Notice there are also four fragrances that are offered on this altar where they will waft into the holy of holies. The Bible says they were sweet spices of stacte, onycha, galbanum, and pure frankincense (refer to the chapter, 'Fervent Prayer Releases the Anointing'). They were to be of equal amounts and tempered by a perfumer. Some was to be crushed even finer to be placed before the ark of testimony where the Lord would meet with the high priest on the Day of Atonement. Some of the incense is crushed extremely fine as specified by the Father of spirits. Making the incense in the prescribed way would cause the Lord to respond favorably. It would be wise for us to consider reverencing this Holy God. It is also said the four spices represent the life, death, burial, and resurrection of Jesus. It was here that another new song came from the Spirit, 'Take Me beyond the Veil.' You can enter with intercessory worship—spirit to Spirit."

The Seventh Revelation of Jesus Christ—the Ark of the Testimony

Exodus 25:10–22, Hebrews 4:9-10

"Here is where your journey, which began at salvation, takes you—the holy of holies. Here is where the covenant is kept. Here you enter into communion and intimacy with your Father-Creator, Elohim. Here is where reverential worship is perfected in His presence. Here you are changed from glory to glory. Waiting in silence, being still to know He is God. Here empowerment, renewal, transformation, and restoration all take place continuously. We are being strengthened with divine might in our innermost man. Daily we are experiencing God's unconditional love, union with Him, and being made perfect in one by love. Is there any greater aspiration or fulfillment in all creation for mankind but this: to be lovers of the Most High God, our Father, and the Lover of our Souls, Jesus? Hallelujah! Glory forever!"

Lavender broke in. "Philippe, that was amazing! I thought my fingers would be aching from all the writing, but wait a minute. Philippe, Philippe!"

Philippe was startled. "What, Lavender?"

"Philippe, I just realized something!" Lavender said.

Philippe asked again, "Are you going to tell me what, Lavender?"

"Yes, yes, yes. Wait a minute! I'm taking off the bandages… I don't need them anymore! I'm healed! It happened while you were sharing. Thank You, Jesus, thank You!"

Lavender had not told Philippe she had an accident or that she picked up the phone with her left hand. She was caught up in getting the information for Jasmine when the Lord began the healing process. It was finalized when Philippe called and confirmed the Scriptures she had just been reading. As she was hearing and writing about the pathway from salvation to dwelling in the presence of the Lord for Jasmine, she didn't realized that she acted by faith when Philippe told her to get pen and paper and started writing normally with her right hand.

Lavender continued, "I'm sorry, Philippe. I was so caught up in getting the information for Jasmine, so engrossed that it didn't even occur to me to tell you I had an accident where the right side of my face and right arm were injured. Philippe, Jesus healed me! Are you hearing me? I just wrote out all the notes as I normally write. I didn't know it until you stopped talking. My fingers aren't aching at all—no pain!"

"Wow! Praise the Lord, Lavender! He said healings would occur when we follow the pathway as laid out. I'm really happy for you!"

"I'm really glad you called, Philippe. You were right. It was ordained of the Lord. Wow!"

She went on, "I'll have to go over this information. I've never heard or seen the pathway into God's presence laid out like this before. This… is… beautiful! Philippe, did your friend give you any kind of a pattern or guideline for following this pathway daily?"

Philippe laughed out loud again. He seemed to be doing that a lot. "Lavender, you are asking me the same question I asked him. My friend left the room when I asked him and then came back with a sheet of paper in his hand. He said, 'The outline on this paper is my personal daily approach to God as I follow this pathway.' He said he's going to put it in his book, and each person can tailor the model to fit their own personality since God made us individuals. He's so funny! He said he thought this was called sharing. Lavender, when he was reading this, the Holy Spirit was confirming every word. I was truly blessed. Are you ready to write again?"

"Yes, I'm ready! This is so exciting! Go ahead," said Lavender.

A Personal Daily Approach to God

Philippe started in, "Praise the Lord! Going back through each of the seven revelations of Jesus Christ, these are some of his thoughts and prayers my friend prays each day. Continue to meditate on the seven revelations yourself to suit these prayers to you personally. His prayers are a guideline for us. My friend shared the following.

"Father of Glory, uncreated, and Love Divine, I bow my knees before You. Jesus my Savior, King, and Lord, I bow my knees before You. Holy Spirit, teacher, and friend, I bow my knees before You. All praise, honor, glory, and power to You for my inseparable union with my heavenly Father through Jesus Christ, my Lord."

The Gate

"Father, I thank You for keeping me alive to see a new day, for Your mercy endures forever. Thank You for the salvation You provided through Jesus Christ, for Your mercy endures forever. Thank You for the resurrection life you've given me through Jesus Christ, Your Son, for Your love endures forever. Thank You that Jesus, the perfect Man, identified with me. With gratitude I worship the Son of Man, my Lord. I humbly bow and obey You, Christ Jesus my King.

I praise You, Elohim, for Your wonderful work of creation and making me in Your image. I praise You for making Your name known in all the earth through signs, wonders, and miracles. I praise You for extending Your Kingdom through us. Let Your will be done in me as it is in heaven."

The Altar of Burnt Offering (the Cross)

"Thank You for Your Holy Spirit who provides me grace to offer my body as a living sacrifice. I thank You for giving me the willingness to crucify my old nature on the cross and be raised up with You by faith into Your resurrection life. Thank You that I am seated in heavenly places in Christ Jesus. Sanctify me with the precious blood of Jesus Christ, setting me apart for holy use. I praise You that I am forgiven, justified (made as if I had never sinned), and have been made the righteousness of God in Christ Jesus. Glory to you, almighty God. All power belongs to You, Lord of Hosts."

The Laver

"Cleanse me, Father, with the washing of the water of Your Word. Sanctify me with Your Word—Your Word is truth. Jesus, I thirst. Jesus, You are the living water. Let Your Word become as honey to my lips, water to my soul, and a lamp to my feet. Teach me, Holy Spirit, how to hide the Word of God in my heart so I will choose not to sin against Him."

The Table of Showbread

"It is written, 'O taste and see that the Lord is good.' Therefore, I yield my soul, knowing Your Word will transform me and conform me to Your will. I desire that Your Word will become my satisfaction. Lord, I delight in Your Word! Show me how to partake of Your Word as my daily bread. Jesus, You are the living bread. Teach me how to feast, meditate, and abide in Your Word until it changes in me from Word to spirit because the letter kills, but the Spirit gives life."

The Gold Lampstand

"I yield my will, my emotions, and my intellect as I am renewed in the spirit of my mind. Glory to God, my mind is being illuminated by the light and power of Your Holy Spirit. Jesus, You are the light of this world. I thank You that every thought I have I take captive and bring into obedience to my Lord Jesus Christ. Here, I am free from the influence of my body and soul. Free from the snares of the world and the wiles of the Devil. Your Spirit gives me life, the ability to make decrees and to create. Here Your word is life. Hallelujah!"

The Altar of Incense

"I thank You, Holy Spirit, for leading my spirit into intercessory worship, where I worship my Father in spirit and truth so that my prayers, supplications, and worship rise before Him as sweet incense, a fragrant aroma. Jesus, You are the fragrant aroma that ascends to my Father. Jesus, You are splendor, radiance, and majesty. You are crowned King of kings and Lord of lords.

Here I magnify You with adoration and exaltation. Sovereign Father, I bring my worshipful offering before You in awe and with reverence. I adore You for Your holy communion. Holy Father, intimacy with You is more precious to me than all the treasures of this world. In Your presence I am being changed from glory to glory! I want to be lost in You! I glorify Your name, for You alone are holy. Blessing and honor and glory and power be to You who sits on the throne and to the Lamb forever and ever! *Amen*!"

The Ark of the Testimony

"God and Father of our Lord Jesus Christ, I approach Your throne of grace in humility, gratitude, and silence led by your Holy Spirit, in Jesus' name. Amen.

"Here your spirit man waits in stillness, listening as your Father speaks to you from above the mercy seat between the wings of the cherubim. Out of a time of intercessory worship in this place my friend was also given these special new songs from the Spirit: 'Take Me beyond the Veil' and 'Prince of Peace Sweet Shalom.'

"Your approach may be different, but the process is generally the same as there is only one pathway into God's presence. You may linger at the altar of burnt offering (the cross), at the laver or the gold lampstand, or perhaps somewhere else along the way. Another person may linger in other areas. Where you linger may even vary from day to day depending upon what the Holy Spirit knows we need each day for preparation. This is the pathway (the way) of which Jesus spoke where we can worship the Father in spirit and in truth. The Father is looking for such worshipers to worship Him. Will you answer His call of desire?"

Philippe continued, "When he finished, my friend said, 'I pray many people will be blessed following this pathway of righteousness.'"

"Philippe, I feel like I'm in heaven."

"Me too. I'm sure Jasmine's going to enjoy this pathway of righteousness."

"Philippe, she surely will. This is glorious, thank you. Please tell your friend thank you. Let him know he's appreciated and so is this wonderful gift he has shared of the pathway. Encourage him to finish his book quickly and to include his songs from the Spirit."

"I will, Lavender. Do let me know how you get on with Jasmine, okay? I am sure my friend will want to hear also. Bye now."

"I will stay in touch. Bye for now, Philippe, and thanks again."

Lavender hung up the phone and sat in silence. What a day this had been! Heaven came down to her through the Son!

Heaven Came Down to You through the Son (Song)

During the writing of this book, this song caused me much concern as I wondered whether I should add it into this chapter. I wrestled with my conscience and decided to exclude it. When the manuscript came back for review, I fasted three days for direction about the overall workup and the book going into the hands of the readers and into their hearts. In my prayer, the impression from Holy Spirit was clear to include the song, so I took it as God's mercy toward me. This song was birthed in hours of prayer and worship and transitioning into singing in tongues. I just used my guitar, but it sounded as if an orchestra and a choir of angels was in the room with me through it all. I can still hear that time of worship resounding in my spirit as if it had just happened now. Here are the words of His song. My conscience is at rest. Praise the Lord.

Heaven Came Down to You through the Son

Heaven came down to you,
Heaven came down through the Son.
Heaven came down to you,
Heaven came down through the Son.
He's the Light of the world, He's Truth—
Darkness cannot stay in His presence.

The Father said light be—
The Son said I am the Light of this world,
When I go you shall be the lights,
The lights are all around.

North, south, east and west,
The lights are everywhere,
They are in you and me, who know the Son,
That God placed the light within Him.

Let us shine, let us shine bright as the Son.

Reflections of Him within will be seen,
As we yield ourselves to righteousness;
Let *holiness* consume us.

A decision has been made; there is no other way,
But the path of righteousness for His name's sake—
Oh the promises they are numerous, all you need to do,
Is believe, the word you read and call on the name of Jesus.
He said ask in My name, this name has already been proven
There is power and authority in the name of Jesus.

There are four ways we'll lift the banner high
Saying that Jesus Christ is Lord,
To the glory of the Father who sent His only Son—
Oh I love the Lord; I love Him with all my heart.
I am not ashamed of Him; oh I love the Lord,
Jesus is His name, there's no other name like Jesus.

There is healing in the name,
Healing in the name, there is healing in the name.
There is peace in the name, peace in the name,
There is peace in the name, provision is in the name;
There's a Provider. There is peace, peace, healing,
Provision in the name. His name is Jesus.

Call him the salvation; it's in the name,
There is salvation in the name. He's our defender,
The defender. He's our protector in the time of trouble,
There's protection in the name.

Oh let's talk about love; lift the banner high,

There is a banner over you and me—
And that banner is love. They call it Nissi.
There is love in the name of Jesus.

Oh peace, peace, peace; there's healing,
Provision, provision, and protection;
There is love, love, sweet love in the name;
Oh there's clothing, He's our righteousness.

Oh Tsidkenu, eh Shalom, Shammah, oh Rophe,
Talk about Rohi, and Raphekah.
Then there's Nissi, the banner over you,
The banner over me—

Oh Jesus is His name, multi, multi, multi name.
Power, power, power in the name,
Healing, healing, healing, and peace.
God has put everything, power-packed
In the name of Jesus, Jesus Christ my Lord—
A name above every name, His name is Jesus.
Call Him Jesus, He shall save His people.
Everywhere I turn this song will be sung,
That Jesus Christ is Lord.
This song will be sung everywhere I go,
That Jesus is Lord indeed.
My Savior divine, He's my righteousness, He's my friend.
Shalom, Shammah, He's my Nissi.

Believe on the Lord and you shall be,
Shall be, you shall be saved.
I believe in Jesus, I believe in Him with my whole heart—

This heart belongs to Him; my whole being belongs to Him.
Spirit, soul, and body belong to You, my Lord.
Take me as I am and build me how You want me to be.
I offer myself to You. Take dominion,
Take dominion over me.

There is none like you in this whole universe
You are the Creator, you're bigger, bigger than the universe.
And that's my God and Jesus my Lord,
Minister unto me by the Holy Spirit.
Teacher, friend, and comforter, Spirit of Truth,
I will put up my ears and my heart to receive every word.

I love You, Lord, with all of my heart.
I turn my eyes to You. I look to You, Jesus,
I will look up, I will look up to You.
Jesus, I love You more, O Savior, Savior divine,

You're my Savior, You're my Savior,
You're my Savior divine.
My eyes are on You morning, noon, and night.
I love You, Lord, I love You, Lord,
I love You, Lord, I love You, Lord,
I love You, Lord, with all of my heart.

New song from the Spirit by Merlin H Oliver July 26, 1995
Islington, London N1© Copyright July, 1995.

JESUS IS THE WAY INTO JOY FOREVERMORE

I do not know a single person who doesn't want joy. Have you ever noticed with happy children it's always a fun time? My friends, Jesus our Lord is full of joy. He offered it to us in the here and now as a foretaste of heaven. Please read this text twice where love and joy is perfected.

> As the Father loved Me, I also have loved you; abide in My love. If you keep My commandments, you will abide in My love, just as I have kept My Father's commandments and abide in His love. These things I have spoken to you, that My joy may remain in you, and that your joy may be full. This is My commandment, that you love one another as I have loved you. Greater love has no one than this, than to lay down one's life for his friends. You are My friends if you do whatever I command you. (John 15:9–14)

In John 6:38 Jesus said, "For I have come down from heaven, not to do My own will, but the will of Him who sent Me."

Jesus spoke not only about being sent to earth but also about finishing the work Father gave Him to do, according to John 4:34.

a. There was a council meeting of the Godhead before the foundations of the world.
b. There was agreement about the decision for Jesus to come to earth.
c. There was purpose to do what was agreed in the council.
d. There was redemption of Adam's children, manifesting God's name, and giving glory to God.
e. There was a bringing the purpose or the work to completion: proactive intercession (John 17:4, 19:30).

Why? All of Adam's children have gone astray like sheep according to Isaiah 53:6, and there is none who does well, as stated in Psalm 14:3. The role of the shepherd is significant in the Bible, from Abel to Jesus. He said He was the good Shepherd and the good Shepherd gives His life for the sheep in John 10:11. Being a good shepherd, His sheep know and hear His voice and follow Him (John 10:27). In other words, they are obedient, loyal, and trusting. The sheep will go wherever the good Shepherd goes: back to the Father's house following His pathway or road map, from heaven to earth, to the cross, and back to heaven to the Father's right hand, where there are pleasures forevermore.

The leading of the Spirit guided me to Psalm 16:11 for the fulfillment of the journey Christ accomplished for us.

> You will show me the path of life; In Your presence is fullness of joy; At Your right hand are pleasures forevermore. (Psalm 16:11)

Isn't it rather strange that the obvious is usually rejected and ridiculed as too unbelievable? Didn't Jesus say He is the way, the truth, and the life?

> Jesus said to him, "I am the way, the truth, and the life. No one comes to the Father except through me." (John 14:6)

He also said,

> It is the Spirit who gives life, the flesh profits nothing, The words that I speak to you are Spirit and they are life. (John 6:63)

This is what John Wesley[12] said of John 6:63—"It is the Spirit—the spiritual meaning of these words, by which God gives life. The flesh—the bare, carnal, literal meaning, profited nothing. The words which I have spoken, they are spirit—Are to be taken in a spiritual sense and, when they are so understood, they are life—That is, a means of spiritual life to the hearers."

Therefore, though there are many ways into the supernatural, there's only one way for the children of Adam to get back to

---

12 Explanation by John Wesley on John 6:63: http://www.biblestudytools.com/commentaries/wesleys-explanatory-notes/john/john-6.html.

the Father's house, and it's through the love gift provided by the Father—the way of the cross traveled by Jesus of Nazareth.

So let's examine the Scripture in Psalm 16:11, "You will show me the path of life; In Your presence is fullness of joy; At Your right hand are pleasures forevermore." How did David know, or did he just pen the words because he felt good and happy, or was it a revelation birthed out of an experience? What was happening to him at that time? Were there circumstances affecting his thoughts? In some of the Psalms, 27 and 63, he let us know he found the way. In Psalm 27 he mentioned one thing he seeks after, and in Psalm 63 he mentioned seeing God's power and glory. The Psalms he wrote were revelatory because they were birthed through night-and-day worship. That's why we find solace in the Psalms.

MINISTRY IN NORTHERN IRELAND

It was amazing how I ended up in Northern Ireland on such short notice. During that time, I was working as a civilian in the British Army.

It was late Friday afternoon on January 31, 1997, and I was tidying up the barracks before I left for the weekend. The other soldiers had gone, and I was alone when the phone rang. I picked up the phone, put the receiver to my ear, and said, "Hello, how can I help you?" On the other end of the line was the founder and director of prayer for all of London.

"Hi, Merlin, how are you?" she said.

I said something like, "Great! How can I help you?"

She said, "I am going to Northern Ireland tomorrow, and I'd like you to come with me."

On hearing that statement, I thought, *She's crazy if she thinks I'm going with her on such short notice. And to add to it, I've never been to Northern Ireland. How would I fit in with all those white folks? I'd stick out like a sore thumb!* I said none of those things to her that I was thinking. Instead I asked, "Why me?"

She responded, "Because God told me to call you, and furthermore you are in the army, and the incident caused by the army in Northern Ireland must be rectified through repentance and forgiveness."

My mind went on another tangent, and I thought to myself, *What took place had nothing to do with me, and the incident was more than twenty-five years ago. I don't see what it has to do with me.*

Again, instead of sharing my thoughts, I said to her, "I do not see the connection concerning me, Could you please explain what you are seeing?" I need to add here, after she mentioned, "God said," she already had my undivided attention.

She said, "It's like this. Though you weren't involved in the incident, you're now working for that branch of the army. Therefore, you are part of what took place. In other words, you are now party to the guilt and bear the guilt. Because of that you can represent your department by standing in the gap."

What she said made sense and was biblically correct, so I responded, "I acknowledge what you are saying. However, it's very short notice for me to prepare."

She responded, "I need you to come even though I know we haven't much time."

I responded, "What do you mean we haven't much time?"

"There's going to be an Orange March on Sunday, February 2, 1997, in London Derry. The march will end at the cenotaph, where some speeches will be given in commemoration for the youths who lost their lives. We need to be there at that moment also, kneeling down next to the cenotaph, repenting and asking God's forgiveness for what took place and asking Him to heal the wounds and hearts of all involved on both sides—the people and the British Army."

Again, what she said made sense, but my mind was seeing one black face in the midst of a sea of white faces in orange costumes! I had no intention of going after my imagination conjured up that second horrible picture. Fear engulfed me.

She continued, "Early tomorrow morning there's a plane leaving for Northern Ireland from Heathrow Airport. Meet me there, okay, Merlin?"

Of course I responded, "Yes."

I hung up the phone and thought to myself, *Wow, what a shocker! A totally different direction*. February 1 is my birthday, and I had other plans. Northern Ireland was not one of them—not in a month of Sundays!

You may be thinking that I didn't protest and just went along with her command. Well, I could tell she had looked into the matter, had it all arranged, and knew exactly what needed to be done. I was part of the prayer team for London, so she had access to me and where I worked. But more importantly, why I didn't refuse is this—God had told her to call me. That I could not ignore.

Why I had to go is very simple. Back in 1992 I was in a mess holistically and needed supernatural intervention. One night while I was lying on my stomach on the floor in tremendous pain (this pain was 24/7), God showed up and the internal conversation went something like this: "For you to be free, you need to cut a covenant with Me of obedience." I imagined for a moment I had a choice, and to be honest, I didn't want to do it because I knew then that whatever He told me to do from that moment forward, I would have to do it. He knew I didn't want to cut that type of covenant with Him.

However, He impressed upon my heart gently. "You need to do it or stay where you are, not growing any more intimate with Me." It didn't take me long to agree to His sovereign terms. Once I relented and made the agreement to do whatever He said, He departed. I assure you agreeing with God's decision was marvelous, beautiful, and wonderful. That's why I found myself at Heathrow Airport the following morning.

I got to the airport and met her at the appointed place. We greeted each other and proceeded to purchase our tickets at the counter. All the while I was still amazed at what was happening, where we were going, and what I might encounter. It wasn't all pleasant thinking. I did a lot of praying.

Finally it was time for us to board our flight. It was a small plane, and it danced on the air turbulence. On the journey I asked the Lord, "What am I doing here?"

His response was, "I'm expanding your territory."

I had watched the expanding of the territory from North London where I lived. It began on a day back in 1992 when I decided, "I will speak truth no matter what the cost." On that initial decision, I felt the forces of darkness encroach upon me with intensity, as if the very life was being squeezed out of me. The intention was for me to become fearful and back out. I refused to be intimidated by the dark forces and pressed in regardless, trusting the Lord.

So while that little plane danced on the air turbulence, on hearing that word from the Lord, I was comforted. After a while, we landed at the airport in Northern Ireland. We collected our luggage and waited for a taxi to take us to our accommodation. I'll tell you again, I felt weird being the only black face there. My comfort was in knowing God wanted me there.

On the way to our prearranged accommodations, I asked the taxi driver why the land was so dry. He said they hadn't had rain for about nine months. The prophet Elijah came to my mind when God told him to pray to cause the rain to come again after three and a half years of drought in Samaria (1 Kings 18:1).

After we arrived at our accommodations, we got busy sticking to the agenda we had while there. There was a large castle not far from where we were staying. We went there first and got up on the wall so we could overlook the entire area. The top of the wall I would guess was beyond six feet wide. We began to pray, and during part of the prayer we asked God to send rain. That Saturday night it rained, praise the Lord! That faith extender boosted my confidence.

We got back to our accommodation, had an evening meal, and prayed some more. Still, the coming Sunday's activity occupied my mind. In the short time we spent there, we got a lot of things done, like visits, shopping, and sightseeing. It was amazing! Ireland is a beautiful country.

One of the events that gave me great joy was the evening service in a Catholic church. The presence of the Lord was glorious. There were many different denominations worshiping together in the church that Saturday evening. After the meeting was over, the father was picking up bits of paper off the floor. His humility touched my heart. I asked him why he was doing it. I think he said something like he was setting an example. I remembered Jesus saying something like that to His disciples about having a servant's heart.

Still, the big moment awaited us on Sunday, the following day.

Sunday, February 2, 1997, arrived. It was rather cold and overcast. Most likely the rain from the previous night had something to do with it. We had breakfast and then went to the assembly room to have a team talk. We expected a large crowd of Orange marchers. The local group that was part of our team gave us information about what to expect.

The local people were friendly, cordial, and hospitable. I appreciated their friendliness for this reason—Montserrat in the West Indies is my birthplace. It is called the Emerald Isle of the West. It is so named because of its Irish connection. They both have lavish greenery. If you happened to look at the Montserrat flag, you would notice the shamrock is part of its design. Also, our island celebrates St. Patrick's Day annually. It's a popular festive celebration on our island. Visitors attend from around the globe. In Montserrat, some of the Irish relics are still visible. One more point of interest, our island dialect is called Irish brogue. We have a lot for which to thank the Irish settlers, irrespective of whatever reason they were sent there. It was a remarkable period in our island's history. I would recommend Montserrat for a vacation spot.

Let's go back to Sunday. After the morning briefing, the group attended service at the Catholic church. The reverence for the Lord Jesus Christ was evident. That dedication I have not seen anywhere else. After all those years, it is still vivid in my mind. After the service, we had some free time. We used it to pray and prepare for the march, when we would be at the cenotaph later that day.

On making our way to the cenotaph and through the large crowd, certain individuals would say different things! Think of it—an unusual face appearing in the vast crowd to me is obvious and the inevitable reaction, agreed? I stayed focused on the set task, at the same time staying positive and expecting good to come out of the purpose. This thought crossed my mind—my face would not be forgotten. This generated a wee internal smile.

When the mayor finished his speech on the incident and the implications for the country, my prayer leader and I made our way through the crowd toward the cenotaph, in the direction where the bouquets of flowers were placed. We knelt down on the cold concrete and offered up our petition of repentance, forgiveness, and reconciliation to the sovereign Lord for the loss and pain that was caused by the army's action. Innocent blood soaked His soil. We prayed, "Forgive us, and remove the pain from all. May the peace of God heal all hearts, especially the mothers, in the name of Jesus." Our prayer was along that line.

It was amazing what happened next. As we rose from our kneeling position, one of the mothers was standing to my left. I remember inviting her attention. I believe what I did next was of the Spirit of God. It was the courage, boldness, and assurance of what I was about to do that caught my attention. I knew it wasn't my doing. I looked directly into her beautiful hazel eyes and asked her a direct question. "Have you forgiven the British Army for the death of your son?" She responded in a crisp, clear, "Yes." I didn't really have to ask her the question. I already saw it in her eyes. The forgiveness in her heart was reflected in her eyes. I believe Father God wanted her to say it openly.

I'll say this about the prayer. When our knees touched that concrete, everything else was forgotten. We were alone with our Creator making our petition. I say this because I believe the same thing was happening to my prayer leader, bless her heart. After all was said and done, we left the area. It was a peaceful day, mission completed, praise the Lord.

We got back to our accommodations, gave thanks, and later drove to the airport to catch our flight back to Heathrow Airport.

I gave thanks for that memorable trip. I commend my excellent, obedient prayer leader for calling me, as Father God knew best who would admirably perform the assignment.

Later that year I immigrated to the United States. A little while later I was attending a pastors' meeting in one of the cities in Niagara County. One of the pastors posed me a question: "Should the US government ask the African Americans' forgiveness for using them as slaves?" I didn't give a direct answer. I asked the Holy Spirit how to respond. In doing that, He responded with what took place in Northern Ireland just a few months earlier. I raised that encounter as a type of what should happen, not just for that situation only, but in all reconciliations—forgive. Nations must come to repentance in forgiveness, as we see throughout the Bible.

Two years later, in 1999, a peace treaty was signed between Britain and Northern Ireland. Would you say that our prayer, and the faithful prayers of many others made with broken hearts and contrite spirits, was heard by a compassionate and forgiving God? There is no doubt in my mind it is so! Praise be to His name!

THE CLOUD AND THE GLORY OF HIS PRESENCE

At some time or other, we look up into the sky and see lots of different cloud formations. Sometimes they are still, and sometimes they are moving. Sometimes they hide the sun, and sometimes they also hold rain particles. Maybe you have heard the saying, "As in the natural, so in the spiritual"? Well, we want to take a closer look at clouds. One in particular, the cloud of His presence, was the guide and covering for Israel in the wilderness.

At the appointed time, all Israel had an open prayer meeting. That prayer meeting was quite long. In fact, it lasted many hundreds of years, from the death of Joseph until just before Moses' encounter at the burning bush. What was it that brought the visitation? God had made a promise to Abraham.

> Then He said to Abram: "Know certainly that your descendants will be strangers in a land that is not theirs, and will serve them, and they will afflict them four hundred years. And also the

> nation whom they serve I will judge; afterward they shall come out with great possessions. (Genesis 15:13–14)

So at the hands of the hard taskmasters, Israel was releasing the cry of affliction to the Lord. A set time for their release was one stipulation God included in the covenant He made with Abraham. When the time arrived, the Bible says,

> Moreover He said, "I am the God of your father—the God of Abraham, the God of Isaac, and the God of Jacob." And Moses hid his face, for he was afraid to look upon God. And the LORD said: "I have surely seen the oppression of My people who are in Egypt, and have heard their cry because of their taskmasters, for I know their sorrows. So I have come down to deliver them out of the hand of the Egyptians, and to bring them up from that land to a good and large land, to a land flowing with milk and honey." (Exodus 3:6–8a)

God appeared to Moses in the burning bush, identified Himself, and explained to Moses why He had come; He had heard their cry of affliction. During the time of the ten plagues, God spoke to Moses. On the journey to Mount Sinai, He was to them "a cloud by day and a fire by night." From Mount Sinai throughout the rest of the Scriptures, His main covering was a cloud. Most likely we are all familiar with the scene after Jesus' baptism when God the Father spoke out of a cloud. Again, He spoke out of a cloud at Jesus' transfiguration on the mount.

There are numerous scriptural references relating to God covering with a cloud, a demonstration of His mercy toward us. The glory of His presence unveiled would overwhelm us. However we come to learn, we must learn to create a holy habitation for Him, and that's done through spirit-led intercessory worship. We are fast approaching the awareness that we must get to the place beyond the lampstand—the altar of incense. It is at this offering when the spirit man cries, "Abba, Father" that the demonic darkness will shift from families, communities, cities, states, nations, and the world. Jesus performed His ministry in spirit and in truth. That's why Satan was doomed to total defeat. He had no chance whatsoever of defeating Jesus. He said, "Greater works we will do," and it's when we seek to minister like Him in spirit and truth that this happens. We will lead Holy Spirit–led lives.

You may have noticed that technology is upgrading its products about every three months. That's a fast turnaround. What is the church world doing when a new person accepts the gift of salvation? Are we just trudging along in the same old format? We must get into a position of taking the lead to avert the encroaching darkness. Take note of this—Israel was on their way out of Egypt en route to an encounter with their covenant-keeping God at Mount Sinai. Just before the God encounter, who got in the way? You got it—Amalek! Therefore, with such strong opposition as we have just mentioned, don't you think it's necessary to get the new saint into God's presence as soon as possible? We might even echo Lavender's prayer to God for Jasmine that new believers will know quickly how to advance into His presence from salvation to the ark of testimony. This is one place where the tides of evil cannot touch us.

We see the natural clouds floating in the sky, and sometimes they hide the sun. In Hebrews, the cloud is called *Anan*, which literally means to cover. In times just before rain we see thunderclouds. Cloud is also used in the case of a great army according to Ezekiel 30:1, 38:9.

About three-fourths of the occurrences of *Anan* refer to the pillar of cloud that directed the Israelites through the desert; it also represented the presence of God over the tabernacle. See Exodus 13:21–22, 14:19, 20, 24, 16:10, 33:9–10, 40:34–38.

King Solomon prayed a memorable prayer of dedication that became a blueprint for the succeeding prophets. At the end of the prayer, God acknowledged it by the appearance of the cloud. The cloud was present in the temple of Solomon.

> Indeed it came to pass, when the trumpeters and singers were as one, to make one sound to be heard in praising and thanking the LORD, and when they lifted up their voice with the trumpets and cymbals and instruments of music, and praised the LORD, saying: "For He is good, For His mercy endures forever," that the house, the house of the LORD, was filled with a cloud, [14] so that the priests could not continue ministering because of the cloud; for the glory of the LORD filled the house of God. (2 Chronicles 5:13–14)

In the following chapter, you will discover how the Scriptures above became known.

AT A HOUSE MEETING IN LAKEVIEW

Back in February 2002, the last Scripture in the previous chapter came forth as part of a new song during a live intercessory worship session. I had been invited to join a prayer group in Lake View in the south towns past Buffalo. I was asked to lead worship, so I took my Fender guitar with me and my little tape recorder. I spent the day fasting, as I often did when it was the first time I was meeting a new team. Throughout the day, the Spirit of God was prompting me that something significant was coming. I had learned to have a recording unit with me. I had learned to adopt that strategy from days of worship back in United Kingdom. I had missed many beautiful new songs from the Spirit there, but once I started playing the guitar, both words and melody flowed.

I arrived at the house, got introduced to everyone, and after a while I sensed we should have communion. We had communion and felt the presence of the Lord increase. I picked up my guitar and started playing. I don't remember the first song, but after a while I heard myself belaboring, going to the water brook to drink of Him—the Living Water. Then the song took off in its own direction. I had reached the place where the Spirit of the Lord took over, and my guitar and I became His instrument.

I enjoyed every moment because the whole session became effortless. We entered into His rest. I had the tape running and then heard the worship shift to a higher level, like a call of the Spirit for all of us to go into a higher place in Him. During that higher place, I heard myself singing the Scripture about "as the singers sing and the musicians play in harmony, then the glory comes as a testimony." We all felt the shift in the atmosphere, and the harmonies were definitely from heaven.

The worship went on for about forty-five minutes in tongues and interpretations. When it was over, the leader preached a short message. But I will tell you now, that wasn't even necessary. What I sensed should have happened was to sit there in silence, basking in His glory. There was no doubt we had had a glorious and holy visitation.

I didn't know where the Scripture I had been singing could be found in the Bible. Eventually I found it in 2 Chronicles 5:11–14. I'll tell you, electricity shot through my body on its discovery. Yes, you could imagine my excitement and gratitude! Spontaneous praise and thanks to Father God was my response! How great is our God, how marvelous and wonderful is He!

The following week I went back, and a similar thing happened again. This time it was about the tabernacle of David being rebuilt. Our God of abundance is coming again through His live worship. I was aware of other prophetic words about this and just knew they are coming to pass. Glory to the Righteous One! Glory to the Ruler of the universe!

The cloud accompanied the presence of God at Mount Sinai. See Exodus 19:9, 16, 24:15–16, 18, Deuteronomy 4:11, 5:22, and Psalm 97:2. During Jesus' transfiguration, the cloud appeared again.

THE GLORY DEPARTED

The glory departed from Israel on more than one occasion. It is of vital importance to know why the glory would depart or leave a people. Something detrimental would have to have occurred, and to think of it is rather frightening. Let me say this with deep concern. It is so easy to take our walk with almighty God for granted. We, in our presumption, think everything is fine because our sentence is delayed. We are familiar with the term *Ichabod* that was given to the son birthed to Phinehas' wife. She died shortly after having the child. That day Israel was defeated in battle by a great slaughter. Israel's defeat caused the Ark to be taken by the enemy (1 Samuel 4:17, 20– 21). This happened during the time when Eli was high priest of Israel.

Some strange things took place prior to the glory departing, and sin was the problem. God, in His love and mercy, sent word to Eli (1 Samuel 2:27–35) as to the impending judgment. Hophni and Phinehas had gone so deep in their transgressions that even honoring their father seemed a strange thing to them. Their ungodly actions caused the enemy to gain the advantage over them. Still, in their deception they entered into battle expecting God to fight for them. There is also the period when the glory departed during the reign of Zedekiah, in the time of Ezekiel the prophet. You can read this account in Ezekiel 11:22–23. It hasn't returned since.

We are still waiting for His reappearance. We have some indication that this reappearance will take place during the millennial period when the temple will be rebuilt according to Ezekiel 43:1–9. God has promised that the glory of this latter house will be greater than the former house. I perceive some supernatural events would have to take place.

> So rend your heart, and not your garments; Return to the LORD your God, For He is gracious and merciful, Slow to anger, and of great kindness; And He relents from doing harm. (Joel 2:13)

> On that day I will raise up the tabernacle of David, which has fallen down, And repair its damages; I will raise up its ruins, And rebuild it as in the days of old. (Amos 9:11)

Here the prophet Amos prophesied of the rebuilding of the tabernacle of worship. God is asking the church to revert to this type of dedicated, genuine worship. Jesus spoke of the worship that is of spirit and truth.

THE ESCHATOLOGICAL SIGNIFICANCE OF THE GLORY

The glory has eschatological significance and importance. Ezekiel 30:3 says the day of the Lord is near, the time of the Gentiles. I tremble at the thought of what that day will be like. I have no idea whatsoever, apart from what prophet Joel is saying—a day of darkness. I could envisage a traumatic moment for countless millions when that day appears. May God help us to live each day as our last!

Joel spoke about the day of the Lord. We are to blow the trumpet and to sound an alarm in His holy mountain.

> Blow the trumpet in Zion, And sound an alarm in My holy mountain! Let all the inhabitants of the land tremble; For the day of the Lord is coming, For it is at hand: A day of darkness and gloominess, A day of clouds and thick darkness, Like the morning clouds spread over the mountains. (Joel 2:1–2)

The great day of the Lord is not about something pleasant. As in Zephaniah 1:15, he speaks of a day of wrath, a day of trouble and distress, a day of devastation and desolation, of darkness and gloominess, a day of clouds and thick darkness.

It is difficult to draw a parallel as to this ominous time span. I remember what it was like just before a hurricane was about to sweep through the island. All of a sudden, everything became quiet—the wind stopped blowing, and the birds stopped singing. Up in the mountains there are trees called the trumpeter. When there's ominous danger, they turn over their leaves so the white underside is seen. When they were showing white, we knew imminent danger was at hand and we would hurry and board up the houses and stay indoors because the hurricane was coming. It was an awful time, not to be remembered. They usually came in the night. The howling wind and incessant rain beating on the house's tin roof was terrifying. The following morning devastation and debris were everywhere. The fierceness of the wind removed the tops of the trees, and in the ocean, muddy water could be seen miles out from shore. I can only imagine what Zephaniah meant about something more disastrous than these occurrences just described.

These Scriptures are in reference to the Son of Man mentioned in the gospels and relate to the worship of Jesus.

> I was watching in the night visions, And behold, One like the Son of Man, Coming with the clouds of heaven! He came to the Ancient of Days, And they brought Him near before Him. Then to Him was given dominion and glory and a

> kingdom, That all peoples, nations, and languages should serve Him. His dominion is an everlasting dominion, Which shall not pass away, And His kingdom the one Which shall not be destroyed. (Daniel 7:13–14)

Here Jesus is speaking to the high priest of His return in Matthew 26:64 where He spoke about sitting at the right hand of power. After the restoration of all things, according to Acts 3:19–21, the Lord will send His Christ. He will come on the clouds of heaven. His coming will be a culmination of the ages for He spoke about reaping and separating the sheep and the goats.

He also spoke of coming with power and great glory. Isaiah spoke of people hiding in the mountains and asking the rocks to fall on them. Therefore, I can only imagine that it would be a terrifying time for the human race, something we should not treat lightly, as if it will never happen, because it will. I recall that Matthew and Luke record Jesus saying it will be like the days of Noah. Society is ominously moving in that direction.

In Acts 1:11, the angels told the onlookers that as they saw Jesus ascend, so shall He return in like manner. So there's no doubt He will be returning according to the Scriptures. Jesus said it Himself, and that's no lie. He can only speak truth. It is imperative that we do not become complacent and think or believe it will never happen.

> Now when He had spoken these things, while they watched, He was taken up, and a cloud received Him out of their sight. (Acts 1:11)

The saints being caught up in a cloud is described in 1 Thessalonians 4:17. The tribes of the earth mourning say,

> Behold, He is coming with clouds, and every eye will see Him, even they who pierced Him. And all the tribes of the earth will mourn because of Him. Even so, Amen. (Revelation 1:7)

Yes, there's hope for those of us who are looking for His appearing. What clues could we glean in the next chapter that it's imminent?

THE END-TIME REAPPEARANCE OF THE GLORY

What moved David, Daniel, and Nehemiah to take action in relation to divine things? What then would move the saints in the church to investigate the restoration of the tabernacle of David that was broken down? It is mentioned that there are three offices to its restoration: the priestly, the prophetic, and the kingly. While this is true, I believe there is an essential element that binds these three offices together into a cohesive alignment. Obedience to God is this element. Obedience to the Word of God is paramount for the glory to come in as the unifying element of these offices. Therefore, the talk of rebuilding the tabernacle has been ongoing for quite some time. This is what Amos prophesied—Israel will be restored.

> On that day I will raise up The tabernacle of David, which has fallen down, And repair its damages; I will raise up its ruins, And rebuild it as in the days of old; That they may possess the remnant of Edom, And all the Gentiles who are

> called by My name," Says the LORD who does this thing. "Behold, the days are coming," says the LORD, "When the plowman shall overtake the reaper, And the treader of grapes him who sows seed; The mountains shall drip with sweet wine, And all the hills shall flow with it. I will bring back the captives of My people Israel; They shall build the waste cities and inhabit them; They shall plant vineyards and drink wine from them; They shall also make gardens and eat fruit from them. (Amos 9:11–14)

Doesn't this sound like an end-time worldwide harvest? However, to gain understanding of its enormity, its importance and eschatological significance, we need to look carefully at the original setting up of the tabernacle by King David.

The Tabernacle of David

David loved the Lord. He set about moving the ark into the tabernacle he prepared. He was an excellent military man, kingly leader, and administrator. When it came to teamwork, he got everyone involved, whether collecting offerings or distributing gifts or organizing people. From what I have observed, he gave gifts to all Israel. Another observation is that after he was afraid to move the ark to Jerusalem, he left it at the home of Obed-Edom, a Levite.

Do you think he was mystified, distraught, and puzzled? I think so. I wouldn't go near that ark. I would send someone every so often to find out how Obed-Edom was doing. Let's say David probably wouldn't even talk to God because he might say the wrong thing. So let's say prayer was redundant also. Imagine David sitting, day after day with his hand under his chin, and tapping on some object with his right hand—the man was a musician! While tapping, he was thinking, *How can I get the ark back to Jerusalem? I had the boys check in on Obed-Edom. He's prospering, so it must be all right, but I still haven't figured out how to move it.* He was contemplating for some time, he then said to himself, *David, you have to think. Rehearse your past. Were you afraid of the lion or the bear? No! Well great! What about Ziklag then? I notice you're hesitating. Well I cried till I couldn't cry anymore, and I knew what made it worse. Those dropouts who were distressed, in debt, and discontented wanted to stone me. Me, of all people! Can you believe it? Yes. I empathize with you… so what did you do after you finished crying like a baby? I went—to—Abiathar—the—priest. I went to Abiathar the priest, that's it! I will go to Abiathar to inquire for me.* Off he went to Abiathar…

Abiathar came back to David with the answer. He waited patiently for the king to speak. David asked, "Abiathar, what did the Lord God of Israel say?"

Abiathar took his time and carefully chose his words so as not to cause any concern for the king. He said, "My king, live forever. He asked a question, my lord."

The king asked, "So, Abiathar, what did He say? No holding back."

"Thank you, my king. He asked if you remembered what He said to Joshua about the word."

David heard what Abiathar said but took a long time to respond because he realized what he had neglected to do. He said, "Thank you, Abiathar, I know what to do. Blessed be the name of the Lord God of Israel."

On his way back after visiting the priest, for the first time since the death of Uzzah, he spoke to the Lord, saying how good God was and His mercy endures forever. He went on to express his sorrow for not taking heed to the words of Moses that stated the requirements written for the king.

> Also it shall be, when he sits on the throne of his kingdom, that he shall write for himself a copy of this law in a book, from the one before the priests, the Levites. And it shall be with him, and he shall read it all the days of his life, that he may learn to fear the Lord his God and be careful to observe all the words of this law and these statutes, that his heart may not be lifted above his brethren, that he may not turn aside from the commandment to the right hand or to the left, and that he may prolong his days in his kingdom, he and his children in the midst of Israel. (Deuteronomy 17:18–20)

From that day forward, David became a student of the Word of God, reading the king's copy of the books of Moses. He sought to know which of the Levites should be dismantling the tabernacle, who should be assembling which pieces of furnishings, and who should be carrying which items; he desired to know the Lord's procedures. David made the discovery in Numbers 4 of the procedures of the tabernacle of worship. There were thirty eight thousand Levites who were thirty years old and older. Of these, he utilized twenty-four thousand to look after the tabernacle, four thousand were gatekeepers, and four thousand praised the Lord with musical instruments, which David said he made for giving praise (1 Chronicles 23:3–5). After that, David was able to move the ark from Obed-Edom's house because he had learned God's proper protocol (order) for holiness.

> He said to them, "You are the heads of the fathers' houses of the Levites; sanctify yourselves, you and your brethren, that you may bring up the ark of the LORD God of Israel to the place I have prepared for it. For because you did not do it the first time, the LORD our God broke out against us, because we did not consult Him about the proper order. So the priests and the Levites sanctified themselves to bring up the ark of the LORD God of Israel. And the children of the Levites bore the ark of God on their shoulders, by its poles, as Moses had commanded according to the word of the LORD." (1 Chronicles 15:12–15)

The Heart of the King

The ark of God was moved and placed in the tabernacle David erected. They offered burnt offerings and peace offerings before God. Later we see the goodness and generosity in the heart of the king when he blesses the people in the name of the Lord. He also distributed to everyone in Israel, man and woman, a loaf of bread, a piece of meat, and a cake of raisins.

Then he appointed some of the Levites to minister before the ark of the Lord, to commemorate, to thank, and to praise the Lord God of Israel (1 Chronicles 16:1–4).

He went on to assemble the Levites into ministering teams. He separated some of the sons of Asaph, Jeduthun, and Heman to be under his authority. The number of them, with their brethren who were instructed in the songs of the Lord, all who were skillful, was 288. They were arranged into twenty-four groups of twelve participants in each group. Each group could minister on the hour, making up the worship around the clock. This description is not in detail. In the book of 1 Chronicles 23–26 there is a detailed arrangement for the divisions of the Levites, the divisions of the priests, other Levites, the musicians, and the gatekeepers.

> All these were under the direction of their father for the music in the house of the LORD, with cymbals, stringed instruments, and harps, for the service of the house of God. Asaph, Jeduthun, and Heman were under the authority of the king. So the number of them, with their brethren who were instructed in the songs of the LORD, all who were skillful, was two hundred and eighty-eight. (1 Chronicles 25:6–7)

David had three specific leaders among the musicians:

a. Asaph was over those who prophesied according to the order of the king (1 Chronicles 25:2b).
b. Jeduthun was over those who prophesied with the harp to give praise and thanks and to praise the Lord (1 Chronicles 25:3).
c. Heman the king's seer in the words of God, to exalt his horn (1 Chronicles 25:5).

It was no small assembly, and it was well organized. This worship went out daily from the tabernacle, and as you can well understand, the presence of the God of Israel was vibrant continually. Not only that, but you could extend the thinking to understand why David was so successful in battle. This type of continuous worship continued into Solomon's reign. In 2 Chronicles 5 it tells of the moving of the tabernacle from the city of David into the temple by the Levites. After they put all the items in place and the Levites began to worship in harmony saying, "For He is good, For His mercy endures forever," the house of the Lord was filled with a cloud. They created a habitation where the Lord God of Israel was pleased to dwell. They could not continue ministering because the glory of the Lord God filled the temple!

It is this type of dedicated intercessory worship (of which the prophets spoke) that God would raise up in the latter days. There are ministries being raised up following these specifications today, and many more are in the process presently. As we continue to mine the word more and do like David did, following biblical patterns, God will honor the work and worship.

Many ministries have realized that part-time Sunday worship is not enough to avert this end-time demonic onslaught. Satan has been busy twenty-four hours a day, seven days a week, for a long time now. I remember when businesses began to open seven days a week—an ominous sign that a day of worship each week was no longer central to our culture. The church is now realizing nothing less than twenty-four hours a day, seven days a week; continuous worship will create the habitation for almighty God to dwell in. Out of the visitations during worship, strategies will be given on how to defeat the enemy, just like David experienced. He inquired of the Lord, who is the supreme strategist.

Three Days of Worship

Oh, how I wished I had kept notes on this particular conference that was held in Palm Springs, California. I think it was in the month of May 1993. It was the first time I had visited America. I remembered the place had lots of palm trees. There were many trees in the hotel complex also. In fact, the palms give a rather peaceful feeling wherever they grow. They seem to give water pools a tranquil appearance growing near oases such as the valley of Baca, Elim, and Beer Sheva.

During the conference in Palm Springs, from what I can remember, this is what took place. The conference had started with the usual registration. We checked into our hotel rooms and attended the first session the same night, and then more meetings continued in the morning.

The worship began, and we quickly entered God's presence. Next some announcements were made, and then the preaching followed. The messages were inspirational, and the anointing increased preacher after preacher. Those of us in this large international gathering sensed the progressive change taking place in the spirit by spontaneous gestures of worship breaking out in different parts of the building. Just before noon, the Holy Spirit came in, and the entire gathering erupted in rapturous worship. That was the end of the preaching. Every time the preachers came onto the platform to preach, the spirit of worship took over. The Holy Spirit must have stayed on the platform because we worshiped the rest of the three days.

I had no complaints. I enjoyed every moment while it lasted. I had never experienced worship that lasted that long. After that time in Palm Springs, we had almost a day's duration of worship after an all-night prayer gathering in North London, UK. We had breakthrough in prayer just after midnight, and then the worship continued until 7:00 Saturday evening. We need to engage in this type of worship today. I also remembered similar worship in a Catholic church in Northern Ireland in February 1997. Night and day prayer and worship make such manifestations of the Holy Spirit's presence possible.

MIDNIGHT PRAYER: CRYING IN THE NIGHT

The Psalmist said,

> At midnight I will rise to give thanks to you, because of your righteous judgments. I am a companion of all who fear you, and of those who keep your precepts. The earth, O Lord, is full of your mercy; teach me your statutes. (Psalm 119:62–64)

Jesus said in the parable of the wise and foolish virgins,

> But while the bridegroom was delayed, they slumbered and slept, And at midnight a cry was heard: "Behold, the bridegroom is coming: go out to meet him!" (Matthew 25:5–6)

I assure you, the bridegroom is coming sooner than we expect. Be in ready mode.

The Priests

May the priests who delight to minister unto the Lord by night (Psalm 134) come forth from the north, south, east, and west and fill the cities of the earth with worship in spirit and in truth in these latter days. These are the ones who will send forth an invitation to enter into the beauty realm of God. These are the ones who rise at midnight and give thanks because they know the process of affliction and its divine purpose. They know the loving fellowship their afflictions produced. Therefore the Lord's name is remembered in the night. These ones know their journey of pilgrimage and made His statutes their songs. They remembered His judgments of old on the gods of a nation out of which God's people (Israel) was delivered. During the time of their affliction, they made His Word their comfort, gaining the knowledge, understanding, wisdom, and comfort His Word gave. They realized that His Word is forever settled in heaven and knew there was deliverance in the future for those who keep His commandments. They know of love manifesting. These are the ones who rise at midnight to give thanks to the Lord.

Deliverance in the Night

We have come to know that from midnight to 6:00 a.m. are crucial hours for deliverance and advancing out of danger. Using the Exodus out of Egypt as an example, God gave Moses a blueprint for deliverance.

> And they shall take some of the blood and put it on the two door posts and on the lintel of the houses where they eat it. (Exodus 12:7)

At the appointed time He would pass through the land. Promise and timing causes a "suddenly." The Lord said:

> About midnight I will go out into the midst of Egypt. (Exodus 11:4b)

He struck the firstborn of man and beast and executed judgment on the gods of Egypt because He is the Lord (Exodus 12:12).

From this we are certain that He visits in the night. Jesus talked about coming as a thief in the night (in reference to the careless ones). He also talked about being alert and watchful. Paul talked about the sleeping ones who needed to awake from the dust so Christ could shine from their hearts. Why all these warnings, you ask? Jesus, Paul, and others were aware of a major demonic onslaught coming against the saints in these latter days. Those who are napping instead of praying and burning the midnight oil need to be awakened quickly.

I pray to Father God that none of us just miss it like the five foolish virgins in Matthew 25:1–13. Notice that they got to the door, but they were on the wrong side! The watching ones or the sons and daughters of Issachar, the Anna's and the Simeon's, are fully aware of what is ahead. They are not wasting their time on minor activities, though they have some importance. They are synchronized with Israel (the spiritual clock) instead. They are the ones who tremble at His Word.

God spoke through Isaiah the prophet, saying,

> I have set watchmen upon your walls, O Jerusalem; they will never hold their peace day or night. You who make mention of the Lord, do not be silent, and give Him no rest till He establishes and till He makes Jerusalem a praise in the earth. (Isaiah 62:6–7)

Jesus also mentioned to cry out to God day and night.

> And shall not God avenge His own elect who cry out day and night to Him, though He bears long with them? "I tell you that He will avenge them speedily. Nevertheless, when the Son of Man comes, will He really find faith on the earth?" (Luke 18:7–8)

Mike Bickle[13] (2004 handout) stated the following regarding God's speedy justice to night and day prayer, and God's judgment on sickness, where healing is the result:

> Divine intervention is made manifest as God's justice, judgment or vengeance. Often we think of judgment strictly as God stopping rebellion and defiance. Stopping rebellion is only one element of justice. God's judgments fell upon Egypt in the days of Moses when he stretched

---

13 Mike Bickle's handout (2004) from International House of Prayer, 3535 E Red Bridge Rd, Kansas City, MO 64137 http://www.ihopkc.org.

> out his rod and the plagues broke in. We also view it as making things right. As an example of judgment or justice; healing is God's judgment, or vengeance on sickness. When the healing occurs God is glorified.

Here's an example of God's speedy judgment on sickness.

The Lady in the Wheelchair

Some believe the ministry of healing ended when the apostolic period ceased. I tend to disagree because in the red writing in the Bible in the gospel of Mark, part of Jesus' commission is for us to heal the sick. I believe it is applicable today. Let me tell you why. There are many ministries that are presently functioning in the healing ministry using the name of Jesus. Once anyone believes and is obedient to Jesus' instructions, the manifestations are inevitable.

Throughout the years in my role of serving other ministries, I have seen many people receive healing based on the faith of one who believes. I am of the opinion that healing will continue until Jesus returns. I also believe that, due to the existence of so many different debilitating diseases, there will always be a need for healers ministering to people who need healing beyond what medications can do. Health problems and disease will always be present in a fallen society.

This brings me to a case in point of something that took place in my past where a lady came out of a wheelchair by the spoken word of God. There was no approaching the individual like there was in the book of Acts 3 when Peter physically held the person and lifted him up. The word of God has the inherent power in it to bring about the outcome the Lord desires.

Early one morning, back in 1994, the Spirit of the Lord impressed upon my heart to visit my sister in Walthamstow, East London, UK. Let me emphasize here that a person needs always to be in a state of readiness or preparedness to respond to these kinds of directives from the Lord, like a soldier who is trained to respond to the alert at any given moment. Doing the will of the Lord at any moment shows the depth of love in the heart of an individual for Him. I never questioned why I should go, and neither did I question my purpose in going. I knew once I received such a directive, it would be of the utmost importance. In addition, I was in a covenant of obedience with the Lord. Wherever He sent me, I would go. However, I didn't get it right every time. In His goodness, there were times when the Lord would remind me of our covenant agreement. It was such a season that was ongoing in my life at that time. So I stopped what I was doing and got myself ready to visit my sister.

London has an excellent transport system where you can get anywhere throughout the city by the bus, tube, and train network. I walked up to manor house, which is not far from where I lived. From Manor House I could take certain buses that went near to my location and then catch another connecting bus to my destination. When I eventually got to my sister's house, I knocked on the door and waited. Eventually the door opened, and we greeted each other. I told her why I had come at that particular time. She said they were getting ready to go out so I could wait in the living room.

Let me tell you briefly about my sister. She has a gentle and loving spirit and is an excellent counselor and advisor. There were times when I was unable to make decisions on personal matters so I would talk it over with her, and out would pop the answer! She is reliable and dependable and an excellent servant of the Lord.

So there I was, still not knowing the purpose for which the Lord had said to go to her house. I only knew that it was a divine moment and something would unfold. On hearing the instruction my sister gave me, I walked in the direction of the living room. The door to the living room was partly ajar. As I got near the door, my spirit man came alive with excitement! It reminded me of the time when Mary visited Elizabeth in the hill country in the city of Judea. When Mary entered the house and greeted Elizabeth, the baby leaped in her womb. The Bible recorded that Elizabeth was filled with the Holy Spirit. It was at the moment I approached that I knew there was something in that living room that had to do with why I was there. As I got around the door, I saw a lady in a wheelchair. It wasn't just my spirit man who was excited. I was totally consumed! Her back was turned toward the door so I had to walk around to see who the person was. I had never seen her before, but I had the thought that she was the mother of my sister's husband. I greeted her and sat on a soft two-seater where I could see her clearly. Again, I was excited and knew she would be healed as now I began to know the purpose I was there—a divine encounter. God was about to do the miraculous because I was sent. His divine presence would bring about His purpose. Praise the Lord.

I took mental note of her condition. Her hands and feet were twisted around and inward into her body. I was wondering to myself, *How could that happen?* Because of the contortion of her hands, she couldn't look after herself!

I didn't waste any time. I began to ask who she was and why she was in the wheelchair. I could tell she was a tall lady and of pleasant features—rather elegant. One of the questions that automatically came out of my mouth was whether she had accepted Jesus Christ as Lord and Savior. I went on to talk about God's goodness even when we find ourselves in difficult situations. We exchanged words, but I stayed in the Scriptures. I mentioned to her Scriptures from Psalm 91, which is about if any plagues came near her dwelling, it was because a door was left open to allow the Enemy in. I intimated a door was left open to allow the Enemy into her life and asked her if she thought that might be a possibility as to why she was in her present condition. She agreed it was possible. I went into Psalm 139 and mentioned about being fearfully and wonderfully made by God and how that was her real image. I shared how God's reality is that she is well and is still perfect, devoid of her wheelchair hindrance. I asked her if she was happy where she was and she said no; she wanted to be free. I then let her know the purpose for which I was there. I told her that God's love for her had brought me there. In the meantime, I was watching her countenance for responses. During our conversation, there was a quiet hush in the room as we were both aware of the divine presence of God.

I then said to her, "You said you want to be free, so I must ask you if there is anything you can think of that may have brought on this hindrance."

She never answered but looked off into the distance. I noted the shifting of her head and her eyes gazing into the distance. I could see she was probing the annals of her memory, so I waited. Finally I asked, "What are you seeing? Do you mind sharing what is coming into your thoughts?"

Instead of a verbal response, tears traced her face. I waited on her, and after some time, she spoke. Out of what she shared, I mentioned to her forgiveness is not an easy thing to do, and God knows her heart better than any human. He had come to extend divine love to her that very moment.

I reminded her that we had never met before and I was sent just because of her because she was so precious in the heart of God. He was there to heal her and set her free. I shared how important it was to God for us to forgive those who have hurt us terribly. He knows and understands how painful it is to forgive. He died on a cross to forgive us. I had to tell her I honestly believed she was in her wheelchair at that moment because she had not forgiven from her heart. I told her if she would be willing to forgive then and there, God would heal her. After some time, she agreed to forgive. I related to her that we would say a prayer of forgiveness together, and when we finished, she would be healed. She agreed.

We said the prayer, and then by the leading of the Holy Spirit, I spoke some more Scriptures and watched as the right hand unfolded back to normal. Next the left hand returned to normal. As I shared more Scriptures, the right foot straightened and then the left foot. During that part of the miracle moment, I was absolutely amazed at seeing the miracle with my own eyes! Her limbs were moving back to normal by the power of the spoken word of Jehovah Rapha! By this time her countenance was aglow with the presence of the Lord. She was examining herself and taking in what the Lord had done. When she finished, the Spirit of the Lord indicated to me that she wasn't ready to get out of the wheelchair at that moment, so I didn't ask her to get up. Instead I said to her, "When you are ready, you will get out of that wheelchair." I didn't have to question whether she would get out of the wheelchair because I had heard what the Spirit said to me and knew she would come out eventually. My assignment was completed, so I said my good-bye to my sister and returned home.

About two weeks later I visited my sister, and the lady was walking. Eleven years later, in 2005, I attended my father's funeral in Preston, Lancashire, England, and she was still walking. All praise, honor, and glory are due to our awesome God! That was an opportunity to glorify God, and it can happen for and through any of us today. Miracles will continue to glorify God!

Oneness Produced by the Glory so the World Knows

In His intercessory prayer in Gethsemane Jesus was belaboring this point for all of the saints—that those the Father had given Him would come into oneness. It seems He emphasized this oneness so any reader would not overlook it. It sure caught my attention to the point where I marveled at the synchronizing of the unity of Father, Jesus, and we mortal, sinful sons of Adam. It is rather difficult to comprehend such a heartfelt and dynamic holy request. I feel like when John the Baptist encountered Jesus and became aware of his own insignificance and he admitted he was not worthy to untie Jesus' sandals. Yet Jesus prayed we would be one. "Help me, God, to comprehend what Jesus meant, because neither am I worthy of such honor."

Jesus said,

> That they may be one, as You, Father, are in Me, and I in You; that they also may be one in Us, that the world may believe that you have sent Me. I in them, and You in Me, that they may be made perfect in one, and that the world may know that you have sent me, and have loved them as you have loved me. (John 17:21–23)

MANIFESTING THE GLORY

How are we to manifest this glory, this radiance, this brilliance, this *Doxa* that commands attention? This glory is in every born-again believer. We could term the saints "producers of the glory," providing we give careful consideration to the word *obedience*. Though this may not have entered your thoughts, we are carriers of the good news and the glory. The glory of God is in us. Therefore, wherever we are, His presence flows out of us and fills the room. It will happen when we follow the seven revelations and apply them personally each day. Take hold of this revelation: Obedience is the key to perfection through faith. Without it, there would be no manifestation.

Let us look at an example of the manifestation of the glory of God. I want us to look specifically at an example where Jesus used the word *glory* in relation to healing. Such an example is in John 11:3–4.

Everyone who opens a Bible could admit they see the word *obedience* written from Genesis through Revelation. However, in my opinion, true obedience has not really impacted us to the degree that our lives have become radically transformed. Only in Jesus did it seem to have this radical effect. I always wondered why. "Obey my commandments," God continually reminds us. I thank God we have a Mediator praying for us this moment. By Holy Spirit's power inside us, we can obey as Jesus did. Thank You, Jesus! You are my High Priest.

Saints, let us purpose in our hearts to *lovingly obey God's commands* and experience the weight of God's glory even in the midst of this present ungodly age.

> For our light affliction, which is but for a moment, is working for us a far more exceeding and eternal weight of glory. (2 Corinthians 4:17)

Let us continue to follow on and do like David said,

> Give unto the Lord glory due unto his name; worship the Lord in the beauty of holiness. (Psalm 29:2)

To Him be glory and honor and power forever! Amen.

The Seventh Trumpet—the Kingdom Proclaimed

What an awesome truth to meditate on. Finally, and at last, the spiritual war is coming to an end. The earth will be restored, and God's original purposes will begin to unfold. Think for a moment. No human since Adam and Eve has known what peace is really like. We all have been harassed in some form or another. The seventh angel sounding its trumpet caused a lifting up of voices in heaven.

> Then the seventh angel sounded: And there were loud voices in heaven, saying, "The kingdoms of this world have become the kingdoms of our Lord and of His Christ, and He shall reign forever and ever!" (Revelation 11:15)

Also, the song of Moses and of the Lamb will be sung because of victory over the beast, over his image, over his mark, and over the number of his name.

> And I saw something like a sea of glass mingled with fire, and those who have the victory over the beast, over his image and over his mark and over the number of his name, standing on the sea of glass, having harps of God. They sing the song of Moses, the servant of God, and the song of the Lamb, saying: "Great and marvelous are Your works, Lord God Almighty! Just and true are Your ways, O King of the saints! Who shall not fear You, O Lord, and glorify Your name? For You alone are holy. For all nations shall come and worship before You, For Your judgments have been manifested. (Revelation 15:2–4)

In Conclusion

In the beginning we read the oath of the Lord, "But truly, as I live, all the earth shall be filled with the glory of the Lord." We have read what Jesus said, "It is the Spirit that gives life; the flesh profits nothing. The words that I speak to you are spirit and they are life." You have also read what was impressed upon my heart, "I want you to know my glory," and the testimonies. In addition, you have read two teachings on how to produce the anointing in "Fervent Prayer Releases the Anointing" and "Heaven Came Down to You through the Son." Also, "A Personal Daily Approach to God" is about how to walk in the Spirit. I believe if we all engage night and day in crying out like Jesus said in Luke 18:7, and what the prophet wrote in Isaiah 62:6–7, I am convinced we will see the glory of God invading the seven mountains of society globally.

Father God, let Your glory fill all the earth, as You have said.

> Then the Lord said: "I have pardoned, according to thy word; but truly, as I live, all the earth shall be filled with the glory of the Lord." (Numbers 14:20–21)

THE GREATEST MISSIONARY

Jesus is the greatest missionary. He left His home in glory, came to earth as a man, defeated Satan, and returned to His Father in heaven victorious over *all.*

Who is a missionary? I believe it is anyone the Father has directed to His Son, who has said yes to the message of salvation, has been baptized in water, and has been filled with His Holy Spirit. Following some boot camp training, within such an individual resides the power to advance God's kingdom. Going to other countries and encountering spiritual forces is inevitable at some point for a person thus prepared by God. The missionary must also enforce the defeat of Satan.

The Command

Jesus came and spoke to them, saying,

> All authority has been given to Me in heaven and on earth. "Go therefore and make disciples of all nations, baptizing them in the name of the Father and of the Son and of the Holy Spirit, teaching them to observe all things that I have commanded you; and lo, I am with you always, even to the end of the age." Amen. (Matthew 28:18–20)

Many have heeded the above command out of obedience and love for their wonderful Jesus and went to foreign lands with great excitement and wonder. Some returned beaten, broken, and bewildered. Sadly, some did not return. Have you ever wondered why? I have.

Having traveled to West Africa, Northern Ireland, North East India, Israel, and other places in the world, I have gained some idea of the different cultural behaviors and beliefs nurtured by these people groups. I have not seen anywhere in the gospels where Jesus went in like the owner and declared a takeover. He had a humble heart and won them over by being and doing. He also had knowledge of the different mind-sets. He never came away beaten, broken, and bewildered. His life wasn't taken from Him unwillingly; He gave it voluntarily. Bear with me. Is it possible that we (the body of Christ) have had some needless casualties on mission fields in the past by not maturing in the command mentioned above to walk as Jesus did until we walk in His authority? Do we try to fulfill this command in our own strength instead of being with Him in it? Jesus ministered in the fullness of the Spirit; we must also minister in the fullness of His Spirit. This writer has shared with you how to live and minister in the Spirit.

Knowledge and Experience

First, observation of Jesus' above command is primary. This command was made after He was resurrected! That, in itself, is a big eye opener and calls for one of those "Wait a minute!" statements. Encapsulated in the command is forty days of fasting and temptation in the wilderness, three and a half years of ministry, accusations, hunger, beatings, buffetings, scourging, and death itself.

Would you say He was prepared? Would you say there was fasting, prayer, and much reliance on God to be successful? I think so! Do you think because we are in the twenty-first century, aided by sophisticated electronic equipment where, at a glance, we can see the happenings in other countries, so that means we don't need to prepare? Absolutely not! Mind-sets are invisible, and so are demons.

Do We Have Authority?

Absolutely, as stated in Luke 10:19! Just having head knowledge of your authority through Christ isn't sufficient. Even if you are in the company of one who has revelation knowledge of this authority, it will not get you by. What about when you are in a one-on-one situation? What would you do? I don't know. You must seek the

Lord for this revelation of your authority for yourself. You will know when it is granted (Luke 24: 45). You may say, "Is it really worth it?" Without a doubt! I can tell you the very day it was revealed to me. It was unforgettable! Even the demons become agitated. Thank You, Lord Jesus, Captain of the Hosts.

Preparation

The Sovereign Lord wants each of us to know our authority in Him through His Son. Knowing this authority and preparation, no territory is out of bounds. Saying all that doesn't mean you can randomly stick a pin in the world map, buy a ticket, and head out! Remember the phrase above, Captain of the Hosts? He is the one who will direct you where He wants you to go. He will notify you well before the departure date to give you time to prepare, gather information, and settle your mind for any "suddenly" on the field. If such a "suddenly" did occur, you would automatically call to Him for help. Whatever the outcome, you would know and not wonder whether it was the will of the Lord because you settled, He called you, and you went in obedience.

A prayer covering should be in place before going, during, and after the journey. If you believe ambush is possible, then so is backlash. This latter usually occurs long after the journey ends. Staying alert at all times isn't being overcautious. It's a command. Herein is your confidence and success. As He would say, "Fear not." Then go as He commands, and you shall surely come back rejoicing.

To Elohim is the entire honor. So let us rise and shine because the glory has been given to us. *You can know God's glory.*

BIBLIOGRAPHY

1. Prayer for Japan—research information came from Moorgate Library, London, England.
2. Definition of glory: A Merriam Webster, *Webster's New Collegiate Dictionary*, Springfield, Massachusetts, U.S.A. 1977, Page (490).
3. Tents of Mercy ministry led by Eitan Shishkoff—http://www.tentsofmercy.org.
4. Pat Robertson, DVD: "God's Plan for America How to Prepare for the Days Ahead." Centerville Turnpike, Virginia Beach, Virginia 23463. The Christian Broadcasting Network, Inc, 2012.
5. Taken from *The Voice of the Martyrs Magazine*, April 2013 issue. Visit http://www.persecution.com Contact: The Voice of the Martyrs P. O. Box 443, Bartlesville, OK 74005-0443. Orders and contributions: 800-747-0085. Ministry information: 877-337-0302. E-mail: thevoice@vom-usa.org
6. The Elijah List mail out September 12, 2005—website http://www.elijahlist.com
7. Recommended Book by Jeanne Guyon, *Experiencing the Depths of Jesus Christ.* Sowers of Seeds, Inc., 1981.

8. Recommended Book or Video by Derek Prince, *Blessing or Curse: You Can Choose.* P.O. Box 6287, Grand Rapids, MI 49516, Chosen Books, 1990. http://www.derekprince.com.
9. Andrew Murray, *The Secret of Intercession.* 30 Hunt Valley Circle, New Kensington, PA 15068: Whitaker, 1995, (Pages 16).
10. Electronic News Letter by Daniel Juster—Tel Aviv, Gay Rights and the Boy Scouts - http://www.tikkunministries.org/newsletters/dj-may13.php.
11. Definition of song: Dictonary.com http://www.ditionary.reference.com/browse/sing
12. Explanation by John Wesley on John 6:63, http://www.biblestudytools.com/commentaries/wesleys-explanatory-notes/john/john-6.html.
13. Mike Bickle's handout (2004) from International House of Prayer, 3535 E Red Bridge Rd, Kansas City, MO 64137 http://www.ihopkc.org.

Recent and past resources: Pastor Benny Hinn's DVD, *The Glory of God's Presence.* P.O. Box 16200, Irving, TX 75016, Benny Hinn Ministries, 2008 http://www.bennyhinn.org.

Book by Guillermo Maldonado, *The Glory of God*, 1030 Hunt Valley Circle, Kensington, PA 15068, Whitaker House, 2012. http://kingjesusministry.org.

Book by Charles Spurgeon, *The Key to Holiness,* 30 Hunt Valley Circle, New Kensington, PA 15068. Whitaker House, 1997.

Book by Andrew Murray, *The Holiest of All* Abridged Edition, An Exposition of the Epistle to the Hebrews. Fort Worth, Texas 76192. Kenneth Copeland Ministries, 1993.

Book by John G. Lake's, *His Life, His Sermons, His Boldness of Faith*. Fort Worth, Texas 76192, Kenneth Copeland Publications, 1994.

GLOSSARY OF TERMS

Baptism of Fire

> John answered, saying to all, "I indeed baptize you with water; but One mightier than I is coming, whose sandal strap I am not worthy to loose. He will baptize you with the Holy Spirit and fire." (Luke 3:16)

This is a baptism of purging, cleansing, consecration, or holy passion that goes deep into our being. Part of the nature of our God is that He is a consuming fire.

Kairos

This is a God-ordained or divine moment in time where all converges in time and in the spirit realm to create a *now* time that must be moved into to be of value. No spectators will profit!

Last Days (End Times)

This is the time spoken of just before Jesus returns. It will be the coming together of all time as we know it. Many fearsome events will take place, as well as the kingdom of God advancing. It is the time of the revelation of Jesus Christ Himself, coming in His glory for His bride!

Red Writing

In some editions of the Bible, all the words Jesus spoke when He lived on this earth (mostly in the gospels of the New Testament) are written in red. This makes it easy to see exactly what He said during His life and ministry.

Songs from the Spirit (Singing in the Spirit)

After you have received salvation and Jesus is your Savior and Lord, the Holy Spirit comes to live inside of you. As you yield to Him, He (the Spirit of God) fills you and flows out of you in many ways. One of the ways is in song. You might sing spontaneously from your heart to Him, write your own song, or sing in an unknown tongue, letting Him be the only one who knows what it means, or He might tell you what it means as you go along.

Speaking in Tongues (Prayer Language, Unknown Tongues, Tongues of Angels)

> Likewise the Spirit also helps our infirmities: for we know not what we should pray for as we ought: but the Spirit Himself makes intercession for us with groanings which cannot be uttered. (Romans 8:26)

After you have received salvation and Jesus is your Savior and Lord, the Holy Spirit comes to live inside of you. As you yield to Him, He (the Spirit of God) fills you and flows out of you in many ways. One of the ways is by helping us pray (note verse above). This also means speaking or praying in an unknown language that only God understands or that angels use and understand (they are God's servants), or that might be another language spoken on earth. What's most important is our yielding to the Holy Spirit of God who lives inside of us so He can be the power that works in us to live free of sin, enabling us to love and give ourselves to God wholeheartedly.

Printed in the United States
By Bookmasters